PSYCHIC ENVELOPES

Forthcoming title to be published by Karnac Books:

Didier Anzieu: *A Skin for Thought*

PSYCHIC ENVELOPES

D. Anzieu   D. Houzel   A. Missenard
M. Enriquez   A. Anzieu   J. Guillaumin
J. Doron   E. Lecourt   T. Nathan

translated by

Daphne Briggs

Karnac Books
London 1990

This translation first published in 1990 by
H. Karnac (Books) Ltd.
58 Gloucester Road
London SW7 4QY

British Library Cataloguing in Publication Data
Psychic envelopes.
  1. Self. Psychological aspects
  I. Anzieu, Didier. II. Les enveloppes psychiques.
  English
  155.2

ISBN 0–946439–60–5

Printed in Great Britain by BPCC Wheatons Ltd, Exeter

CONTENTS

CHAPTER ONE

Formal signifiers and the ego-skin

Didier Anzieu   1

(I) Three cases   1

(II) Formal signifiers and signifiers of demarcation   11
> *(1) Linguistic signifiers and signifiers*
> *of demarcation   11*
> *(2) Formal signifiers, pictograms, twilight*
> *states   15*

(III) Characteristics of formal signifiers   16

(IV) Classification of formal signifiers   17

(V) Formal signifiers and functions of the ego-skin   19

(VI) The transformations of formal signifiers   22

(VII) Interpretation   23

(VIII) The role of formal signifiers   25

CHAPTER TWO

The concept of psychic envelope

Didier Houzel   27

(I) The genesis of the concept 28

(II) The properties of the psychic envelope 42

    (1) Its structure 42
    (2) Its plastic qualities 49
    (3) Its functions 51

(III) Conclusion 55

CHAPTER THREE

**The dream envelope
and the phantasy of a 'common psyche'**

André Missenard   59

(I) Working on the dream 59

(II) Dreams 'from above', dreams 'from below' 62

    *(1) A dream of RL, confronted with a
        difficult reality 62*
    (2) A dream of a depressed analysand 64
    (3) Dreams of a patient with a somatic illness 66
    (4) The dream envelope at work 67

(III) Dreams and psychic functioning in common 69

    (1) The mother, the dream and the baby 69
    (2) A transferential dream by Sarah 72
    (3) Dreaming one's patient: 'I dream for us' 74
    (4) Psychic functioning in common 77
    (5) Return to the cases 80

(IV) Dreams in common 81

    (1) Family dreams 81
    (2) One dream for two 84
    (3) Dreams in a group, dreams of a group 89

CHAPTER FOUR

The memory envelope and its holes

Micheline Enriquez   95

(I) The need for recall   95

(II) Obstacles to the discovery of historicity   98

(III) Sarah, or the decomposed past   101

(IV) Theoretical perspectives   112

    (1) Memory that can neither be remembered
        nor forgotten   112
    (2) Forgetful and memorable memory   115
    (3) Collective cultural memory   117
    (4) Attacks on memory   118

CHAPTER FIVE

The hysterical envelope

Annie Anzieu   121

(I) The hysteric and his mother   122

    (1) Hysterical defences   122
    (2) The case of Mrs G   123
    (3) Features of the hysterical character   125

(II) Maternal depression   126

    (1) Psychotic depression   128
    (2) Narcissistic depression   129
    (3) Accidental depression   133
    (4) The aetiology of hysteria   134

(III) The excitation envelope   136

    (1) Its contradictions   136
    (2) A reactive violence   138
    (3) The carry-over into sexuality   140
    (4) The death instinct   141
    (5) Displacement inwards of excitation   142
    (6) The multiplicity of identifications   143

CHAPTER SIX

The psychic envelopes of the psychoanalyst: some suggestions for applying the theory of psychic envelopes to the study of the psychoanalyst's functioning
Jean Guillaumin 147

(I) General competence of the envelopes model:
   problematics retained here   147

(II) A metapsychology of the analyst in terms
   of psychic envelopes?   153
   (1) General schema   154
   *(2) Early cathexis of the relationship
   between verbal signifier
   and strangeness   157*
   (3) Complementary conditions   158

(III) 'Professional disorders' of the psychoanalyst
   from the point of view of the envelopes   161

(IV) Psychoanalysis, envelopes and creativity   179
   (1) The work of creation   179
   *(2) Two types of relationship with creativity
   in the psychoanalyst   181*

CHAPTER SEVEN

Modifications of the psychic envelope in creative work
Jack Doron 191

(I) Introduction   191

(II) Clinical studies   193

(III) Modifications of the ego-skin in creative work   200

(IV) The creation of psychic operators   204
   (1) Thinking by means of shapes   204
   (2) The psychic portrait (Doron, 1984)   205

Conclusion   207

CHAPTER EIGHT

The musical envelope
  Édith Lecourt   211

(I) The problematic of sonority and the notion
    of envelope   211

(II) The sonorous bath   213

(III) The first human exchange   214

(IV) The sonorous cavity   214
        (1) Mythology   217
        (2) Music   217
        (3) Clinical work   217

(V) Sounds of the front, sounds of the behind   218

(VI) The sonorous musico-verbal envelope   223

(VII) The contemporary musical envelope   227

(VIII) Pathologies of the musical envelope   229

CHAPTER NINE

Two dream representations of the ego-skin
  Tobie Nathan   237

(I) Skin and anger   237

(II) The skin, an 'as-if': the case of 'Patroclus'   239

(III) The fear-skin: the case of 'Deimos'   246

(IV) Conclusions—hypotheses   253

Bibliography   257

List of cases   269

Index of proper names   271

PSYCHIC ENVELOPES

CHAPTER ONE

Formal signifiers
and the ego-skin

D. Anzieu

(I) THREE CASES

Definitions

I understand 'form' in the first sense of the word, as 'an aggregate of the contours of an object; result of the organization of its parts', i.e. as configuration or shape. The adjective 'formal' relates to form as defined in this way, for example in the sense of formal logic, which studies the form of arguments without considering their contents. A formal signifier could therefore be understood as signifier of configuration. But that is a static view. The configurations in question undergo deformations or produce transformations that result from their structure and from influences brought to bear on it. We are therefore dealing with signifiers that relate to changes in form. These signifiers are psychic representatives not only of certain instincts, but also of various forms of organization of the self and the ego. On this account they appear to belong to the general category of representatives of things, most especially representations of space and bodily states in general. But is space a thing? Is it not rather the container of all things? In this sense, formal signifiers are pri-

1

marily representations of psychic containers. But each possesses a property, a mode of operation, that generates a transformation within them, and whose failures only produce deformations. They compose the elements of a formal logic appropriate to the primary processes and to an archaic psychic topography. This brings them close to what Gibello has called representatives of transformation, in connection with cognitive mental operations. But the violent and specific anxieties that they denote turn them either into restraints upon the acquisition of the first semiotic systems, themselves preconditions for access to language and word representatives, or into sources of alterations in the functioning of these systems.

Marie

Marie, a young unmarried woman some thirty years of age, came into my office looking distraught. She sat facing me for her weekly session, which we had just agreed upon after several preliminary interviews, while she was waiting for me to have a vacancy to take her into psychoanalysis. After several suicide attempts since adolescence, she had embarked upon a first psychoanalysis, whose interruption had been followed by a fresh suicide attempt. Reading my book on the ego-skin (*Le Moi-Peau*) had made her decide to consult me. On this day Marie was having difficulty in speaking. Her hands rose to the level of her shoulders as though, failing to find a resting-place, they were floating in space. Her mouth opened without being able to articulate anything. She finally managed to communicate the bodily sensation that was distressing her: her skin was shrinking, this was driving her mad, and she was afraid of losing her identity. I was surprised, having never been confronted with such a symptom. I did not immediately remember that she had told me during the preliminary interviews that she had previously suffered from the obsessive feeling that she was an old woman who was shrivelling up. Now it was the whole of the skin of her trunk and neck that was shrivelling, for her four limbs were not involved. This feeling was accompanied by sensations of suffocation and disappearing. Elasticity is one of the properties of the skin: when the latter is separated from the flesh that keeps it spread, it hardens. I wondered what separation was at work here, and what distortion of the ego was being conveyed by this subjective deformation of the skin.

Marie asked me if it was true that her skin was getting smaller. I replied that I saw her intact. She began to speak more normally.

MARIE: It's horrible; I feel I am a skin of troubles; nothing else is going to be left.

I offered her an interpretation that seemed quite soon to have had three defects: hasty, intellectual, and reassuring:

ME: This shrunken square of skin is what is left of your mother's skin, that imprisons you and that you have now to tear off.

Marie burst into tears and cried, 'I know very well that I must detach myself from my mother; but if I have no skin left, I shall dissolve into space.'

ME: You must get rid of this maternal skin so that a skin of your own can grow.

At her request I granted her an extra meeting for the day after next; the psychoanalytic process was now under way.

Marie arrived for her session in a helpless state, for the shrinking skin sensation had returned to her. She had floated in space all day. She no longer had boundaries. Her suffering was unbearable.

My countertransference echoed the transference: I felt that I had 'been given short notice', and I offered her a comparison that was more of a suggestion than an interpretation.

ME: You are like a sloughing snake that abandons its old skin in order to have a new one.

Marie associated to her mother as to a snake that constantly bit her and poisoned her life. Then she went on to describe the web of constraints that her mother had spun around her. The sensation of skin shrinkage diminished, and Marie was able to leave me assured of a new supplementary session soon.

After her departure I received my next patient. I was aware that I was having difficulty in keeping my attention on him. I was thinking about Marie's suffering. I reproached myself for 'obliterating' my patient from my mind in favour of thinking about Marie. This reproach made me find the interpretation I wanted: this shrinking skin was the realization of a wish to obliterate herself. This wish had already been translated into her numerous suicide attempts: a wish that was not her own, but was imputed to her mother, in whose psychic economy Marie had played the role of a persecuted–persecuting bad object throughout her childhood. This mother reproached Marie for being 'bad', for using her, for 'killing' her with her recriminations and illnesses, for having deformed her woman's body (whence came Marie's identification with the shrivelled skin of an old woman) through a pregnancy that the mother had certainly desired, but which had begun during a fit of anger with her husband. Marie was a disappointment for her parents because she was born a second girl when they had wanted a boy. Her mother, a rigid superego figure, insisted that everything was done out of duty, not for pleasure; she systematically failed to take Marie's wishes into account.

At the beginning of the following session I conveyed my interpretation to Marie about a circular wish for obliteration between her mother and herself; she immediately acknowledged its accuracy. She described a number of situations in which her mother had not made room for her wishes. I could then complete my interpretation by involving one of the principles that govern the archaic functioning of thought: either one or the other—you cannot make room for yourself without taking it from someone else; either you dispossess them or you obliterate yourself. She recognized herself in that; but she protested: with me she had the feeling that we could exist, both of us, 'because', she insisted, 'you *occupy your place* and not mine'.

ME: You are learning to live together, just like politicians.

She laughed. I remembered that she had mentioned physical difficulties in recognizing symmetry between the right and left parts of her body. I added:

ME: . . . your right and your left living together. She laughed again. She recovered her sense of humour, which was her best defence mechanism, except in periods of great disturbance. I could stop the session there.

At the next meeting the symptom of the shrunken skin had almost completely disappeared. Marie returned of her own accord to my explanation in terms of self-obliteration, adding a detail that she had not yet communicated: her skin shrunk by re-entering the navel, in a movement that Marie experienced as real; she was later to add: 'like water rushes down the drain'. This detail is important because it reveals the nature and violence of the movement she experienced, i.e. the instinct at work: her self-destructiveness had the patient's ego-skin for its object; for its source it had the umbilical cord, through which the mother took back what she had given during her pregnancy; and it aimed to deny the existence of a shared skin between mother and baby in the sense of first psychic envelope; this shared skin was torn away, swallowed up and expelled.

ME: It is the reverse, the negation of birth: you were returning to a previous nothingness, to the unborn state.

MARIE: I do everything in reverse. My life is a river that flows upstream from the estuary to its source. There is a Greek myth about an old person who got younger, became an adolescent again, a child, a baby, and then nothing at all.

ME: This sensation of a skin that obliterates itself doesn't tally with your own wishes. It is the fulfillment in your imagination of your mother's supposed wish, a way of pleasing her by disappearing and at the same time of hurting her.

MARIE: I do feel inhabited by desires that are not my own. It is true that Mother would have been pained if I had disappeared.

Commentary

Here is an example of what I call a formal signifier. It is a signifier whose spatial dimension is essential: here, a skin of troubles. This spatial signifier conveys metaphorically a particular configuration of psychic space, the source of an appalling pain; to lose one's skin is to lose the boundaries of the self, to lose the cohesion of the pieces that make it up, to lose the feeling of identity. What is more, this formal signifier is the vector of a psychic operation that is not of a dynamic or economic order but topographical—shrinkage. This operation is a version of a more general transformation: involution, or evolution in reverse. The Nirvana principle here at work involves the tendency to reduce towards zero not the quantitative tension internal to the self, but the envelope of the self. Here the instinctual conflict is played out primarily on the body, which confirms the notion of an 'archaic hysteria' proposed by Joyce McDougall (1986) and allows the patient to displace certain violent archaic affects, such as the distress of abandonment and destructive rage, from the psyche into the body. In Marie's case, this somatization developed in three stages: skin allergies in infancy; then feeling that she had the shrivelled skin of an old woman; and, finally, the hallucination of a shrinking skin. Here there is an obvious relationship between faults in the ego and distortions in tactile sensations.

This episode of bodily hallucinosis was followed by some others during Marie's treatment. They worried me mildly in so far as I had from then on a conceptual basis for understanding them (her psychic economy functioned 'in reverse') and a technique for dealing with them (putting into words what she could not express except in gestures, movements and postures). When my effort at interpretation came at the right moment, she would emerge from her somatic conversion, begin once more to look at me and ask me to 'say some more'. This bath of words reconstituted Marie's sonorous envelope for her, both as an envelope of cohesion— which is to say that it maintained her bodily shape—and as an envelope of meaning (and here we find the two functions of the body image, according to G. Pankow: to provide a spatial form and to gain experience of dynamic contents endowed with meaning). Later on Marie was to speak of an impression of 'table linen' (i.e., she had by then been spread with a table-cloth, covered and enveloped).

But the image that thus came to light caused her severe psychic suffering. She became resistant to any further engagement in a psychoanalysis that was so painful, above all if I was only going to occupy myself with her in order to drop her afterwards. This fear turned out to be a repetition in the transference of the principal traumatic episode of her early childhood, an early hospitalization far from her family, a trauma that we had to work on for several months.

In this treatment we were dealing with other formal signifiers, typical of narcissistic faults, but which from then onwards alternated with linguistic signifiers, typical of neurotic disturbances. The first of these accompanied the recall of this early hospitalization and the intense anxiety of being abandoned that had flooded her: 'It won't work' [ça ne va pas marcher]. Marie herself analysed the triple meaning of this formula:

1. A bone disorder had brought about a two months' hospitalization, then kept her immobilized at home for two years, when she began to walk, and it was feared that she would not be able to regain that function: 'she will never walk [marcher] again'.
2. A number of people whom she had trusted, starting with her mother, had subsequently let her down—that is, they had 'fooled her [faire marcher]'.
3. Marie was worried today, as she engaged in the analytical process, in the way she had worried as a little child in hospital: will this type of treatment 'work [marcher]?' My countertransference reacted to this intense transference as though it were a challenge to rise to: I was convinced that by adopting the techniques of traditional analysis, Marie's treatment could be made to work.

I had to analyse firmly and with perseverance the aggressive and self-destructive use that Marie unconsciously made of her transferential repetitions by putting them at the service of a negative therapeutic reaction.

Nathalie

Observation of Nathalie helps to illustrate a principle that accounts for the importance of formal signifiers: space has psychic properties. There is nothing surprising in this, for space is created by our own minds, and we only find what we have put there. In other words, to use an expression used by Sami-Ali, space is an imaginary reality.

Before it becomes a setting that contains objects, space is not differentiated from the objects that occupy it. Even the expression 'from the objects that occupy it' has no meaning. This lack of differentiation between an object and the place occupied by it in space is the cause of one of the most archaic anxieties that the mind has to face—the anxiety of seeing an object that moves tear out the part of space in which it was located, take it with it, and encounter other objects into which it crashes, destroying their place.

Nathalie, a teacher some 40 years of age, approached me for a third psychoanalytic psychotherapy, because she had read my work on the ego-skin and thought that I could help her. We had several preliminary sessons in which she brought me a lot of material, and in which she described, lucidly and coolly, what intense and archaic anxieties she had: a nameless terror older than words that left her prostrate, mute and suicidal; pain from a skin that was thrashed, or murdered; suffering from being torn away, abandoned or falling into the abyss; a longing for death as an absolute regression to a Nirvana from which all suffering would be excluded; a desire to find herself at the bottom of water where she could not fall any further, and where she would dissolve into the infinite space of the sea; fear of becoming a whirling sandstorm (which reminded me of the novel *The Woman of the Sands* by Abe Kobo). At the same time I was astonished that she did not actually experience any of these anxieties in her sessions.

This transference of a symptom into the treatment did eventually take place. Nathalie externalized not her anxieties but her defence against them by withdrawal. It was an almost completely silent session on her part, during which none of the interpretations that I attempted to offer had any effect. The moment of separation was difficult; she refused to rise. She finally asked me for a glass of water, which I brought for her, and this enabled her to leave. She telephoned on the following day to ask whether there was any point in continuing her treatment; I replied that she had at last transferred into it her fundamental difficulty in communicating, and that we could work on this problem in the next session.

In the meantime I thought about what astronomers could project into space in the broadest sense of the word—black holes, for example, analogues of the black holes in the mind that tormented my patient. Or, again, about Einstein's theme of the curvature of light, which, instead of being propelled in a straight line, bends in the vicinity either of those black holes in which it is in danger of being swallowed up, or of the great mass of stars that exert their pull upon it.

Nathalie arrived for her session. She had read a biography of Einstein. She explained that she had thought a lot about the last session, and she said to me, 'Basically, when I communicate with you I aim at you with my communication, but on the way it bends, gets lost in space, and does not reach you'. Thus the two of us had resorted simultaneously and without conferring to the same thought about an inflection of communication which stopped it from reaching the person it was aimed at. Here the formal signifier was "a straight line that bends'. Her discovery had enabled both Nathalie and me to be sensitive to the distortions of communication between us and to the frequent need to take corrective measures.

Gérard

Gérard is a social worker some thirty years of age. He is in psychoanalysis three times a week, lying on the couch. In the first part of his treatment he transferred onto me the image of a father who was a good technician, but taciturn. Then the transference swung into the maternal register. Two elements came to light. At the beginning his mother had breast-fed him generously, at the risk to the baby of being suffocated by his own avidity. Then, as the child grew, she talked to him in an imprecise, vague and general way, and she bought him clothes that were too big so that they would last longer. The more Gérard explored this register in his sessions, the more he felt a need for intense physical activities outside, in order to develop his breathing, threatened by over-greedy feeding, and to tighten up his muscular girdle (instead of being afloat in clothes that were too big for him). He went on to training on his back, lifting heavier and heavier dumb-bells. For rather a long time I wondered what he was trying to tell me in this way about his lying-down position on my couch. In the end we made the link with the earliest painful memory that he retained from his infancy, and about which he had so far spoken in a manner that was too vague and general for us to decipher its meaning. Lying down in his little bed, he spent an interminable time getting to sleep because he could see facing him on a pedestal table an apple that he wanted someone to give him, but he was unable, and did not even know how, to say that he wanted it. His mother, who received communications as badly as she gave them out, did not react, failing to understand the meaning of his crying, which she allowed to continue until Gérard fell into an exhausted sleep. This was a good example of how the prohibition on touching remained too confused and the containing function of the mother too imprecise to allow the child's mind, feeling secure in its ego-skin, to renounce tactile communication for a linguistic exchange supported by mutual understanding. Practising with dumb-bells was to strengthen and allow sufficient growth in at least one of his arms to enable him to succeed in taking the apple for himself. Such was the unconscious underlying scenario for Gérard's effort to develop a muscular second skin. Here the formal signifier was, therefore, 'an arm extends'.

These three examples are unlike one another because they are taken from different psycho-pathological organizations. Marie is in a borderline state. Nathalie has gone through several autistic episodes in her life. Gérard is normally neurotic. 'My skin is shrinking' conveys the fear of loss of the boundaries between the psychic ego and the body ego and between the self and the environment: the self-destructive instinct is at work there. 'A straight line bends' expresses all the anguish of loss of contact with the primordial object and the deformation of psychic space, as well as the communications that take place there: the attachment instinct is frustrated. 'An arm extends' belongs to the dialectic of weaning and the early Oedipus complex: the desirable apple symbolizes the feeding breast; the arm that extends, erection; the instinct at work is libidinal.

(II) FORMAL SIGNIFIERS
AND SIGNIFIERS OF DEMARCATION

(1) Linguistic signifiers
and signifiers of demarcation

Despite my initial reticence about using the term 'signifier' outside the field of language, I have been convinced by G. Rosolato's (1984) arguments in his article 'Destin du signifiant', repeated at the beginning of his work *Éléments de l'interprétation* (1985). Assimilating the signifier to Bion's alpha element and enlarging the notion, he distinguishes properly linguistic signifiers (articulated to a signified and referring to a referent, they are constitutive of signs) and those that he calls signifiers of demarcation, which he relates to representations of things in Freud's sense. These signifiers originate in early infancy and could precede the acquisition of language; their 'weight of impregnation' bears heavily upon psychic functioning. They allow impressions, sensations and ordeals that are too early or too intense to be put into words that can be committed to memory. To take up the semiotic distinction between sense and reference, it is they that give *sense* to non-verbal communication. They impose themselves on the psyche as ineffable. After the event they can assume value as a sign by fixation to a given signified and thus acquire *reference*.

I would agree with Rosolato about the aim of psychoanalytic interpretation when he writes, 'Thanks to speech, the translation of these [enigmatic signifiers of demarcation] by means of linguistic signifiers is the major function of psychoanalysis' (Rosolato, 1985, p. 9).

I would add several points that seem to me implicit in Rosolato's thinking: linguistic signifiers, i.e. phonemes, are of a fixed and limited number, while their combinations are of an indefinite number; these combinations of signifiers are articulated to the diversity of semantemes, i.e. of signifieds, by means of more or less purely conventional links. By contrast, signifiers of demarcation seem to be unlimited in number. But the formal signifiers that are important for understanding any one person's psychopathology are of a restricted number and are the object of psychoanalytic investigation. Rosolato points out two characteristics that allow them to be identified: their repetition and their incongruity. The articulation of a signifier of demarcation to the sensations of images–affects that posed problems for the infantile psyche do not spring from a collective convention but from an idiosyncratic link, whose individual specificity requires recognition and being brought to light by the work of interpretation.

All the same—and herein lies a fundamental characteristic of signifiers in general, whether they are linguistic or of demarcation—they develop by differentiating themselves in the form of oppositions, marked out by the presence or absence of a distinctive pertinent feature. Thus, following Freud's article (1925h) on 'Negation', Rosolato proposed the following list of pairs of opposites for signifiers of demarcation (their sequence and concatenation were intended to be both logical and chronological, but it would be useful to discuss their order and exhaustiveness in greater detail): pleasure/displeasure–pain; good/bad; presence/absence; inside/outside; passivity/activity; self/others (p. 76).

Still following Rosolato, the signifier of demarcation is delimited (demarcated) as a figure on a background (ibid.). While I agree with its importance, the figure–background scheme does not seem to me to be capable on its own of exhausting the richness and diversity of these signifiers: in my view it is no more than a particular instance of a more general difficulty: the fragility of the differentiation between two-dimensional and three-dimensional space. Other effects of this relative lack of differentiation could be found among the signifiers that I call formal, and other types of lack of differentiation should be taken into account (I have cited for Nathalie the lack of differentiation between straight line/bent line).

I would agree with Rosolato when he states that 'it is signifiers that are our objects in a continuous interaction between sensations whose impact is perceptual, the initial innate responses of the baby, and the anticipatory attention of the mother to signifiers of demarcation' (p. 32). But I am less in agreement when he is content to outline a very classical list of these 'objects' which seem to be (but he does not formulate it that way) primary signifiers: the breast, the anal object, the gaze, the voice, the phallus. The signifiers that I prefer to call 'formal' are, in effect, constitutive not so much of 'objects', which form the fundamental unconscious psychic contents, as of psychic containers. Rosolato's thinking remains silent about the role and vicissitudes of the distinctive opposition of container/contained.

By contrast, it is absolutely explicit about the characteristic spatial dimension in the register of the signifier of demarcation: 'Memory of experiences of analogical type that were had during infancy, images that have remained sheltered from language, relations between different sensorial stimuli . . . that embody relations with other people, with the mother of early infancy, in bodily contact, or a spatial position, a kind of bearing, a closeness' (p. 44). Rosolato underlines the importance of the analogical body language that permits understanding without words, which ensures community with others by means of the interplay of sympathies and adherences: 'here therefore there is certainly an area of reciprocal identification, properly somatic and tactile' (p. 69).

The only example of a signifier of demarcation that I have found in Rosolato's work is not taken from a psychoanalytic treatment. It is Freud's famous observation of his grandson Ernst, involving a game with a cotton reel. 'It is the mother's absence that is metaphorized by little objects thrown aside, by the cotton reel. . . . The only common, analogical point is that of a body (an object) that disappears. The object marked out in this way is a signifier of demarcation' (p. 79). Metaphorical mental activity first of all substitutes one pair of oppositions (appearance/disappearance) for another (present/absent) in a system of communication that is non-verbal (throwing away of objects), then pre-verbal (the sonorous modulation of O); then it substitutes a pair of linguistic signifiers (the phonemes O and A) for the pair of signifiers of demarcation (the cotton reel that disappears and reappears). 'One could therefore say that the 'representative' of the representation' [Freud's *Vorstellungsrepräsentant*], *qua* 'material' element . . . and formal support of the representation (representative that gives the re-presentation), is the signifier of demarcation' (p. 80).

In this Freudian example, the signifier of demarcation constitutes a normal stage of the baby's psychological development, accentuated by the acquisition of reversibility in the operation proper to this signifier. Translated into linguistic signifiers, the signifier of demarcation of the game with the cotton reel could be expressed thus: a body disappears and reappears. There seems to be a considerable difference in structure from the formal signifiers of which I gave examples above: 'the skin shrinks', 'a straight line bends', 'an arm extends', which are component parts of pathological mental organizations with which our psychoanalytic practice confronts us. The transformation of these signifiers is a deformation of irreversible character. The work of psychoanalytic interpretation notably aims to bring reversibility into this operation: by regenerating, through the skin of words that the psychoanalyst weaves, the skin can once more become a global and consistent envelope; the message that followed a curved line can be received correctly if the sender or the receiver shifts sufficiently; the distant object that the arm cannot reach can come closer if one learns to walk (to go to get it) and to speak (to ask to have it).

Rosolato adheres to the expression 'signifier of demarcation' for his double sense of delimitation and separation. In effect this signifier delimits representations; it thereby gives an identity to objects by endowing them with a form that can on the one hand, transform itself (according to the perspective adopted on the object), and on the other hand can fit together with others (according to this author, fitting together is fundamentally equivalent for the signifier of demarcation to the double articulation proper to the linguistic signifier). At the same time, the signifier of demarcation is accompanied by an awareness of difference from the referent, which makes it available to enter into a process of symbolization.

(2)   Formal signifiers, pictograms, twilight states

Formal signifiers are related to the pictograms that Piera Castoriadis-Aulagnier, in *La violence de l'interprétation* (1975), regards as typical of the original level of the psyche, or, rather, they constitute a first stage in the symbolization of these pictograms. They arise from what Joyce McDougall (1986) calls 'archaic hysteria', which she has studied especially with patients presenting various psychosomatic illnesses. She draws attention to what is at stake with the signifiers that I call formal: they represent a struggle for psychic survival. She illustrates this with the case of a patient who had rid her psychic ego of all hostile thoughts towards an intrusive mother and a retiring father in order to preserve refined, non-bodily links with them, so that her 'distress could only be expressed in an archaic and non-symbolic manner, by somatic dysfunctioning' (p. 42). 'This is why we do not encounter those compromise solutions to sexual and oedipal problems proper to neurosis, but a primitive sexualization involving the whole body, which offers itself as site for the conflict' (p. 14).

The formal signifier is inscribed within the setting of an original phantasy requirement, which J. McDougall translates thus: 'One body between two, one psyche between two' (in other words, 'a being missing half of itself'), which is another way of describing what I mean by the ego-skin, but an ego-skin confronted with a severely conflictual maternal imago—'promise of life and threat of death'. The split in this imago goes hand-in-hand with the split in the psychic ego and the body ego. Still more dreadful than the phantasy of a mother with the penis, 'the representation which the mother has of her own sex, and which she transmits to her child, relates to the image of a boundless void' (p. 15). The formal signifier is an attempt to delimit this void as well as being an imaginary realization of the various ways in which the body ego of the child could feel itself sucked in by this void.

Another consequence of the disturbance of the ego that underlies the formal signifier is that it cannot be repressed, since the ego does not yet have repression at its disposal, which it tends to impose upon itself in the form of a hallucinatory experience. What Freud described in 1900 for the dream in the last chapter of *The Interpretation of Dreams* (1900a) also applies to the formal signifier: not only is there a retrogressive movement in the psychic apparatus from the motor pole towards the perceptual pole, but this topographical regression is also accompanied by a twilight state, intermediate between waking and sleeping. The formal signifier is often experienced by the patient as a particularly distressing dream, like a waking nightmare.

(III)   CHARACTERISTICS OF FORMAL SIGNIFIERS

The formal signifier has a different structure from a phantasy. The phantasy scenario characteristic of neurosis is constructed on the model of the sentence, which it puts into essentially visual images, and it is therefore later than or contemporary with the acquisition of language: it includes a subject, a verb, and a complementary object; the subject and object are persons (or animals that stand for them); there is usually also a spectator of the action, who represents the subject of the statement in so far as he is distinct from the subject of what is stated; the action takes place in a three-dimensional space. The instinctual cathexis is made up of sexuality and aggressiveness. The typical example is 'a child is being beaten', with the implication: by his father.

By contrast, formal signifiers:

- are made up of images that are proprioceptive, tactile, coenesthetic, kinesthetic, postural, or to do with balance; they have nothing to do with the distance sense organs (sight and hearing);

- when put into words, they are limited to the verbal syntagma, i.e. to a grammatical subject and a verb; the sentence that translates them has no complement;

- the verb is usually reflexive; it avoids the active as well as the passive voice;

- the grammatical subject is an isolated physical shape or a piece of a living body, not an entire person;

• it is uncertain whether the subject is qualified by a possessive adjective (my) or by an impersonal article (the, a);

• it does not involve a scene either in the theatrical sense or in the architectural sense, but a transformation of a geometrical or physical characteristic of a body (in the general sense of a portion of space), a transformation that brings about distortion or even destruction of its shape;

• this transformation takes place without a spectator, and it is often felt by the patient as alien to himself;

• it takes place in a two-dimensional space;

• these transformations are primarily due to various types of confusion between inside/outside (while the action in phantasy scenarios is due to confusion between imaginary/real);

• formal signifiers are monotonous, repetitive and identical in any given patient (they do not give rise to variations, as happens in phantasy with its permutations of places and persons);

• the pathological formal signifier undergoes a distortion that is felt to be irreversible, and which fuels the negative therapeutic reaction.

(IV) CLASSIFICATION OF FORMAL SIGNIFIERS

In a first category of formal signifiers, a spatial configuration is at work or undergoes an irreversible modification, whose paradigm seems to me to be: a shared skin is torn away. Here are some examples:

• a vertical axis is reversed;

• a support collapses;

• a surface puckers, or a band twists;

• a plane surface buckles and whirls;

• a flat surface undulates;

- a bubble closes in on itself;
- a volume flattens out;
- a pierced bag leaks;
- a hole sucks in.

A second category relates to the basic states of matter:

- a solid body is passed through;
- a gaseous body explodes;
- a liquid body pours out or is agitated.

A third category introduces the reversibility of the transformation:

- an orifice opens and closes;
- an object disappears and reappears;
- a cavity empties and is replenished;
- a glove turns inside out.

A fourth category introduces the fitting together of signifiers:

- a boundary intervenes;
- a cover goes on top;
- a pocket stores;
- different perspectives are juxtaposed.

A fifth category brings into play the symmetry or dissymmetry of the transformation and presupposes that individuation has been achieved:

- my double leaves me or controls me;
- my shadow accompanies me, or I accompany my shadow;
- my inside is sought/found outside; an external being is preserved inside.

A sixth category adumbrates the passage of formal signifiers into phantasy scenarios supported by linguistic organization:

- an object that approaches persecutes me;
- an object that goes away abandons me.

(V) FORMAL SIGNIFIERS
AND FUNCTIONS OF THE EGO-SKIN

My grid of the nine functions of the ego-skin permits an interpretation of formal signifiers.

The toxic or self-destructive function is illustrated by Marie's case quoted above: the sensation of skin shrinkage translated a psychic impulse to obliterate herself.

The function of support or maintenance was the first to be reestablished in this patient after three months of constant internal struggle on her part and mine against her suicidal temptations. She recovered not only a global skin, but she experienced more particularly, and for the first time in an intense way, the feeling of having a back, of being able to be backed up and stand on her own two feet. The wish to die and its attendant anxiety disappeared. What was still missing can perhaps be localized on her body image: from then on she possessed a spinal column and a skin, but there was not yet any flesh between the two. This absence of living and life-giving flesh was translated into a prolonged anorexia: she had nothing but skin on her bones. Psychoanalytic work on psychic containers and their self-destruction must not make us lose sight of parallel work on the need for the primordial object and on the effect of its lack.

To remedy this emaciation, which was on the verge of becoming catastrophic, Marie, with my support, took the decision to be hospitalized and in this way to put an end to this impulse to refuse to take anything from an object that could only be bad.

The containing function of the ego-skin was metaphorized by Noémie in the form of a small shaggy animal that I could not immediately identify. Tucked away in her bag, it accompanied her all the time, night and day; it 'slept with her in her lap'. After an initial period of persecuted mistrust of the analyst, she marked her entry into a therapeutic alliance by showing me this koala and asking me to keep it on my person for the duration of her sessions. The koala, like the kangaroo, is a marsupial; the young are suckled and held by the mother in a furry pouch on her abdomen. When the mother gets up on her

hind legs, the little one can explore the outside world by looking around while remaining not only protected but curled up in
the warmth and softness of this fold of the maternal skin.
Noémie, who is an adult, thus behaved as though in child psychotherapy. Since I accepted entering into this sort of non-
verbal game, Noémie continued to use me as an auxiliary ego
by going on to propose another activity, playful, more evolved,
and this time verbal, that I also accepted—to read her a little
illustrated book for children that told the story of an opossum,
another marsupial, of whom one does not know whether it is he
who sees things upside-down or whether it is the others who
are wrong about him and who understand the expression of his
emotions upside-down. By means of a toy and then a reading,
she brought me the representation of an ego-pouch, which put
me in the picture about which functions of the ego-skin we
should work on.

The function of excitation-screen gives rise to formal signifiers
around the themes of an ego-skin–eggshell (or sea-shell), of an
ego-skin–carapace (or crustacean shell), and of a muscular ego-
skin. I shall borrow an example, developed by Didier Houzel
(1985) in his article 'Le monde tourbillonnaire de l'autisme'. The
formal signifier at work in the autistic child could be formulated
thus: a surface folds back on itself and whirls. Lacking a normal
excitation-screen, the autistic person somehow folds instinct back
upon himself, confounding its source with its object. Houzel proposes as a topological model the 3-torus, which corresponds in
three-dimensional space to what the Möbius ring is in two-dimensional space.

Where the ego-skin's function of individuation is concerned, I
shall confine myself to the following example, taken from Marie's
treatment. She was afaid to see the whole of herself in a mirror,
because she was afraid that she would not recognize herself—or,
rather, that what she would see would indeed be her body, but
topped by her mother's head, with the latter's cold, closed, mute
and deadening face that she generally presented to her on her
return from school, and whose memory she said drove her mad.
Here the formal signifier expresses itself quite naturally in a
sentence with a double meaning: 'I have lost my head'.

Where the function of intersensoriality or of consensuality is concerned—i.e. the function of constituting object constancy by putting sense data coming from different sense organs into contact with one another—I shall mention a particularly distressing psychodrama on the theme that the organs of the body (the nose, mouth, eyes, ears and anus) secede, and each wants to function on its own account, in an anarchy that was so dramatic, concretizing the mechanism of dismantlement described by Meltzer, that the group leader felt himself obliged to take on the role of the skin, which reunited the whole in an envelope. The last verse of Shakespeare's 23rd sonnet, taken up by Masud Khan (1971), provides a formal signifier that is typical of the intersensorial correspondences dear to writers: 'To hear with eyes'.

The ego-skin's function of supporting sexual excitation is evident in the formal signifier cited above in connection with Gérard: an arm extends. This was a masculine signifier. A feminine signifier would be: the hymen is perforated. According to Annie Anzieu, the skin that is shared between the mother and the little girl is first of all imbued with narcissistic libido, and then with sexual object libido. The daughter's approach to the Oedipus complex requires this shared skin to be perforated and torn, so that the little girl can have her own envelope, fit to contain her dawning desires for her father. The holes convey a presentiment of defloration, while the hymen is then imbued with a desire for penetration by the father. The skin that was shared between mother and daughter is thus reduced to an erotized part, the hymen, a membrane shared between the two of them, through which the father passes, the common object of their desires.

The ego-skin's proper function—the libidinal recharge of psychic functioning and the maintenance of internal energetic tension and its unequal distribution among the psychic subsystems—corresponds to the skin as the sensorimotor tonus's permanent surface of stimulation by external excitations. I have already drawn attention to the two failures of this function in my book *Le Moi-Peau*: 'the dread of explosion of the psychic apparatus under the effects of an overload of excitation (epileptic fit, for example), and the dread of Nirvana faced with what would be the fulfilment of the wish to reduce tension to zero' (D. Anzieu, 1985, p. 104). In Samuel Beckett's first novel, mainly written during his psychoanalysis with Bion in London in 1935–36, the character of Murphy, who gives his name to the work, veers between these two extremes: initial retreat from the external physical and social world into the bliss of rocking himself, and a final suicidal explosion from a gas pipe that had been connected up with water tubing.

Finally, the function of inscribing traces itself veers between two extremes: a trace so deeply engraved that it becomes indelible and deadly—the condemned man of Kafka's *Penal Colony* (1914–19); the maternal curse 'You are bad' that pursued Marie— and a trace so fragile that it could be obliterated and definitively lost (whence the fear of falling asleep, and the comfort afforded by the sensitive film of the dream; whence also holes in the memory).

(VI) THE TRANSFORMATIONS
OF FORMAL SIGNIFIERS

Among the formal signifiers already mentioned, those in the last category are all pathological and are signs of a fault or alteration in the psychic envelope: shrinking, curving, flattening out, undulation, sucking-in, whirling, falling, emptying, tearing-out, piercing, explosion; one could consider them as variants or specifications of mechanisms of psychotic defence that are active as much against psychic containers as against their contents: fragmentation, ripping, pulverization etc.

Among the formal signifiers in the third, fourth and fifth categories it is fitting to mention those that Gibello has called representatives of transformation. They are more widespread, more 'normal', more inconspicuous in the material of sessions: overlaying, fitting things together, unsticking, dividing in two, inversion of meaning, tracing, opening/closing, converging, distancing, perspective, separating. . . .

Two of these transformations are particularly important for the development of the mind and would require a special study:

• symmetry on the three planes of Euclidian space: vertical, horizontal, and sagittal;

- reflexivity, at first tactile, olfactory and auditory; then visual and, finally, intellectual.

(VII) INTERPRETATION

The interpretation of formal signifiers is an integral part of the more general work of psychoanalytic interpretation of psychic containers, and it has a specificity that distinguishes it from work that bears upon the contents. Here are several elements of it:

- The distortions of the psychoanalytic setting demanded or inflicted by the patient should be used to reveal the organization of his psychic envelopes.

- It is appropriate to lead the patient to describe the particular configuration of his envelopes (which are generally preconscious) and, if necessary, to name this configuration for him (if it has remained unconscious and if he cannot express it except in gestures, postures, etc.—i.e. in non-verbal material).

- Awareness of the container is a step towards understanding the faults in the functioning of the ego from which the patient is suffering and which can then be connected with particularities of his psychic container. Until the faulty function of the ego has been restored, the psychoanalyst may be led to supply it provisionally in the capacity of auxiliary ego.

- While waiting for this understanding to take effect, the psychoanalyst takes it that these faults can be understood, which reinforces the hope that the patient places in the psychoanalysis and counterbalances the resistance that the negative therapeutic reaction produces, which is all the more intense because the altered functions of the ego permit little control over it.

- The next stage is the construction of the traumas that occurred in the early relationship between the infant and the maternal environment, which have:

1. produced distortions in the psychic envelopes (for example,

confusions between the envelope that receives excitation and the envelope that receives communication;

2. prevented the stirrings of phantasy from developing (one notices their re-establishment when it has been possible to analyse the distortion of the envelope).

• These original traumas notably involve alterations in the distinctive primary oppositions: sensorial, kinesthetic and rhythmic. Although it is non-verbal, this must be regarded as psychoanalytic material in the same way as dreams, phantasies and slips of the tongue, which are structured by language.

• The distortions of communications emitted and received by the patient during sessions should be understood as transferences of containers.

• Interpretation of the container belongs to the topographical perspective, not to the dynamic or economic ones: it is talked about in terms of psychic space, of confusion of objects and their place in space, of deformation of space in the vicinity of objects, of difficulty in bringing together different sorts of sensations etc. upon the same object, the psychoanalyst.

• The patient solicits the personal involvement of the psychoanalyst, and up to a certain point this is necessary for psychoanalytic work on formal signifiers to go well. The countertransference is intensified in its double polarity of attachment and rejection, of love and hate. Interpretation in the first person ('Here is how I personally feel the situation with you . . .') uses the experience of the countertransference as a means of communicating an understanding to the patient.

• With patients such as these, the task is not so much one of analysing as of helping them to operate syntheses. Thus, if the analyst involves himself sufficiently, and in a manner that is sufficiently controlled, the psychoanalytic situation allows them at last to *live* the structuring experiences that they have not had in their infancy: the game with the cotton reel (Marie), transitional area (Nathalie); being alone in someone's presence; access to truthful talk; the effort to get onto the same wavelength etc.

(VIII)   THE ROLE OF FORMAL SIGNIFIERS

In conclusion I would like to emphasize the following points:

- formal signifiers are pertinent for describing the construction of the ego and the self;

- they are readily metaphorized;

- they allow psychic envelopes and their alterations to be identified;

- they are imbued above all with the instincts for attachment and self-destruction;

- their identification is useful to the psychoanalyst for the interpretation of alterations in psychic space and the functions of the ego before interpreting the instinctual conflict.

- a boundary intervenes;

CHAPTER TWO

The concept of psychic envelope

D. Houzel

T he thirst for knowledge leads us to mark out fields of experience in such a way that the invariants we register can be referred to fields whose laws of functioning they define. Wanting to know without reference to lines of demarcation would inevitably lead into an endless accumulation of *ad hoc* rules, such as can be observed in globalizing explanatory systems that refuse to delimit their field of validity.

The individual need to construct a coherence and an identity corresponds to the epistomological necessity to delimit our field of knowledge. This presupposes a capacity to differentiate what properly belongs to us, what belongs to other people and what belongs to the perceptual world.

This epistemological necessity has led philosophers to take an interest in the boundary between two fields of experience: empirical knowledge, which depends upon perceptual experience, and intimate knowledge, which is not mediated by the senses. Philosophy refers intimate knowledge to awareness of the self as opposed to palpable awareness, or else to intellectual intuition as opposed to palpable intuition (Fichte, Schelling). The individual need to carve out a coherence and an identity has led philosophy and then psychology to define concepts of 'self', 'subject', or 'ego'.

Psychoanalysis also finds this double necessity in its practice as well as in its theoretical elaboration. One could even consider it as the field in which these two necessities meet. Here the epistemological need takes the form of drawing the boundary between an interior, or an internal psychic world, and an external or perceptual world. The internal world defines the field of validity of psychoanalytic exploration, which must be radically distinguished from the field of validity of the experimental sciences. In it, the demand for personal identity takes the form of psychic work both in the analysand and the analyst, to sort out what belongs to the psychic world of one or other of them, what belongs to the internal psychic world, and what belongs to the perceptual world.

It is the plane of demarcation between the internal world and the external world, between the internal psychic world and the psychic world of other people, that I have called 'psychic envelope'. I shall stop right at the beginning to review the genesis of the concept in psychoanalytic theory.

(I)   THE GENESIS OF THE CONCEPT

(A)   It seems that D. Anzieu (1974; 1976) was the first psychoanalyst to use the term 'envelope' to describe the frontier structures that are at issue here. Their existence had nonetheless been registered in the early days of psychoanalysis. The psychoanalytic discovery was made almost entirely within the field of neurosis. This could account for the fact that for a long time analysts were more preoccupied with the contents of the mind than with its container. Conscious and unconscious phantasies, affects, representations of things, representations of words, internal objects, etc.—such were the pieces of material submitted to psychoanalytic investigation. Before there could be interest in the container, we had to wait until analysis was better settled on its foundations and had dared to tackle new forms of psychopathology. Child psychoanalysis, psychoanalysis of psychotics and borderline patients, group psychoanalysis and more recently family psychoanalysis have drawn attention to the limiting, enveloping and containing structures, precisely because these new analytic situations were confronting psychoanalysts with possible flaws in these structures.

(B)   Yet psychoanalysis itself could not have come into being without the question of the envelope being raised. I think it is useful to examine the first analytical texts from this angle by locating them within the dynamic process of Freud's discovery and in the light of his long epistolary relationship with Fliess, which allowed Freud to elaborate the discoveries he was making not only with his patients but also in himself. There the question of a limiting and containing structure of the mind took the form of the concept of 'ego'. The emergence of this concept itself sheds light upon the deeper meaning of the psychic envelope. That is why I propose to stop here, in order to consider it in the light of what we know about the evolution of Freud's relationship to Fliess at that time.

It is in fact worth noting that until 1895 Freud did not use the term 'ego' except in a sense very close to that of the philosophy or psychology of his day. Littré gives it the following definition: 'the human person in so far as it is at one and the same time subject and object of thought'. When the term ego appeared in Freud, it was in a very similar sense: see the psychoanalytic texts of 1893[1] and 1894.[2] He used it to describe persons who were self-aware and capable of associating their thoughts in an uninterrupted chain, as opposed to split 'psychic groups' made up of 'representations of painful contrasts' or 'irreconcilable representations'. The ego did not yet have a precise metapsychological meaning.

(c)   Everything changed in 1895; in manuscript G (January 1895) Freud spoke of the 'boundary of the ego'. In manuscript H (24/1/1895) he described paranoid projection as an expulsion from the ego of what was no longer tolerable within it. But it was in the 'Project for a scientific psychology' (1950a [1895]), drafted in autumn 1895, that Freud explicitly introduced the ego as an organization charged with a precise psychic function: to contain psychic excitation and to block the free flow of quantities of excitation inside the mind. What had happened for Freud to arrive at a metapsychological definition from a quasi-philosophical and globalist conception of the ego, attributing to the ego the role of an organization charged with topographical and economic significance?

If we can trust Max Schur (1966), in the correspondence between Freud and Fliess in summer 1894, signs of ambivalence in the relationship between the two friends can be found—a relationship that he called 'quasi-transferential'. But the Emma affair was to bring things to a head during the winter of 1895 and threaten Freud with having to proceed with an abrupt de-idealization of Fliess. The hypothesis that I would propose is that this process led Freud to raise the question of the psychic envelope with a sort of urgency, as though to contain the emotional storm stirred up in him by his relationship with Fliess during the Emma affair. He was to conduct this enquiry in two ways: on the one hand through the dream of 'Irma's injection', the first dream of which he gave us a systematic interpretation, and which inaugurated the work that was to lead to *The Interpretation of Dreams* (1900a); and, on the other hand, through writing the 'Project for a scientific psychology' (1950a [1895]), a text in which he defined the ego with precision as a psychological organization, giving it the meaning of a containing and limiting structure.

Emma was a young woman whom Freud treated by psychoanalysis for troubles that he judged to be of a hysterical nature. In February 1895 he called Fliess to her bedside because he was afraid that he was overlooking an organic complaint. Fliess diagnosed disorders of the oto-rhino-laryngeal sphere and performed a sinus trepanation on Emma. Following this intervention the patient became increasingly ill, until another specialist removed from the operated sinus a band of gauze several tens of centimetres long that Fliess had inadvertently left *in situ*. The aftermath of the removal of this foreign body was complicated: Emma had a severe and life-threatening haemorrhage, and she had another serious haemorrhage several weeks later, before overcoming this dramatic episode. Freud informed Fliess of all this in a long letter dated 8 March 1895. Fliess took it very badly, going so far as to demand retractions by the Viennese doctors who had blamed his intervention as being responsible for Emma's poor state of health. The correspondence that Freud addressed to him during this period bears witness to the emotional storm that the episode had caused to break over their relationship, which he had to still by assuring Fliess of his continuing friendship and admiration.

During the night of 23–24 July 1895 he had the dream of 'Irma's injection'. He wrote it down and analysed it in detail when he woke up. He obviously sensed its importance. Max Schur has clearly identified the Irma of the dream with the Emma of the drama. In *The Interpretation of Dreams* (1900a) Freud gave us the interpretation of this dream, which led him to define the central axis of his theory of the dream—namely, the dream as hallucinatory fulfilment of a wish. Here, he said, the dream-wish was to exculpate himself from Irma's ill health. Schur adds to this interpretation the wish to exculpate his friend Fliess.

I propose to make a transferential reading of the dream of 'Irma's injection', by locating it as far as possible within the dynamic of Freud's 'quasi-transferential' relationship with Fliess. Viewed from this perspective, the latent meaning of the dream could be expressed as follows: 'my solution consists in the psychic exploration of the inner world; it owes nothing to the medical hypotheses of Fliess, founded upon biology'.

Here is the account that Freud has left us of his dream:

A large hall—numerous guests, whom we were receiving. Among them was Irma. I at once took her to one side, as though to answer her letter and to reproach her for not having accepted my 'solution' yet. I said to her: 'If you still get pains, it's really only your fault'. She replied: 'If you only knew what pains I've got now in my throat and stomach and abdomen—it's choking me'—I was alarmed and looked at her. She looked pale and puffy. I thought to myself that after all I must be missing some organic trouble. I took her to the window and looked down her throat, and she showed signs of recalcitrance, like women with artificial dentures. I thought to myself that there was really no need for her to do that.—She then opened her mouth properly, and on the right I found a big white patch; at another place I saw extensive whitish-grey scabs upon some remarkable curly structures which were evidently modelled on the turbinal bones of the nose.—I at once called in Dr M, and he repeated the examination and confirmed it. . . . Dr M looked quite different from usual; he was very pale, he walked with a limp and his chin was clean-shaven. . . . My friend Otto was now standing beside her as well, and my friend Leopold was percussing her through her bodice and saying: 'She has a dull area low down on the left.' He also indicated that a portion of the skin on the left shoulder was infiltrated. (I noticed this, just as he did, in spite of her dress.) . . . M said: 'There's no doubt it's an infection, but no matter; dysentery will supervene and the toxin will be eliminated.' . . . We were directly aware, too, of the origin of the infection. Not long before, when she was feeling unwell, my friend Otto had given her an injection of a preparation of propyl, propyls . . . propionic acid . . . trimethylamin (and I saw before me the formula for this printed in heavy type). . . . Injections of that sort ought not to be made so thoughtlessly. . . . And probably the syringe had not been clean.'

I suggest that the great hall where all the dream took place represents a psychic container, in which the dreamer could stage and activate all his internal objects: 'numerous guests, whom we were receiving'. Freud's preoccupation with Irma's (Emma's) health appeared there explicitly, but the latent meaning of the dream seems to me to become clear if one regards Irma not as a direct representation of Emma, but as a personification of a feminine part of Freud, which submits passively to Fliess's solutions and which consequently held back from a deeper engagement in the psychoanalytic exploration of the mind. Freud reproaches this feminine-Irma part for not having yet accepted his 'solution'. The problem posed by the dream could be formulated thus: 'how is a passive feminine transference to Fliess to be resolved?'

The doctors who intervene in the dream, M (clearly identified with Breuer; and Freud said he made him think of his brother Emmanuel), Otto and Leopold, are so many images of masculine identifications. M represents a paternal image, an image of authority, but one who propounds absurd theories; might this not be the personification of Fliess qua paternal transferential object? Freud says of Otto that he was a brilliant friend, but superficial; while Leopold was a reflective and profound friend. Are these not two images of Freud himself? One is that of a brilliant and ambitious but superficial young doctor whom he can reproach with grave errors like having advised the use of cocaine to his friend von Fleischl, thereby hastening his end, and of having prescribed too much sulphonate to his patient Mathilde, which brought about her death. The figure of Otto also seems directly linked with Fliess, making a therapeutic error and establishing false theories about sexuality (Fliess had recently spoken to Freud about trimethylamin as an important sexual substance). Leopold, by contrast, would represent the reflective and profound aspects of a Freud who takes the time to examine his patient in depth and discovers her internal suffering (the dull area low down on the left), thanks to a patient labour of observation and analysis.

Several indications refer to the analytic method itself. 'In spite of her dress' seems to indicate the purely psychic method of analysis without physical contact; Freud ties in the zone of skin infiltrated at the level of the left shoulder to his own rheumatism of the shoulder revived the previous evening by the work of writing up Irma's (Emma's) case; this indication alludes to notation as an integral part of analytical work.

Thus therefore the dream of 'Irma's injection' seems to have had the function of containing violent transferential emotions which disturbed Freud's relationship with Fliess, but which, as in any transference, surely had much deeper roots. This containing function should be understood in the sense in which Bion later described it, namely as a process of deep-seated transformation which allows unthinkable sensations and emotions to become thinkable and be contained in an activity of thought, instead of being purely and simply evacuated in action or deflected into somatic afflictions, or breaching the boundary between the internal and external worlds in a hallucinatory activity. I shall return to this essential point, but I would emphasize here that this containing function of the dream is figured by a container on a scale commensurate with the emotions and conflicts that required elaboration, the great hall containing lots of guests.

In this connection it is interesting to note the contrast between the beginning and the end of the dream. At the beginning this large container is the place where a scene full of life unfolds with many characters, whom I propose to regard as so many objects belonging to the dreamer's psychic world. At the end, a chemical formula was written in bold type. This all suggests that something had not found a place in the three-dimensional container of the dream and remained in the form of an abstract and two-dimensional formula while awaiting figuration charged with psychic life. I think this something is to be found in the direction of the maternal transference.

The maternal object and maternal transference scarcely appear in the narrative of the dream and the interpretation I have offered of it, even though one could hypothesize that the very setting of the dream, the great hall, might be their representation. They do not appear directly in the commentaries that Freud gives on the dream, but a footnote alludes to them in an enigmatic way: 'There is at least', he wrote, 'one spot in every dream at which it is unplumbable—a navel, as it were, that is its point of contact with the unknown'. I would suggest that there is in this note an implicit reference to a problem that had not been resolved by the dream: how to undo the passive–feminine transference without cutting himself off from his dependent relationship upon the maternal object—the 'feeding breast', as Melanie Klein would say. It is, in my view, this unresolved problem that inspired the writing of the 'Project for a scientific psychology' (1950a [1895]), one of the texts in which Freud explicitly raises the question of the baby's dependent relationship on the mother. Freud still needed Fliess as an object of maternal transference, as D. Anzieu (1975) has stressed: 'Freud felt the unconscious, whose corpus he undertook to establish, as being the body of the misdemeanour from which he needed to exonerate himself, for it symbolically represents and metaphorically contains the desired body of the unknown mother.' The 'Project' seems to me to be a final attempt to bend himself to Fliess's wishes and his biological solution, which here represents the umbilical tie to the maternal object.

(D) In this text Freud defined for the first time a limiting and containing organization of the mind, the ego. Here is the complex definition that he gives of it:

> In fact, however, with the hypotheses of '*wishful attraction*' and of the inclination to *repression* we have already touched on a state of ψ which has not yet been discussed. For these two processes indicate that an organization has been formed in ψ whose presence interferes with passages [of quantity] which on

the first occasion occurred in a particular way [i.e. accompanied by satisfaction or pain]. This organization is called the 'ego'. It can easily be depicted if we consider that the regularly repeated reception of endogenous $Q\eta$ in certain neurones (of the nucleus) and the facilitating effect proceeding thence will produce a group of neurones which is constantly cathected and thus corresponds to the *vehicle of the store* required by the secondary function. Thus the ego is to be defined as the totality of the ψ cathexes, at the given time, in which a permanent component is distinguished from a changing one. It is easy to see that the facilitations between ψ neurones are a part of the ego's possessions, as representing possibilities, if the ego is altered, for determining its extent in the next few moments.

The functions of the ego as envelope, as described in the 'Project', can be summed up in the following characteristics:

(1)   The ego is formed by differentiation of one part of the mind. In the 'Project' it is a 'group of neurones which is constantly cathected and thus corresponds to the *vehicle of the store* required by the secondary function'. Later, in *The Ego and the Id* (1923b), it was to become a differentiation of the part of the id that enters into contact with external reality.

(2)   The ego is the seat of the function of 'judgement', which allows a discharge of the mind from inside outwards to be avoided:

Thus *judging* is a ψ process which is only made possible by inhibition by the ego and which is evoked by the dissimilarity between the *wishful cathexis* of a memory and a perceptual cathexis that is similar to it. It can be inferred from this that coincidence between the two cathexes becomes a biological signal for ending the act of thought and for allowing discharge to begin. Their non-coincidence gives the impetus for the activity of thought, which is terminated once more with their coincidence.

This activity of judgement is as necessary to avoid inopportune and ineffectual motor discharges as it is to avoid hallucination:

It [the ego] learns first that it must not cathect the motor images, so that discharge results, until certain conditions have been fulfilled from the direction of the perception. It learns further that it must not cathect the wishful idea beyond a certain amount since otherwise it would deceive itself in a hallucinatory manner. If, however, it respects these two barriers and directs its attention to the new perceptions, it has a prospect of attaining the satisfaction it is seeking.

(3)   The ego is the agent of 'repression', which protects the mind from being breached from outside. The 'tendency to repression' permits avoidance of a breach of the 'contact barriers' and invasion of the mind by an excessive quantity of excitation, whose affective connotation is pain. The ego can struggle against suffering linked to an external stimulus, as well as against the memory of such a stimulus, which, this time, attacks the internal ψ system, thanks to what Freud called 'side cathexes', i.e. facilitations operating in deflection. The ego can deflect a quantity of excitation from a facilitation that leads to a 'key neurone', and therefore to an effect of unpleasure—a sufficient amount of excitation to avoid the affect of unpleasure. This is how Freud defined 'repression' at that time.

(4)   The ego is endowed with the function of attention. Freud gave a description that is very close to what Bion was much later to describe as the 'containing' function. Bion (1970), moreover, took a close interest in attention, which he made one of the essential functions of the analyst in the analytic situation.

Right at the beginning Freud introduced attention as a function of the ego, which permits the timely recognition of a painful perception—that is, a perception from which an excessive quantity of excitation emanates, a source of displeasure—in such a way as to avoid displeasure by activating side cathexes. This he called 'primary defence'. One can see in this aspect of 'attention' the first beginnings of what was much later to become the function of excitation-screen destined to protect the psychic apparatus from a traumatic overflow.

Then he said that 'attention', as a cathexis coming from the ego, is necessary for the satisfaction of desire, for it allows perceptions of the desired object to be cathected. Thus 'attention' is defined as a cathexis of the ω neurones (or 'perceptual' neurones) by the ego, producing what he called a 'thought interest' commensurate with 'affective interest'.

But 'attention' also serves to contain excessively violent affects:

thus it is the ego's business not to permit any release of affect, because this at the same time permits a primary process. Its best instrument for this purpose is the mechanism of attention. If a cathexis releasing unpleasure were able to evade this, then the ego would come into action against it too late.

Following the neuronal model of the 'Project', Freud described 'attention' as a cathexis from the ego of the ω neurones, perceptual neurones, which have been cathected with an energy coming from an external stimulus. 'Attention' therefore functions by means of a hypercathexis of the ω neurones. Here the attention is turned towards perceptions coming from the outside world, with the specific biological aim of recognizing the object of satisfaction. But 'attention' can be applied to memories, that is, to the internal world; this is the case when the ego's cathexis turns away from the first neurones cathected by the stimulus from the external world, to direct itself towards the furthest neurones yet reached by perceptual excitation: Freud wrote that

it is certain that more and remoter neurones are cathected now than when there is a merely associative process without attention. Here too the current will eventually end in certain terminal cathexes or in a single one. The outcome of the attention will be that instead of the perception one or several *mnemic* cathexes appear (linked with the initial neurone by association).

Here there is a new aspect of the ego, defined by this function of 'attention': the ego is in contact with the external world and the internal world at the same time. Is this not the property of a frontier?

In short, the ego of the 'Project' is an organization that blocks the free flow of energy and prevents breaching of the 'contact barriers'; which delimits the external perceptual world from the internal psychic world by means of its function of 'judgement';

which protects the psyche from a traumatic overflow from outside by means of its function of 'repression'; and which exhibits a double sensitivity by virtue of its function of 'attention', turned on the one hand towards the perceptual world (outside), and on the other towards the world of memories (inside). Finally, it is formed by differentiation of a group of ψ neurones that remain cathected with psychic energy from inside the body in a manner that is permanent for some people and temporary for others.

(E)   Strachey[3] noted that after the 'Project' (1950a [1895]) Freud abandoned the theory of the ego and was not to take it up again until some twenty years later. During this period he devoted himself to the contents of the psyche rather than to its container. For Strachey the structural study of the mind of the 'Project' was a defensive description, 'pre-id'—that is, prior to the description of its instinctual contents which Freud was later to call the 'id'. The resurgence of the theory of the ego in 1914 was to take on a new meaning, that of a 'post-id' description. I think that if one situates the emergence of the concept of ego in the 'Project' within the dynamic of Freud's discovery that had its background in his quasi-transferential relationship to Fliess, then the contrast between the ego of the 'Project' and the ego of the second topography fades, except in so far as the biological form of the model of the 'Project' partly masks its deep metapsychological meaning. If one allows, as I have proposed, that this biological form was to a large extent a concession to Fliess, dictated by the imperious necessity to safeguard a maternal aspect of the transference, a transferential womb, one can see that this attempt was without immediate future and could only disappoint him. Instead of the great hall of the dream of 'Irma's injection', capable of containing all his internal objects and representing the maternal envelope, he had had to construct a whole machinery, as he wrote to his friend: '. . . I had the feeling I was actually facing a machine that was eager to function on its own' (letter to Fliess, 20/10/95). His attempt was akin to the construction of a 'false self', as described by Winnicott, namely a personality constructed not from the inside but from the outside, to answer to the mother's wishes; it is also akin to the 'second skin' described by E. Bick as being a substitute for the 'psychic skin' when the maternal container is unsatisfactory. Freud very soon abandoned the model of the 'Project'; in February 1896 he substituted the term 'metapsychology' for 'psychology', which he had used to describe the model of the 'Project', thereby clearly marking his abandonment of the biological envelope that he had thought he had to give his thinking. This abandonment must not be understood as a renunciation of reference to the body, but from then on reference to the body was no longer made through biological analogies; it was made through the theory of anaclisis, which is quite another matter.

It is interesting to note that the resurgence of the metapsychological theory of the ego can be observed in 'On narcissism: an introduction' (1914c), which Freud wrote in response to Jung's criticisms of his theory of the libido. Thus once again it was violent turbulence in a relationship with one of his closest collaborators, loaded with transferential and countertransferential meaning, that drew his attention back towards the organization charged with containing and delimiting the mind. From then on this preoccupation never left him. In 1915 he discovered the role of identification in the formation of the ego—*Mourning and Melancholia* (1917c [1915]). During the 1920s the second topography provided the opportunity to develop a structural theory of the ego, which, as Strachey emphasized, returned essentially to the basic ideas of the 'Project', while transposing them into a new language and model that were purely metapsychological. Let us note that he now insisted upon the ego's dependence upon the body and the significance of the surface of the psychic apparatus: 'The ego is first and foremost a bodily ego; it is not merely a surface entity, but is itself the projection of a surface' (*The Ego and the Id*, 1923b).

(F) With the exception of Nunberg and especially Federn, few psychoanalysts contemporary with Freud took up the study of the ego from this perspective. It would only be fair in a study of the concept of psychic envelope to pay homage to the work of Paul Federn, who introduced the notion of the 'frontier of the ego' and who studied its variations in psychoses, dreams, and states of falling asleep and waking up.

The American school of Ego Psychology (Kris, Hartmann and Löwenstein) has only retained the adaptive role of the ego and has made the ego into an autonomous organization, fuelled by a desexualized energy. There is no need to insist upon the total rupture of this conception of the ego with that of Freud and with that of the current that led towards the concept of psychic envelope.

For Jacques Lacan, the ego is reduced to the sum of the subject's identifications, as Freud described in *The Ego and the Id* (1923b). It is, he says, '. . . the superimposition of the different mantles borrowed from what I shall call the bric-à-brac of its store of accessories' (Lacan, 1978, p. 187). But in this view this imaginary bric-à-brac masks the truth of the subject, which is of a symbolic order. The analyst's work consists in identifying these imaginary levels of the psyche, which Lacan feels are necessarily alienating, to allow the truth of the subject to come through. He certainly recognizes the ego's dependence upon the body, but only to denounce it as a decoy, which leads him to describe in moving terms a psychic world that is tragically riven:

> His body image is the principle of any unity that he perceives in objects. Now, he cannot perceive the unity even of this image except from outside, and in an anticipated fashion. Because of this dual relationship he has with himself, it is always around the wandering shadow of his world. Objects will all have a fundamentally anthropomorphic character, shall we even say egomorphic. Man's ideal unity, which is never attained as such, and escapes him at every moment, is evoked at every moment in this perception. The object is never definitively his ultimate object, unless it be in certain exceptional experiences. But it then presents itself as an object from which man is irremediably separated, and which confronts him with the very figure of his dehiscence within the world—an object which of its essence destroys him, pains him, which he cannot join up with, and in which he cannot truly find his reconciliation, his adherence to the world, and his perfect complementarity on the plane of desire. Desire has a radically torn character. [Ibid., p. 198]

What Lacan proposes is obviously the very opposite of the formation of a psychic envelope. It would be more like an anchoring point on an impersonal verb from which the whole of the subject's organization would be suspended, like a mobile from its point of attachment. It is striking to note that his reading of the dream of 'Irma's injection' is accentuated in precisely the opposite way to what I have proposed. Where I see the dreamer's internal world peopled with living psychic objects, Lacan sees an 'imaginary chaos'. Where I see two-dimensional elements that the dream cannot elaborate, Lacan sees the 'I of the subject', a curious 'I' because it is acephalous and totally impersonal. He writes,

> In the dream of Irma's injection, it is at the moment when the dreamer's world is plunged into the greatest imaginary chaos that discourse comes into play, discourse as such, independently of its meaning, because it is a senseless discourse. It appears when the subject decomposes and disappears. In this dream the fundamentally acephalous character of the subject is recognized once a certain limit has been passed. This point is designated by the AZ^4 of the formula for trimethylamin. This is where the I of the subject is at this moment. And it is not without humour or hesitation that I have proposed that you should see the last word of the dream in this, since it is almost a joke. At the point at which the hydra has lost its heads, a voice that is no more than nobody's voice makes the formula of trimethylamin come up, as the last word about what it is about, the word of everything. And this word means nothing unless it is that it is a word. [Ibid., p. 202]

Lacan's model diverges from the model of the psychic envelope by virtue of its topological properties; the three-dimensionality of the great hall contrasts with the two-dimensionality of the chemical formula written in heavy type; the ramified structure of signifiers of the symbolic order contrasts with the density of the psychic envelope.

Melanie Klein did not propose a theory of the psychic envelope. She did assume the existence of an early ego that was capable from birth of forming relationships with external objects and introjecting them in order to build up an internal world. One would be wrong, however, to reduce her thinking about the containing structures of the mind to a theory of the early ego already formed at the outset, like Athena springing fully armed from the head of Zeus. Melanie Klein was describing an early ego that is poorly integrated, fragile and ready to split, even to disintegrate. It needs to internalize a good object in order to become stable and integrated:

> The feeling of containing an unharmed nipple and breast—although co-existing with phantasies of a breast devoured and therefore in bits—has the effect that splitting and projecting are not *predominantly* related to fragmented parts of the personality but to more coherent parts of the self. This implies that the ego is not exposed to a fatal weakening by dispersal and for this reason is more capable of repeatedly undoing splitting and achieving integration and synthesis in its relation to objects ['On identification', 1955]

On the other hand, the description she gave in 1946 of the mechanism of projective identification ('Notes on some schizoid mechanisms') as a splitting of a part of the self that is projected into the object, is an essential conceptual instrument for our understanding both of the genesis of the psychic envelope and of its states of dehiscence.

It remains true, however, that her conception of the early ego made her avoid certain questions concerning the genesis of the psychic container. It seems to me that it was partly in reaction to this monadological position that Winnicott proposed his concepts of transitional object and phenomenon (1951), of true and false self (1960) and of potential space (1971).

(II)   THE PROPERTIES
OF THE PSYCHIC ENVELOPE

(1)   Its structure

The analytic approach is not deductive. It is based upon a very specific experience, that of the treatment, which strictly depends upon the analytic setting. The whole of the dynamic phenomena observable in the course of treatment within this setting constitute the analytic experience. Theory must endeavour to describe this experience with the greatest possible rigour. The concept of psychic envelope has grown out of an effort to theorize the analytical experience. Didier Anzieu has recently demonstrated the homeomorphism between the analytic setting and the psychic envelope, when everything happens as though the patient were projecting his own psychic envelope onto the setting of the session.[5]

In order to understand its structure, it is indispensable to refer to this analytical experience, and especially the analysis of the setting, upon which Bleger insisted. Analysis of the contents of the mind depends above all upon elaboration of the transference, whereas analysis of the setting depends more upon elaboration of the countertransference. Here we must take countertransference in the sense of a primitive communication of elements of the patient's mind that are evacuated into the analyst, as Paula Heimann described.[6]

The analyst, listening to his patient's transference and his own countertransference, perceives the psychic envelope as a structure of great complexity that cannot be reduced to a sack containing the elements of the mind. His experience of the skin is the best guide to help him to find his bearings in the analysis of this complex structure, but for this it is necessary that he envisage this experience from a very particular angle, namely from the inside. This does not involve making analogies between the biological skin, as described by histologists, and the psychic skin. It involves being sensitive to the most intimate aspects of our experience of the skin and endeavouring to elaborate this experience mentally. It is in this sense that one can say that the psychic skin depends upon the bodily skin. The skin in question is indeed the skin in which we live, but in the sense in which one says 'feeling happy in one's skin' or 'wanting to jump out of one's skin'. This is not the skin seen by the anatomist. As I have maintained in another work,[7] the psychoanalytic link with the body is of a metaphorical and not an analogical kind.

The most general structural properties of the psychic envelope that we can recognize by following this route are the following: belonging; connexity; compacity.

(a) Belonging

The psychic envelope defines the belonging of psychic elements to a given space: internal psychic space; perceptual space; other people's psychic space.

(b)   Connexity

The psychic envelope is connected, that is, one can join up any two of its points by a line entirely enclosed within itself.

(c)   Compacity

The notion of compacity is not easy to illustrate by intuitive examples. The essential idea is that of the possibility of covering space, called compact, by a finite number of what one could regard as pieces of construction of the said space, 'open topographical spaces'. A discrete infinite space is not compact. In this respect, as I have said above, the psychic envelope is distinct from the network of signifiers described by Lacan.

The properties of connexity and compacity give the psychic envelope the requisite form of continuity for its specific functions. This continuous structure must permit communication among its spaces at the same time as it delimits spaces—that is, it must have qualities of permeability.

The psychic envelope must not be conceived of in a static manner, but rather as a dynamic system that permits a synthesis to be made of the dynamic and topographical points of view, i.e. of concepts of force and shape. There is no psychic force that does not mould itself to a given shape, and no shape that is not supported by an underlying dynamic. The psychic envelope could be compared with a field of force, like that which spreads out around a magnet and organizes surrounding iron filings into precise shapes along its lines of force. The concept of 'attractor' seems to me to be applicable to this aspect of the psychic envelope: if one represents a dynamic system by a space whose every point is furnished with a vector that represents the force that is exerting itself at that point at an instant t, then an attractor would be an invariant sub-space of the dynamic system. It is, in some sense, a shape in which the force at work is being moulded, following its curvature and points of inflection. For example, a valley is an attractor for the flow of water.

The concept of attractor allows a better understanding of Bion and Bick's descriptions that make the nipple–breast the container of primitive oral instincts. The nipple–breast does not contain, in the sense of a receptacle, but it allows a stable form, and therefore a meaning, to be given to the baby's oral instincts; it is an attractor for the dynamic system of these instincts and in this sense it contains them. This poses the problem of the preconception of the object, here the breast, as Bion postulates it. The attractor–object is in fact preconceived, not in the sense of an internal image, but in the sense of an object that comes to complete the dynamic development of the instincts, to stabilize their development, and thus to avoid a psychic explosion (a generalized catastrophe, in the words of René Thom).

The study of the first object relations, which baby observation permits, as well as psychoanalytic treatment of very archaic states like infantile autism, have led me to hypothesize that the psychic envelope is made up of three sheets, which I call 'film', 'membrane', and 'habitation'.[8]

The film

I suggest that instinct can be represented by a non-orientable manifold.[9] The construction of the Möbius strip is familiar; it is possible to imagine the same sort of construction with a greater number of dimensions, such as the construction of the 3-torus: take a cube, in imagination stick its upper to its lower face and its right to its left face, and we get a torus in three dimensions, or a '3-torus', plunged in a four-dimensional space. In such a manifold, everything that leaves the upper face (of the initial cube) enters simultaneously by its lower face; everything that leaves by its right face simultaneously enters by its left face. It is impossible for an inhabitant of such a world to distinguish an inside and an outside. Yet it is not a limitless world.

I suppose that the primitive psychic envelope, which I call 'film', is formed by a non-orientable manifold. I have recently suggested a model of infantile autism based on this conception: the autistic child would be faced with unthinkable anxieties connected with a world such as this, bent back on itself and totally unmasterable. The possibility of treating such children by psychoanalysis would depend upon the analyst's capacity to allow himself to be drawn, without losing himself, into the whirling autistic world, and little by little to give meaning to the child's anxieties, which would have the effect of opening up the psychic envelope and giving it an orientation, so that an inside/outside distinction becomes possible.[10]

Until this opening has been made, what can we say about the 'film', which I give this name to underline its formation by the effect of the surface tension of the instinctual dynamic?[11] Nothing. It is absolutely necessary that it should be loaded with a minimum of representations for it to be thinkable. Instinct, Freud said, 'appears to us as a limiting concept between the psychic and the somatic'. The 'film' is also a limiting concept, not representable in itself. The first representations that can be attached to this sheet of the psychic envelope are very close to body functioning, like a woman patient's phantasy of urinating endlessly in an interminable stream. But one can also find traces of the whirling functioning of the world that is enclosed in the 'film' in certain transferential phantasies, for example the same patient's phantasy in which, during her sessions, I left by a concealed door at the back of the room, behind her, in order to reappear threateningly in the picture that hung on the wall in front of her.

The membrane

Like M. Mahler and F. Tustin, I suppose that the first mode of object relationship is symbiotic in nature. Subject and object are included in a single symbiotic membrane. But within this shared membrane there would already be a privileged direction, represented by an axis linking the subject to the object, which in the baby's primitive relationship to the mother is concretized by the axis tongue–nipple–breast.

David Rosenfeld[12] has recently hypothesized a first form of body scheme that he calls 'primitive psychotic body scheme', in which the self is represented as a system of pipes filled with liquids and gas, in the manner of the arterial and veinous systems; phantasies of spilling away and haemorrhaging are associated with this representation; the elaboration of these phantasies is conveyed by a feeling of the increasing consistency of the psychic contents. Frances Tustin has taken up this model[13] to describe an evolutionary stage in autistic children's construction of their identity. She suggests that this is a more elementary stage of body image than that described by E. Bick, which is the image of the body contained within a skin. I think this image of the primitive body is associated with the first stages of construction of the 'membrane': every opening in a direction of the 'film' would give rise to a tubular system, each branch of which would be oriented according to the axis of relationship to a part-object. A second stage would consist in the gathering together of the whole of this tubular system within a single container.

The weaving of the membrane emphasizes the importance both of the trace and of the function of the psychic skin as surface of inscription, upon which D. Anzieu has insisted. The trace represents the opening of a non-orientable world and the delimitation of a psychic space; it is the beginning of symbol formation, which will continue life by going on consolidating the psychic world and its envelope.

We must suppose that the opening-up of the baby's psychic world takes place in two phases: in a first maternal phase the agent of the opening is the mother's 'capacity for reverie'; in a second paternal phase the agent of opening would be the paternal object, which comes to open up the mother/baby symbiosis in order to guarantee each their own identity, without either tearing the baby away from the mother or cutting him off from his symbiotic roots.

Habitation

To differentiate 'habitation' from 'membrane', I shall borrow the distinction between 'field theory' and 'construction theory' from the physician Nicola Cabibo.[14] In the first type of theory, a phenomenon is described not by the elements that constitute it, but by a field of vectors, each point in space being associated with an oriented and determinate size. Construction theories, by contrast, describe a phenomenon by its component elements, which are considered as stable and invariant according to their localization in the space of reference. The 'habitation' is the aspect of the psychic envelope that could be described in terms of construction theory.

I define the 'habitation' as a sheet of the psychic envelope methodically constructed from perceptual and motor material according to the temporal and spatial reference points of our Euclidian world, in a coherent and stable arrangement whose texture and form are precisely linked with these qualities of stability and coherence.

From a genetic point of view, in order to describe the construction of the 'habitation', there would be room to take up Piaget's descriptions of the development of the intelligence from the sensori-motor stage to the hypothetico-deductive stage. The 'habitation', the outermost sheet of the psychic envelope, contains the 'membrane' in a tangential relationship. This inclusion of the 'membrane' within the 'habitation' is necessary for the coherence of the psychic envelope. In analytical treatment, the 'habitation' is represented by the time–space of the session, the rhythm of the session, the fundamental rule, etc., a setting that is necessary if the membrane is to be woven.

But the 'habitation' can be more or less empty, out of contact with the 'membrane', and consequently out of contact with instinctual and emotional life. Winnicott has described the 'false self', Hélène Deutsch the 'as-if personality', Meltzer 'superficiality', E. Bick the 'second skin', which are so many forms of 'empty habitation'.

This three-layered psychic envelope delimits a triple frontier:[15] a frontier with the internal space of external objects, a frontier with the internal space of internal objects, and a frontier with the perceptual world. I have already insisted upon the frontiers with external objects and with the perceptual world. I would add, following Meltzer, the frontier between the internal space of the self and the internal space of internal objects, which it is necessary to suppose in order to specify a form of narcissistic introjection of 'self-objects' with which the self identifies by a sort of projective identification into internal objects, different from true introjective identification that allows the internal objects their share of mystery, of the unknown, and of the unexplored.

(2) Its plastic qualities

I would formulate the hypothesis that the most primitive levels of psychic bisexuality depend upon the adequate qualities of the psychic envelope, which permit the different parts of the self to be contained and promote their integration. Everything happens as though the psychic envelope's qualities of receptivity and suppleness were located at its maternal pole, while its qualities of consistency and solidity were located at its paternal pole. I call these qualities 'plastic qualities'. A good matching of maternal and paternal aspects would be necessary for the formation of a psychic envelope with the requisite plastic qualities. The two polarities can be split into a hard aspect that is devoid of any receptivity and is not deformable, and a soft aspect that is devoid of shape and inconsistent. They can also enter into a destructive opposition, whether the maternal component engulfs the paternal component, which it succeeds in destroying or gumming up; or whether the paternal component violently attacks the maternal component and tears it. In all these cases the psychic envelope would be marked with the same seal, it would be split into hard and soft aspects that are devoid of proper shape, or torn.

According to Bion, the prototype of the 'container' is the maternal breast, 'breast' being understood as representing all the communications between baby and mother. The experience of feeding functions as an axis of reference for this primitive communication, and the breast is its most figurable aspect. But mother/baby communication includes many features other than mere satisfaction of the need for food. As Esther Bick said, 'the optimal (containing) object is the nipple-in-the-mouth together with the mother's way of holding and talking and her familiar smell'.[16] From a psychic point of view the experience of the breast involves the internalization of a good object into the internal world, a good object that is the basis of the coherence of the self and source of psychic life; but it also involves the formation of the psychic envelope, which must happen before any internalization can take place. One could therefore say metaphorically that the plastic qualities of the psychic envelope depend upon the plastic qualities of the breast in its guise as 'container'. According to whether the infant experiences contact with a supple but consistent container or, conversely, with an infinitely deformable container, or, again, a breachable container, or one that is too tense and lacks elasticity, he will form a psychic envelope that is supple and consistent, or inconsistent and without proper shape, or torn, or rigid. It seems to me that it is here that the first elements of bisexuality and integration of the two polarities—maternal and paternal— are located.

In fact, everything happens as though the container's qualities of receptivity and suppleness were located at its maternal pole while its qualities of consistency and solidity were located at its paternal pole. Frances Tustin has related these two masculine and feminine aspects of the first container to representations of the nipple and the breast, respectively. In phantasy the nipple supports the paternal components of the container, while the breast supports its maternal components. The nipple, firm and erectile, stands as mediator between the baby's instinct and his object; it distils satisfaction and prevents the breaching and omnipotent possession of the breast; it forces the baby to participate actively in the search for satisfaction. In all these functions it is like a precursor of the paternal function, and in some sense marks the place of mediation between instinct and object, between need and satisfaction. Frances Tustin has shown the deep split between these two aspects in early infantile autism, a split represented by a phantasy of a broken nipple, torn from the breast. This split prevents the formation of a true psychic skin and blocks the processes of internalization. She has insisted in the treatment of these children upon the importance of the work of integration of contrasted sensual qualities—dry and wet, rough and smooth, hard and soft etc.—contrasted qualities that she relates to a double paternal and maternal polarity.

I think it is useful to consider integration of the bisexuality of the psychic envelope not only in its economic aspects, i.e., the reciprocal apportioning of the paternal and maternal aspects, but also in its topographical aspects; everything happens as though the maternal container had to be reinforced by the infusion of paternal components into its structure, without being rigidified —somewhat the way in which, from an anatomical point of view, the teguments that envelop the breast are reinforced by fibrous structures converging upon the nipple, fibrous structures that ensure its shape and consistency.

(3) Its functions

The formulations from the 'Project' (1950a [1895]) that I have mentioned are essentially energetic. The concept of envelope is a geometrical[17] or a topographical one. The energetic functions of the ego of the 'Project' must therefore be transformed in order to discover the functions of the psychic envelope. I propose the following equivalences:

1. The ego blocks the free flow of psychic energy; this corresponds to the psychic envelope that contains internal objects, a function of 'containment', in which one can see both the psychic envelope's capacity to prevent the dispersal of internal objects in a boundaryless space and its capacity to connect internal objects among themselves into a coherent grouping.

2. The ego protects the mind from being breached by an excessive quantity of energy coming from the external world; this corresponds to the psychic envelope's function as 'excitation screen'.

3. By means of its function of 'judgement' the ego delimits the perceptual world and the imaginary world; this corresponds to the psychic envelope's role as frontier between external and internal worlds.

4. By means of its function of 'attention' the ego is sensitive to excitation coming from perception, and to memories awakened by perception. This corresponds to the psychic envelope's connection by its external face with objects of the perceptual world, and by its internal face with those of the internal world.

5. The ego results from a cathexis of certain neurones by an energy coming from inside the body, which corresponds to the formation of the psychic envelope by means of a differentiation of the surface of the mind in contact with the external world.

One can therefore extract five functions from the ego of the 'Project', once it is disencumbered of its neuronal 'machinery': containment; excitation screen; delimitation of the internal psychic world and the perceptual world; double connection with the internal world and the external world; and differentiation of the surface of the self. These functions are also to be found in the descriptions of authors who, since the 1960s, have introduced the concepts of 'container' (Bion), psychic skin (Bick), 'ego-skin', and 'psychic envelope' (D. Anzieu).

Bion insists upon the functions of containment, linking and delimitation. Taking up the study of projective identification, he was led to define what he called a 'container–contained' relationship (*Learning from Experience*, 1962), for which he used the notation ($♀♂$). Its prototype is the baby's psychic relationship with the mother, figured by the relationship between the mouth and the nipple/breast. The infant projects into his mother's mind elements of sensorial origin that Bion christened 'β elements', which are non-thinkable elements, incapable of being linked one with the other, and only fit to be agglomerated into what the author calls a 'β screen'. These elements are dealt with by the mother's mind, by her 'capacity for reverie', in such a way that they become thinkable, take on meaning, and can be linked with one another to form what Bion calls a 'contact barrier', taking up a term from the 'Project' which designates a semi-permeable membrane that divides psychic phenomena into two groups, conscious and unconscious.

Without developing Bion's theory of thinking any further, I would emphasize the dynamic and organizing role of the container, which is not confined to a passive function, but which brings about a veritable transformation of psychic elements. The first container is an external object, the nipple/breast in the Kleinian sense, or indeed the mother's 'capacity for reverie'. The transformation of β elements by this external container is a precondition for the infant's ability to introject thinkable elements into a psychic space. The membrane formed by α elements fulfils a role close to that of the preconscious of the first topography, but Bion makes us understand its process of formation, which necessarily involves the mediation of an external containing object. He shows us its dynamic role of 'mental skin', as he called it (*Second Thoughts*, 1967), namely a function of organizing the elements of the mind, while Freud's preconscious had an essentially economic definition.

Esther Bick defined the 'psychic skin' in an article published in 1968.[18] The following quotation sums up the functions that she attributes to it:

The thesis is that in its most primitive form the parts of the personality are felt to have no binding force amongst themselves and must therefore be held together in a way that is experienced by them passively, by the skin functioning as a boundary. But this internal function of containing the parts of the self is dependent initially on the introjection of an external object, experienced as capable of fulfilling this function. Later, identification with this function of the object supersedes the unintegrated state and gives rise to the fantasy of internal and external spaces. Only then the stage is set for the operation of primal splitting and idealization of self and object as described by Melanie Klein. Until the containing functions have been introjected, the concept of a space within the self cannot arise. Introjection, i.e. construction of an object in an internal space, is therefore impaired. In its absence, the function of projective identification will necessarily continue unabated and all the confusions of identity attending it will be manifest. The stage of primal splitting and idealization of self and object can now be seen to rest on this earlier process of containment of self and object by their representative 'skins'.

This quotation defines, in a very condensed manner, several functions of the 'psychic skin':

• It contains psychic objects, both in the sense of preventing them from spilling out into an unbounded space and in the sense of permitting connections between them. This latter aspect of the psychic skin differentiates the true psychic skin from the 'second skin', which only has the power to collect together the parts of the personality, without this aspect of connection between the parts.

• The function of excitation screen is not explicitly stated by Bick. However, one can see its equivalent in the role of the psychic skin in establishing the first splitting-and-idealization of self and object, which, in Melanie Klein's theory, plays the role of protecting the internal world from all inassimilable intrusions.

- The function of delimitation between internal and external world is clearly described by the phrase: 'until the containing functions have been introjected, the concept of a space within the self cannot arise'.

- It seems to me that the two last aspects I have mentioned of the ego of the 'Project'—the ego's connection by its internal face with the intrapsychic world and by its external face with the perceptual world, and the ego's formation through differentiation of the surface of the mind—are condensed by Esther Bick when she said that the earliest process of containment of self and object takes place through their respective skins.

D. Anzieu initially recognized three functions of the 'ego-skin' in his first article in 1974: 'A function as containing and unifying envelope of the ego, a function as barrier that protects the mind, and a function as filter of exchanges and inscription of the first traces. . . .' He later differentiated other functions. Thus in 1984 he described seven functions of the 'ego-skin':

1. A function of maintaining the mind, which corresponds to what Winnicott called 'holding': 'The ego-skin is a part of the mother—especially her hands—that has been internalized and keeps the mind in a functioning state, at least during waking, in the same way as the mother keeps the baby's body in a state of unity and solidity during the same time'.

2. A function of container: 'just as the skin envelops the whole body, the ego-skin seeks to envelop the whole of the psychic apparatus, an effort that subsequently proves to be misconceived, but which is necessary at the beginning. The ego-skin is represented as a husk, and the instinctual id as its kernel: each of these two terms needs the other. The ego-skin is not a container unless it has instincts to contain, to localize in their bodily sources, and later on to differentiate.'

3. A function of excitation screen.

4. A function of individuation: 'the ego-skin ensures a function of individuation of the self, which affords the latter the feeling of being a unique being.'

5. A function of intersensoriality, which leads to the construction of 'common sense': 'the ego-skin is a psychic surface that interconnects sensations of different sorts and makes them stand out as figures on this primary ground that the tactile envelope is.'

6. A function of support for sexual excitation: '... on the basis of which erogenous zones can be localized and the difference between the sexes can be envisaged.'

7. A function of libidinal recharge, which Anzieu links with a function of inscribing tactile sensorial traces.

In his recent work on the ego-skin that appeared in 1985 he differentiated two further functions:

8. A function of inscribing tactile sensorial traces, which is thenceforward clearly distingished from the function of libidinal recharge. He relates this function to the concepts of 'pictogram' proposed by P. Castoriadis-Aulagnier in 1975 and 'shield of Perseus' proposed by F. Pasche in 1971, as well as the function of presenting the object described by Winnicott in 1962.

9. A self-destructive function: '... negative function of the ego-skin, an anti-function that is in some sense in the service of Thanatos. . . .'

(III) CONCLUSION

Out of a concern for rigour it seemed to me necessary to tackle the study of the concept of psychic envelope in as formal a manner as possible. However, I hope this formalism does not mask the richness and fecundity of the concept. It is often on the interfaces of several fields of experience, or several fields of knowledge, that new facts or new ideas spring up. The psychic envelope is by nature located on the boundaries of different individual psychic spaces, which makes it into a complex and very rich structure. But the concept itself is located at the intersection of several different analytical and epistemological fields, which doubtless accounts for its fecundity. I shall do no more than mention these various fields.

In individual treatment, whether of children, adolescents or adults, the concept of psychic envelope subsumes at one and the same time aspects of the analysand's mental functioning, aspects of the analytic setting, and aspects of the countertransference.

The extension of psychoanalysis to group situations, family therapy and institutions confronts the analyst with new aspects of mental functioning, which lead to the definition of supra-individual psychic envelopes—group, family and institutional.

It is doubtless no accident that we are part of a general movement in modern thought, which in a certain sense ties up with presocratic philosophy by challenging both the positivism of the last century and the rigid structuralism of the first half of this century. In taking an interest in the fluctuations of psychic phenomena, in the wave fronts of the dynamic systems that underlie them and in the deformations of the interfaces between psychic spaces that result, psychoanalysis is no more than following the same movement. This is a movement of letting go in which the spirit accepts losing mastery of its object of knowledge in order to allow itself to be surprised by the unexpected and be questioned by change.

The deductivist ideal of Hilbert's programme (1917), ruined by Gödel's theorem (1931), has been replaced by theoretical models that are often more descriptive than explanatory, but which allow the infinite variety of forms and happenings to scintillate without imprisoning them within a narrow determinism: catastrophe theory[19] and turbulence theory with its strange attractors,[20] fractal object theory[21] and the theory of order through fluctuation.[22] Psychoanalysis has contributed to preparing the mind for this epistemological upheaval, and it is only fair that it should reap its fruits.

NOTES

1. A case of successful treatment by hypnotism (1892–93); Some points for a comparative study of organic and hysterical motor paralyses (1893c); Charcot (1893f).

2. The neuro-psychoses of defence (1894a).

3. In *The Standard Edition of the Complete Psychological Works of Sigmund Freud, Vol. 1* (London: The Hogarth Press, 1966), pp. 283–293.

4. Lacan uses AZ to designate nitrogen in the chemical formula, whose symbol is, of course, N.

5. Cadre psychanalytique et enveloppes psychiques, *Journal de la Psychanalyse de l'enfant, 2* (1986): 12–24.

6. On countertransference, *International Journal of Psycho-Analysis, 31* (1950).

7. Interprétation: Métaphore ou analogie, *Journal de la psychanalyse de l'enfant, 1* (1986): 159–173.

8. Le monde tourbillonnaire de l'autisme, *Lieux de l'enfance, 3* (1985): 169–183.

9. In topology the term 'manifold' designates a generalization of the notion of surface.

10. Le monde tourbillonnaire de l'autisme (note 8 above).

11. D. Anzieu has recently described the ego-skin as a sensitive surface capable of registering traces and inscriptions, under the name of 'dream film' in *Le Moi-Peau* (Paris: Dunod, 1985).

12. Esquema corporal psycotico, *Psicoanalisis, 4* (1982): 383–404; Hypochondrias, somatic delusion and body scheme in psychoanalytic practice, *International Journal of Psycho-Analysis, 65* (1984): 377–387.

13. The development of 'I-ness', in *Autistic Barriers in Neurotic Patients* (London: Karnac Books, 1986), pp. 215–236.

14. L'unification des forces fondamentales, *La Recherche, 148* (1983): 1216–1224.

15. Cf. D. Houzel, L'Évolution du concept d'espace psychique dans l'oeuvre de Mélanie Klein et de ses successeurs, in *Melanie Klein aujourd'hui* (Lyon: Cesura Press, 1985), pp. 123–138.

16. The experience of the skin in early object relations, *International Journal of Psycho-Analysis, 49* (1968): 484–486; this quotation is from the French version, in D. Meltzer et al., *Explorations dans le monde de l'autisme*, trans. G. & M. Haag, L. Iselin, A. Maufras du Chatellier & G. Nagler (Paris: Payot, 1980).

17. In differential geometry, a manifold tangent at each of its points with one of the manifolds of the family in question is defined as the 'envelope' of a family of manifolds dependent upon a parameter.

18. See note 16 above.

19. R. Thom, *Stabilité structurelle et morphogenèse* (Paris: Ediscience, 1972); *Modèles mathématiques de la morphogenèse* (Paris: Christian Bougois, 1980).

20. D. Ruelle & F. Takens, On the nature of turbulence, *Communications in Mathematical Physics, 30* (1971): 167.

21. B. Mandelbrot, *Les objets fractals: forme, hasard et dimension* 2nd ed. (Paris: Flammarion, 1985).
22. I. Prigogine & I. Stengers, *La nouvelle alliance* (Paris: Gallimard, 1979).

CHAPTER THREE

The dream envelope
and the phantasy
of a 'common psyche'

A. Missenard

(I) WORKING ON THE DREAM

The goddess Thetis held her son Achilles by the heel to plunge him in the waters of the Styx so that he would lose in them the 'humanity' and fragility that he had inherited from his father. Siegfried became invulnerable by bathing in the blood of a vanquished dragon; but a lime leaf prevented the blood from spreading over his back. For one the heel, and for the other the back remained vulnerable zones, through which these heroes met their deaths.

People who function on the basis of heroic identifications, like airmen, and especially fighting airmen, conduct their dangerous lives on the basis of a feeling of invulnerability, which is transformed into a feeling of security after a long, difficult, and selective apprenticeship for their professions. Metapsychological reflection reveals that these feelings are indissociable from a 'narcissistic envelope' that is grafted onto the ideal maternal ego,

---

This paper takes up a previous article published under the title, Rêves de l'un, rêves de l'autre. *Psychiatrie, 4* (1985): 67.

the first links, and a feeling of omnipotence, but which cannot be separated from the negative narcissism that marks the origin of the hero's vocation.

When a flying accident happens with no bodily, if not emotional, damage, it often precipitates a traumatic neurosis: the scene of the accident is relived in racing thoughts by day and in dreams by night. It is possible to demonstrate (Missenard, 1979) that the accident functioned as a wild interpretation. In fact it presented the airman, on the level of reality, with the representation of an unconscious scenario that was central to his psychic organization and vocation: it figures an 'explosive encounter', which I have called his 'original annihilation'. The narcissistic envelope is torn, the organizing phantasy can no longer be contained within the psyche, and mastery of space outside is no longer wished for. Positive narcissism threatens to pour out through the breach like a haemorrhage.

The dream that repeats not the accident itself but the instant that preceded it is an attempt to link up two times: the one before, with its feeling of invulnerability, and the one afterwards, when the reality of death was confused with the phantasies that had underlain love of the profession. The dream is an attempt to repair the breach, not only an attempt to master the outrush of excitation—an insufficient economic perspective on its own—but a 'repeat' on the psychic plane of what had composed the subject; he was confirming afresh that he was appropriating this relationship to death that had been wished upon him from the very beginning. The resort and return to phantasy are an attempt at symbolization by means of images—the dream—and words—the narrative that is made of it. In parallel, the social aeronautic body aims to reinstall the accident victim in the common body of the collectivity by means of its presence and action after the accident, to relocate him as an equal connected to the group, its ideals, its heroes, and those who embody them.

Symbolic and identificatory references form the setting within which, in the dreams of traumatic neurosis, a repetitive return to the primary, the phantastic, and the life and death instincts (which have suddenly been threatened with being unbound) is actualized until they can be elaborated.

Here elaboration means sublimation that will ensure that the instinctual will be transformed and partly taken up into an activity with social value, giving the subject a social identity and a symbolic identification (inscribed in the *socius*). Here therefore dream has an envelope function that is not only a topographical function but also a function of transforming and elaborating the fundamental unconscious conflict, with the aim of reconstituting the subject's narcissistic organization.

These remarks about traumatic dreams repeat my earlier propositions and tie in with those of D. Anzieu (1984). For him, the dream envelope takes on three functions: that of a containing sack, a protective barrier, and an active membrane.

The present work is centred upon the last of these functions.[1] As an active membrane, the dream establishes communication between the various parts of the psychic apparatus, while at the same time transforming the material it is dealing with. In its form, this comes from the preconscious—the dream we hear is always a narrative—but it proceeds from psychic reality, which forms the nucleus of the unconscious and has its own origins and fixation points.

Working on the dream means working on psychic reality, its sources and the limits of its knowledge. Can one go beyond the 'navel' of the dream, that stopping-point where, for Freud (1900a), the dreamer's associations stop? Is this 'beyond' accessible? What represents the 'mycelium' from which the 'mushroom' of the dream is produced?

Working on the dream also means attending closely to the situation it emerged from, namely the interlocutor to whom it is reported—and the transference that underlies that relationship—that is to say, the treatment setting or any other context (family, group, early mother–baby relationship) that produces the dream: people dreamt long before analysis. At present analysts find a place in some of these settings outside individual treatment and can study the dream by placing themselves actually within the conditions of its genesis.

Between the setting and psychic reality . . . comes dream. This will be our work space while we tackle this envelope of communication and psychic transformation.

This research has been stimulated by remarks of Freud, mentioning at the end of *The Interpretation of Dreams* (1900a) the 'obscure forces' that animate the psyche, and, in 1925, 'sexual matters' located in 'the darkest unconscious' which date 'from primitive times' and are not unconnected with 'myths, stories, folklore, and legends'. This latter article ('Some additional notes on dream-interpretation as a whole', 1925i) contains an invitation to work afresh on the question of repression in order to shed a stronger light upon the dark and perhaps inaccessible zones. For the oldest memories 'are not lost, but transformed. . . .'

(II)   DREAMS 'FROM ABOVE', DREAMS 'FROM BELOW'

(1)   A dream of RL, confronted with a difficult reality

Treatment is the setting within which the function of the dream and its work of transformation can best be discerned.

Here is a dream of an analysand, RL, who had been in analysis for a long time. He was a scientist who had suddenly been entrusted with work placed under his sole responsibility, and he felt overwhelmed and helpless in the face of the task he had to accomplish:

'I was with friends from my student days. I needed a printed pamphlet on a question of work. Some of them had one, from whom I had borrowed it the day before. None of them wanted to lend it to me. They gave good reasons: some, that they had never had it, others, that they did not have it now. There I was just standing there among them, wondering why they were treating me in this way.

Among these people was Renée Lucie Bailly: she had already given me something for this work I had to do'.

Associations allowed the problem to be located around the prohibition on thinking. The feminine character's initials, RLB, revealed that the dreamer, whose surname initial is L, was framed on one side by a student friend, an engineer like himself, who died young from an illness, and on the other side by a sort of big brother, protective and affectionate, who had been very successful in his professional and affective life.

This dream, which can be understood at several levels, will be the object of two observations here:

1. It constitutes the staging of the analysand's private theatre. It allows different components of his psyche to be seen at a single glance: certain organizations (the superego, the ego-ideal), and behind these his major conflicts and the castration phantasy; in the dream the latter take the place of the prohibition on thinking and the feeling of impotence that were invading the patient's psychic space in waking life. In the dream, the major phantasy only occupied a restricted place, and the patient had retreated from it; a work of elaboration could begin.

2. The dream shows that the patient's current difficulties were referring him to an underlying conflict. The representation of a dead friend (whose surname initial was R) was certainly associated with the incapacity to think, but also with a fraternal friend (B). Each of them was represented, together with the dreamer (RL), in the name of a woman friend who 'had given him something'. In this dream, the subject was no longer under the spell of the mortal prohibition on thinking, as he was in his symptom; he found his roots again, and his major identificatory reference-points.

The dream provided a figuration of the different elements of the patient's conflict—desires, prohibitions and phantasies that had come into play when faced with the task to be accomplished and blocked the capacity to think and create. Dream is a staging of the different planes of psychic space. It is also a secondary elaboration leading to a narrative, starting from which what could be called a tertiary elaboration will be made, one of associations and significant chains that the dreamer will pursue in the context of his transferential relationship.

A general communication is made by means of links of contiguity (figurations in psychic space) and of continuity (associations between present and past, desires and prohibitions, phantasies, organizations): what was separated and dissociated in the subject is brought together by the dream; it brings together something of his name and his roots and what constitutes him in the conflict.

The dream enlightened the patient RL about his beginnings as well as about his initials, and no doubt to a sufficient degree because the day after the dream he was able to get to work and in his turn become creative and take initiatives. This dream that was provoked by a difficult vital situation set in motion phantasy impulses that had previously been illuminated by his treatment (castration phantasy, a link with two male figures and representation of an 'englobing' maternal figure).

The dream's figuration puts the recent situation at work in communication with the subject's unconscious problematic. An elaboration takes place whose elements the dream has provided; it allows the patient to confront a difficult reality in another way.

(2)   A dream of a depressed analysand

In some cases, the question arises whether the analytic process not only gives access to an unconscious problematic, but also produces modifications in unconscious organizations. Some dreams allow this question to be answered, such as that of an analysand who had been depressed for several months.

'I was in a town at night, in the fog and gloom; this town had a mediaeval appearance, there were only a few rare lights; the atmosphere was sinister.

I was at the edge of the town; I got out of the car I was in with my girlfriend G. I entered the deserted town. I went into a house, which was my analyst's (although I didn't recognize it). I was alone, and I thought I would be caught out, since I was afraid I would be blamed for being there and having gone in without having the right to.

I got out of the house without being apprehended. Outside, a crime had been committed, there was a body and blood on the ground. I returned to the car where my girlfriend G had continued to wait for me.'

The period of the depression had been marked up to that moment by insistent (and conscious) fantasies in which the dreamer and his mother died together in a car accident that he had caused. The dream put an end to the repetition of these fantasies; it marked the beginning of a reorganization of unconscious functioning, which led to a separation/distinction from the maternal psyche that had been impossible up to then. These modifications at depth, figured by the dream, heralded a clinical improvement that was confirmed in the course of the succeeding months.

The different significant lines to which this dream led were at the heart of the dreamer's unconscious and concerned his origins, birth and place in his mother's unconscious wishes as an extension in phantasy of his father's violence.

This dream is a transformation in so far as it represents the dreamer in an aggressive penetration in which death is present, and he risks being blamed for it. However, in the dream he has been able to detach himself from it.

In fact his dream represents a collection of distinct spaces, the town, the house and the car with his girlfriend. But these spaces are arranged in a particular way relative to one another: the house is in the town, the town has discernible limits (being surrounded by walls), and the dreamer and the car with his girlfriend are on the edge of this dead town, which the dreamer can enter and leave again. The dreamer is no longer shut up in this town, any more than he was from then on in his relationship with his primary object. The dream provides him with a new figuration of the organization of his psyche.

This reorganization undoubtedly had to be confirmed during the phase of progressive improvement that ensued: the dream returned spontaneously to the analysand's thoughts, as though the recomposition of his psyche with the same materials—but differently—needed to be reaffirmed; as though the separation from the phantasy organization that was figured at the centre of the dead town had to be repeated and gone over again.

For the battles continued for a long time. Even when victory seemed to have been won, occupation of the territory had to be confirmed. At other times the struggle was conveyed by a succession of successes and setbacks. The phantasy organization included impulses that were opposed to one another and which took the lead in turns, according to the whim of the day, and in function also of their own dynamic. Thus a dream that stressed the specific features that made a love object desirable, behind a risk that was rapidly sketched in, was followed the next day by another dream that put to the fore a representation that was threatening in every way, and behind which the object of desire was barely outlined.

(3)   Dreams of a patient with a somatic illness

Not all dreams have this function of communication, transformation and elaboration. In the context of somatic illnesses outside treatment, some cancers given a harsh, multiple, and restrictive treatment make patients live through a dramatic experience that is reflected in dreams. At an overwhelming point in treatment, pain, the feeling of the precariousness of existence, the threat of death, and the temptation to give up the struggle produce a psychic regression.

The dreams of a woman who was ill in this way were then composed of elementary signs, of lines, circles and geometrical shapes reminiscent of the paintings of Mondrian and Kandinsky; making one think, from the outside, of children's first drawings. In this way the patient was undoubtedly transcribing in her dreams the mode of psychic functioning into which her illness had led her; we should undoubtedly see the geometrical signs as the only forms of psychic inscription that the regression permitted. It does not then seem possible that a work of transformation was going on in these dreams comparable with what has been described above.

On the contrary, this work was resumed later on, when the sick woman's dreams were composed of figures, admittedly monstrous and menacing, but nonetheless with a human appearance, which gradually peopled her dream universe.

Some time later there came a dream of 'a breast from which a baby emerged', then a 'a text written with a coloured ink of which one part was visible and the other hidden'.

Here one can follow with the successive stages of the illness and its treatment, the reconstitution of the dream's functions of figuration and elaboration, from elementary traces to the evocation of an inscription which, as in every psyche, included one part that is visible and one that is inaccessible.

At certain points in a very serious illness and its incapacitating treatment, dreams unveil regressive psychic formations that are archaic forms of thought and that undoubtedly correspond to early moments of development, when thought is composed of collective and composite characters, and when everything in it is 'monstrous' (Gribinski, 1982).

Are these dreams without a narrative, with minimal secondarization, and no use of preconscious material, not 'prehistoric' dreams, corresponding to relations with the mother 'before time' (Pontalis, 1977)? They are in any case at the limit of the expressible, made up only of figures. 'The figural' (Dayan, 1985) is an original form of thought by means of images, corresponding to the pictogram and memories before language, and it demands a particular sort of interpretation in treatment, since the function of these dreams is to create a first psychic space.

Thus we are exploring further what Freud (1900) called the navel of the dream—what could be nothing other than the site of the 'unknown' in the relationship with the mother, as Rosolato (1978) remarked, stressing in addition that the navel is a vestigial mark, the centre of the body and sign of a stopped-up fissure. To which I would add that this navel—and the figures that are sketched behind it—is undoubtedly a boundary, a frontier zone, but is even more a common zone where something of the mother and the baby merge so that in treatment it is impossible to tell them apart for a long time.

It is easy to imagine that in certain treatments without dreams, their appearance marks a decisive step and access to a new form of thought.[2]

(4) The dream envelope at work

This latter category of dreams is therefore additional to the two that Freud (1925) distinguished as dreams 'from above' and dreams 'from below'.

Dreams 'from above' are made up of everyday material (or intentions) which, after instinctual reinforcement, seek to represent and resolve a problem or conflict encountered during waking life by integrating the difficulty into an underlying unconscious organization. The RLB dream is an example of this: faced with the work expected of him and the responsibilities that had devolved upon him, the dreamer had felt impotent—which was figured in the dream by the image of his friend R, who had died of an illness. But the dream also produced the representation of big brother who was affectionate and protective, and the whole thing was inscribed within the name of a woman friend, an image of reassuring security. By means of the dream, the problem encountered in the dreamer's life mobilized not only the castration phantasy, but also the other dimensions of the psyche into which this phantasy linked: a figure of an accessible father/brother and an englobing maternal imago that was also loving and generous. The problem he encountered was integrated into the dreamer's general unconscious dynamic at an advanced point in his analysis. Thus a psychic envelope was reconstituted, and thus the breach threatened by the event had been plugged (cf. Anzieu, 1985).

Dreams 'from below' result from the unconscious activity that is going on ceaselessly all day long. The dream is a manifestation of this activity: by means of preconscious representations that are then accessible (day residues) a wish is illustrated that, unconscious until then, could only remain repressed. The saying that 'the best dreams are forgotten dreams' reflects the conception according to which the remembered dream is indeed the guardian of sleep, and according to which psychic functioning aims to keep the instinctual dynamic and the infantile field beyond the reach of representation.

In the dream the dominant unconscious conflict is revealed and the envelope is established which separates two zones of the psyche when the repressed instinctual impulses tend to surface again. In the dream the modifications that the instinctual dynamic has undergone during extreme moments of psychic transformation are also revealed; the dream of the 'dead town' is an example of this.

Whether there have been external events with traumatic effects, or whether the 'events' were internal, both types of dream ensure the transformations necessary for the psychic envelope to fulfil its functions of boundary, communication and transformation.

The dream envelope performs a work of regulation that can be identified on all three metapsychological levels. Thus on the topographical plane it sets the limits between two zones of the psychic apparatus. On the economic plane, making visual (dream image) and/or verbal (dream narrative) representation ensures the transformation of unconscious affects and wishes. On the dynamic plane, dreams—from above and from below—ensure a figuration of the unconscious conflicts and repressed desires of the unconscious psychic organization.

The dream envelope, as D. Anzieu (1985) has emphasized, reconstructs the psychic envelope: the dream weaves again what life has unravelled of the ego-skin.

(III)   DREAMS AND PSYCHIC FUNCTIONING
IN COMMON

The analyst sometimes finds himself these days in a position of listening, elaborating, intervening and/or interpreting in settings other than treatment.

(1)   The mother, the dream and the baby

This case, reported by L. Kreisler (*Revue du Centre Alfred-Binet*, July 1984), involves a baby four months old brought by his mother for consultation because of serious trouble sleeping (agitation with crying, a disharmonious development, and feeding difficulties. At the start of anaesthesia his mother had gone seriously into shock and had nearly died; he himself was born in an apparent state of death but was revived.

Taking a history revealed that the mother had had a phantom pregnancy a year earlier, and that when she was six months pregnant she had lost a sister aged 18 to a violent death; that in the seventh month a brother had a sudden grave illness that put his life in danger; and that a year earlier an elder sister had had to suffer the death of a baby *in utero*. Finally, the mother had had to spend the last months of her pregnancy in bed to avoid a premature delivery. This was her first pregnancy. The consultation revealed a woman objectifying things by describing them from a medical point of view and denying all affect, attending to her baby in a maladroit and rigid way, a baby who was agitated, sometimes fretful and sometimes screaming.

During this consultation, Kreisler questioned the organicity of the troubles that the mother and her paediatrician had insisted upon and mentioned that the current 'indisposition' (and not illness) could without doubt 'benefit from a better understanding of the events and the situation'.

At the second consultation a fortnight later (with father and mother) the troubles had disappeared, the baby was calm and played. The mother could express that when her sister had died she had been afraid she would have a miscarriage and had done her utmost to 'lock away her grief'. And she spontaneously brought a dream:

'A meal, the big family table where no-one was missing. Jeanne (the dead sister) chatted and laughed; no-one was surprised; and yet everyone knew that she was really dead.'

In addition to its clinical effects upon the baby, the therapeutic consultation had brought about the lifting of a massive repression and a transformation of psychic functioning which the dream revealed: the lost object is recognized from then on both in her presence and in her absence.

What therefore are the place and function of the dream relative to the changes that Kreisler's consultation brought about?

The baby's arrival had coincided with the sister's disappearance. Guyotat (1980) has demonstrated the impact of such coincidences: the historical event undoubtedly had the effect of actualizing the mother's ancient death wishes towards her sister and correlatively towards her baby, and to block, as Aulagnier (1975) specified, the necessary repression of the latter. This hypothesis makes sense of the fact that the only (or one of the only) remaining defensive outcome was a massive repression, since what happened prevented any signifier being able from then on to establish a counter-cathexis that would favour repression. The situation was to all intents and purposes traumatic, and the event was the equivalent of a wild interpretation that put its finger precisely upon what should have remained repressed.

What is more, after a baby's birth the mother and infant remain partially indistinct, as during pregnancy, and constitute a single functional unit (cf. below). The baby can still express in his body functioning the psychic dynamic that animates his mother and which she makes him share. In contact with this, the baby then manifests what his mother unconsciously feels about him: 'that he should and should not be'. This mode of functioning had, moreover, been encouraged by the investigations of the first paediatrician consulted.

Kreisler's intervention restored a psychic dimension to this functioning, a dimension that gave due place to affect, unconscious wishes and to the events that had happened. It allowed the functioning to be 'psychized'; it replaced the 'indisposition' in history.

The young mother's dream conveyed how this change had taken place. One could formulate it thus: 'I know very well (that she is dead), but all the same (that she is alive)'. A denial and a splitting were at work in the dream about the sister, whom the baby need no longer replace in the mother's psyche.

The dream reveals progress that resulted from the transferential link that the mother established with Kreisler; it also affords a glimpse into the uncertainties that weighed upon the patient's future: mourning and the evolution of the splitting.

In this episode, the baby was entirely taken up into his mother's psychic dynamic.[3] Between mother and baby it was not so much a matter of psychic communication as one of communion. The baby and mother were still in the phantasy of a 'common skin' (Anzieu, 1985).

The dream reveals a reorganization of the maternal psyche, which was fit from then on to contain what had previously had to remain separated.

(2)   A transferential dream by Sarah

During treatment, dreams reflect the state of the transference and the imaginary representations that the analyst and the analysand bear.

A patient, Sarah, began a session by expressing the sense of lassitude that she felt, of no longer being able to 'save her face'. In the dream that she then reported, 'she felt that she was in danger of being enclosed in a space from which she could not escape. Finally, after having for a long time been taken for a stranger by the people of the house—where the dream took place—little by little they recognized her.'

For the analyst the dream was soon fairly clear: it conveyed the—ongoing—loss of imaginary maternal identifications in a depressive movement that had begun some time ago (I was going to 'lose face'). In the dream other identifications emerged that had so far been repressed. But this dream was not separable from the point in treatment when it happened: it followed upon a period during which, in her life, the patient had sought to make herself recognizable as a woman, sexual and desirable—while at the same time doubting her capacity to succeed in so doing—and no longer as mother–spouse who took all the duties and responsibilities upon herself.

This dream is not separable either from the transferential ground upon which it was drawn, namely the transference of patient and analyst as they were registered since the beginning of this second analysis. For the patient the analyst was at one and the same time, separately and successively, a paternal and a maternal figure, a figure of a man and of an analyst, i.e. referring to a certain theory and the rules of conduct of the treatment.

For the analyst the patient was the child who in some ways subsisted in her, a woman who could also be desired, a mother who had lived under the aegis of an omnipotence that was both satisfying and progressively inhibiting of all sexuality (as the husband gradually became a maternal substitute) and finally an object that installed itself in the analyst's psyche.

The dynamic of the session of the dream could be schematized by means of an intervention by the analyst and the patient's associations. In fact in asking her what 'losing face' meant to her, the analyst was also considering this woman's dominant problematic. How could she reintegrate her sexual desires and abandon the laws her mother imposed? When a woman becomes a pubescent girl, she must exclude herself from all relations with the men of her family, or else she loses face in her mother's eyes. The patient's associations made her shortly afterwards talk about rules—those that reigned in her family of origin, but also her rules of womanhood, and the rules of functioning of the analysis and its setting.

The dream, the analyst's intervention, the patient's associations and the evolution of this treatment are not ultimately separable from what I termed above the 'transferential ground'. In the avowedly disymmetrical analytic relationship, each of the two none the less has a part of themselves in the other, which is necessary for its proper functioning. The proposition, obvious for the patient, also arises in the acceptance of certain patients rather than others into treatment, since the answer to the question is not only to be found under the heading of 'indications' for treatment—at least not without considerably widening its scope. What results is a merging of mutual cathexes, a phantasy complementarity (at multiple levels), and a common fabric of relationship. On this common ground, analyst and analysand obviously distinguish themselves from one another. In the case just cited, the analyst considered on the basis of experience that this treatment would have in all probability to pass through the inevitable defile of a depressive moment, contemporaneous with essential changes—a defile that he could envisage to the extent that he could identify its motive, necessity and function. At the same time there are representations of the other levels of the patient's functioning and of her other dimensions.

But it must be stressed that there is also a shift within the analyst's psyche: the level of material expressed by the analysand and what it evokes in the listener must be distinguished from that of elaboration and theoretical working over of the case, which might rather be called the level of the analyst's 'theoretico–clinical reverie'. The patient's dream and the 'analyst's reverie'—are these not the expression of two psychic organizations that are interlinked and sometimes deeply merged?

(3)   Dreaming one's patient:
'I dream for us'

There are treatments in which the privileged place of dream
sheds an even clearer light upon the analytical process and the
particularities of psychic work in analysis; this is the case when
the analyst dreams of his patient.

Gérard's analysis with Jennie had been going on for several
years. During the period in question, Gérard was being rather
boring during his sessions. My colleague Jennie reported:

'During one session I nodded off for an instant and had a
dream: Gérard had his head in the hollow of my shoulder.'

Jennie gave the following commentary:

'This seemed to me to be an oedipal dream. It led me back to
the patient's history. Social circumstances had sent his father
away for years on end during his childhood. He was then alone
with his mother. After that his father had returned and had
died rather soon afterwards. The dominant material at this
period of his treatment was illustrated by dreams of a stormy
sea with terrifying waves, where he was on a path with a sheer
drop, in a situation of danger; he needed rescue; the transference was positive and was fairly strong but restrained; from
that doubtless stemmed his incapacity to dream of other phantasies than these representations of a terrifying sea.'

In the transfero-countertransferential dynamic, it was possible
to relate this dream to the repetitive insistence in the treatment
material upon menancing progenital maternal imagos, and to
make the hypothesis that the analyst's dream responded to this
material by an oedipal dramatization. Expression of resistance
returned to the patient, and figuration of the transference came
to the analyst in her dream.

From another point of view, this dream was a confirmation for
the analyst about the functioning of this patient, with whom it
was not useful to accept any old imago representations that he
presented during sessions. In the analyst's psyche this dream was
an elaboration of the problematic of the case, in a manner that
was quasi-analogous in its effects to what would have happened if
the patient had had the same dream (and had dared to express it)

himself. From this perspective, the analyst is much more than a 'thinking apparatus' or mute setting: she functions as part of the patient's psyche, as in a situation of transitional exchanges between a mother and her baby.

What was inaccessible for the patient in an oedipal relationship had become representable, if not in his own psyche, at least in that of his analyst. And this obviously constitutes an elaboration.

Things subsequently changed in the patient's life: in his social and professional life; in his love life: a brief adventure, but important for him—the first outside his marriage. In his dreams, he saw himself received at a reception at his analyst's house; on the couch, his bodily attitude, which had up to that point been altogether rigid, loosened up and was liberated.

A question arises. For this dream to have had clinical and dynamic effects on the patient's evolution, was it enough for his unconscious desire to become representable in his analyst's thought? For this question to be answered, other considerations are necessary about the process thus observed and about the dream's action mechanism. This dream expresses not only the patient's oedipal desire, but also the dreamer's countertransference. She was effectively attached to this patient; she 'liked him a lot'—he was gentle, he had intellectualizing and rationalizing defences that she understood well and supported . . . admittedly.

But this patient also put her in touch with many things: with the problem that her own child self had in her life; with the care (and nostalgia for care) to be given, and tenderness; with the child that she had been and who had missed out on a certain tenderness, but also . . . with all her father's line: this patient bore the two first names of the analyst's grandfathers and had broken all links with his own paternal grandparents; and with her own analysis, for in her treatment she had encountered difficulties in letting herself go . . . like this patient. For her, he was at one and the same time the possible/impossible and desired child, the oedipal lover, her own father's line, and the analysand that she had been for her own analyst.

This dream had therefore made her work on herself. The material on which she did this work was not only ascribable to the psychoanalytic Oedipus theory as basic structure of the psyche. The material was also the *materia* peculiar to psychoanalysis, that of the transference–countertransference, what J. P. Valabrega (1980) designated as the 'transferred', and the repetitive links that weave what I call a 'common psyche'⁴ between analyst and patient. This dream of Jennie's should be related to clinical observations in which two psyches are strictly interdependent: in certain psychotic states the patient functions as though one part of himself had remained in the other, and this system determines the links that will develop for the whole of life (P. Aulagnier, 1985). In the conjoint therapy of a mother and her schizophrenic daughter, M.-Th. Couchoud (1986) could demonstrate the modalities of the historical and phantasy installation of an 'intersubjective topography': by means of her delusion the child had an essential function in maintaining a denial that was indispensable to her mother.

Other recent propositions also point in the same direction: J. J. Baranès (1986) has proposed to take a 'transgenerational topography' into account in understanding certain clinical cases.

The notion of a phantasy of a 'common psyche' does not seem unjustified to describe the underlying process in the case of Jennie and her patient. With her dream, Jennie was in fact able to analyse the significant representations and chains that were at work in the analytic relationship both for Gérard and herself: what she meant to him—behind the frightening imagos that he put to the forefront of the material in sessions—which he could not yet discern; and what he meant for her, also, across her own personal history. Mutual links were woven there, whose threads crisscrossed and constituted the back-cloth of this treatment; the transference circulated by means of these threads.

In the course of the analytic work, Jennie had not been unaware of unconscious desire for Gérard; he had awoken something that had been slumbering in her. Jennie's dream revealed the existence and origin of the wishes that were then remobilized: the 'hollow of my shoulder' is as much a representation of an erotic tie as a tender relationship. In the immediate present

Gérard could not be aware of the unconscious desire that animated him and was in some way present in Jennie.

By contrast, when Jennie had reworked this dream and had let herself be drawn into this theoretico-clinical reverie—self-analysis, elaboration—Gérard in turn could benefit from the effects of Jennie's interpretative elaboration. In so far as Jennie had transformed and taken back what belonged to her in this analytical relationship by linking it with her private sources—that which the dream of desire illustrated at this particular point in the development of the treatment—something that could be called a common psyche and had unconsciously been welded between analyst and analysand could be undone.

If the analysis had brought alive something of the patient's past—his oedipal organization and his first links with his mother—it also stirred up corresponding wishes in the analyst. 'I dream for you', as a remark borrowed from Jennie, could have been the heading of this paragraph. This formulation also ties in with shamanic practices as reported by T. Nathan (1986, p. 162): the shaman, in an isolated part of the world,[5] 'does not dream for himself', but for his client.

Under the circumstances, 'I dream for us' seemed most pertinent to me here: Jennie's dream was also one that Gérard had in him; their psychic sharing was indicated there.

If the dream figures the unconscious psychic organization that develops between the two partners of the 'analyst–analysand' couple, the text of the dream symbolizes it—namely, 'what connects two parts that are separate and correspond'.

(4) Psychic functioning in common

Functioning of this sort suggests to me an early psychic functioning, a relationship in which mother and infant are not psychically as distinct as they are bodily separate, in which the infant's first identificatory reference points are established only gradually, and in which the baby's 'feeling–pleasure–suffering' is bound up with what the mother feels, notably because she had this baby inside and then outside her, and with the mode of functioning that preceded birth, namely a sharing of the type 'one psyche for two' that still continues after birth during the first period of maternal preoccupation. At this time, mother and baby have both in some sense to accomplish their 'mutual formation'. The mother, who often (especially after a first pregnancy) lives with and for this baby who was expected/has arrived and is the image of what she herself was for her own mother as a baby, must establish that this baby is also an other, whose reactions she must accommodate, adapt to, and fit in with, an other who will gradually have his or her own psychic space, which the mother can discover and explore, and in which she recognizes the specificity of her baby and the feeling of her own creative capacity. It is also a time in which communication between mother and infant uses channels of intuition, empathy and perception of the other's unconscious impulses (we will see the function of projective identifications later on). This can be experienced in the light of the dominant pleasure of admiration for 'the wonderful baby' (and for herself for having made him), or of hatred for finding, for instance, that he is separate in a body that is no longer hers, something that dashes and nullifies the phantasies that his presence *in utero* had allowed her to dream.

I mention this mode of functioning as a structural model that could be characterized by various concepts.

(A) *Primary narcissism* is conceived not as auto-cathexis of a monad that can be found again in sleep, but as a 'dual unity' or functioning of a whole within which two poles can be distinguished: parental narcissism directed towards the baby is potentially transformed there into mutual cathexis, in which each of the two poles reinforces the other's narcissism in a way that is analogous to what their relationship to the baby can be for some pregnant women, affording them an intense feeling of completeness.[6] This primary narcissism cannot be separated from underlying negative narcissism: 'wonderful babies' get killed.

(B) *Primary seduction* was described by Laplanche (1985): in the hands of his first seducer, the baby is plunged into a bath of 'enigmatic signifiers' whose sexual meanings are all the more prominent for the baby because they elude her who is giving them out. Original repression is instituted on the basis of these functionings, to which is added the 'violence of interpretation' of the maternal 'mouthpiece' (Aulagnier, 1975).

(c) From this moment onwards *identifications* spread out over a wide area. If the mother's explicit and/or implicit reference to the man/the baby's father, to her own father, to the 'father of her personal prehistory', and to the ideals within her is undoubtedly present, is already making its mark upon the mother's functioning in relation to the baby, and will make a still greater mark later on, other identificatory signs will gradually emerge that will serve as the baby's first points of reference: the pictogram that springs from the 'zone-object' space common to mother and baby, the orificial reference-points by means of which the 'different' can gradually be distinguished from the 'common', and the various spaces—the envelopes—cutaneous, sonorous and respiratory (Anzieu, 1985), in which for an initial period what belongs to one (*infans*) is indissociable from what belongs to the other.

This makes sense of those first 'feelings of existing' that emerge from confusion within a postnatal womb that prepares for psychological birth after chronological birth (Haag, 1985). It also makes sense of 'shared meanings' (Tustin, cited by Haag), phantasies of a 'common skin' (Anzieu, 1984), and the skin identifications (Bick, 1968) that are encountered especially but not only in the treatment of children. And it makes sense of P. Castoriadis-Aulagnier's need (1975) to propose the category of original alongside secondary and primary (phantasies) as the psychic site of the common and first identificatory reference-points by means of which what lies in store for the baby in a confused universe and will make him present can be distinguished.

These propositions are not in contradiction with what Melanie Klein put forward. Projective identification should be considered in its projective aspect: it is 'the experience of the "self" lived out inside the object', and the anxieties and phantasies inside this claustrum. In its identificatory aspect it is the appropriation of the qualities and capacities of the object that has been penetrated in phantasy. On the basis of these propositions, treatment becomes a space in which the analyst's psyche that receives the projections can 'think unconsciously' and perceive personal phantasies and dreams coming from his unconscious that give him information about the emotional meaning of the situation (Meltzer, 1984). F. Bégoin emphasizes that the basis of the analyst's work is 'introjection' and 'rumination' of the other's desire, whence arises a thought that is 'original' and 'as fleeting as dream'.

Jennie's dream illustrates such a functioning, although used by her in a noticeably different way technically and theoretically. In fact, she never envisaged the prospect of revealing the analyst's dream to the patient. She used the dream associatively to elucidate the countertransference (considered as quite a different thing from 'response to the transference').

(D)   The function of a common psyche leads on to developing on a clinical and metapsychological plane the earlier propositions of E. Bick evoking *original unity*. This concept, taken up by Abello and Perez-Sanchez, describes a stage previous to the paranoid–schizoid position and would permit the first projective identifications. Original unity is the womb of thought: in certain treatments it must first be reconstituted before the latter can unfold. The dream is an envelope between that of imaginary unity and that of the treatment. For Abello and Perez-Sanchez the analyst, like the mother, dreams the patient in his thought; treatment is also an envelope that contains psychoanalyst and patient together, in the same way as the 'original family group' contains mother and baby.

Some manifestations of the common psyche are of a pathological order. Thus M.-Th. Couchoud (1985) demonstrated that, for the artist, maternal seduction and sexuality are absent from the dyad; the baby is neither desired nor 'seduced' by the mother.

(5)   Return to the cases

The case of Jennie and her patient lead to the proposition of a common psyche, as it can be identified in treatment at the most representative moments of the analytic process.

In the case reported by Kreisler, psychic functioning in common would be better characterized by the formula 'one psyche for two'—the psyche being the mother's, which left no room for the infant, as such, in a community of functioning. In mother–baby exchanges no psychic space was made for the baby. He only counted as an object in the maternal dynamic, clad with phantasies and the characteristics of the lost love object: his only job was to represent it. The dream marked the end of this split and at the same time the return of the image of her dead sister to the maternal psyche.

In M.-Th. Couchoud's case, the sick girl and her delusion occupied an active place in the denial necessary for the mother, itself the consequence of an impossible repression. Work in Sarah's treatment led to particularities in the transferential relationship: here the common psyche was less a work of transformation by means of a desire unrecognized by the patient passing into the analyst's unconscious than the fabric of relationship derived from the mutual cathexes of analyst and analysand, which formed the back-cloth of the treatment. The dream is moment and site of actualization, of associative elaboration and of analysis by the analyst—at least in his presence—both of this common transferential fabric and of the roots whence it has sprung for both of them. This work will allow the patient to grasp what properly belongs to her from this actualization of past material, or at any rate to grasp it differently. Here the dream is the most significant extreme point of encounter, of holding in common, and of analysis of transferences (and resistance).

(IV) DREAMS IN COMMON

(1) Family dreams

I owe the three following dreams to Anne-Marie Blanchard (reported during an interview preparatory to an eventual family therapy). They are dreams reported by three members of one family: father, mother and their second son (out of three surviving boys).

At the beginning of the session, the son, a young man of 23, kept returning obsessively to his wish that the therapists would help him find work in a photographic laboratory. He also wanted to know what they thought about his wish to make black-and-white photographs rather than colour ones. Was he behind his times (this is one of the major symptoms, taking all his rituals into account)?

The mother butted in: she, at any rate, for her part, dreams in colour, and it is splendid.

The boy then reported a dream; he was in a tavern, or a cavern, or a cave. The walls were covered with candles, or were of candle wax; they melted, and this quickly made a compact block, with no space, and with stalactites.

The father then described his dream that night: he was in front of a big pipe leading to a water reservoir, and it seemed he had to go into this reservoir and transport water to repair something, but the pipe was too narrow, and he could only get his head into it.

The mother then reported an old dream that she called pre-monitory: during her first pregnancy (and she added that it had been a twin pregnancy; one month before delivery a little girl had died, and the other was born but died soon afterwards), she had dreamt that she gave birth to a child without a head.

For Anne-Marie Blanchard these intra-uterine phantasies in common expressed very well the position of each individual and of the group faced with the eventual birth of the new group-family-therapists.

One therefore finds not only in a couple but also in a family a 'shared phantasy organization' that functions like an unconscious psyche common to all.

Its genesis is easy to understand: the arrival of a baby has mobilizing effects upon the unconscious of each of its parents and eventually brings about changes in the couple's ties. A new family psychic fabric therefore develops on which the baby's psyche will be founded. This will be marked by the trace of parental ties and phantasies, by the trace of the most archaic phantasies and the ideals supported by psychic functioning, and also traces of earlier family lines and events that marked them: dramas, rejections, losses, secrets, disappearances, etc., whose phantoms haunt the unconscious of each of them.

The dream that derives from the very origins of psychic life, at the navel, is linked with what I am here calling a 'shared phantasy organization', in which the subject's psyche finds itself included even before it has become distinct, and on which the family system of unconscious relationships is founded.

This psychic functioning in common is therefore very different from the first representation that Freud offered of a collective psychic organization, in which the figure of the leader (or one of his characteristics, or an idea) took the place of the ego-ideal in each individual and united the whole into a single body. On the contrary, this functioning is somewhat analogous to that conveyed by Jennie's dream: there, an unconscious communication by one had a mobilizing effect on the other's unconscious wishes. In a family the children are assigned a place, not only in the lineage, but also in phantasy: some that occupy, for example, the place of a rejected object in the parents' unconscious desire will be marked out by an unspoken pact to become the scapegoat of the family, upon whom rejections and misfortunes will be heaped with a clear conscience by everyone.

Jennie's dream conveyed nothing other than the functioning of the unconscious between two persons who were in a position to relive buried desires, not in order to proceed towards their fulfilment—something to which family organization also tends—but in order to analyse them.

In a family, with a dream that is exchanged, a sign can be made or a representation given of the dreamer's unconscious functioning, and of the place that he occupies in the common phantasy organization, without knowing much about what he is transmitting. He sends out a message destined for 'good listeners'.

Here there is doubtless an element of the dream functioning as cultural creativity, an aesthetic work that J. Gillaumin regards as a 'collective institution'. The dream, like the work of art, would be the elaboration of relationships into which the subject entered with imago objects, which have a definite relationship with the world, or the public. In a family, the dream is there for those to whom it speaks, like a work of art, for those who can listen not with the ears of reason but with the antennae of their unconscious desire—a shared and/or complementary desire.

The dreams reported by Anne-Marie Blanchard are indeed also the common envelope within which the entire family—at this particular moment in its history—was united, recognized itself, and stifled, at the same time as it revealed, by means of its link with the therapist, the wish to disengage from it.

(2)   One dream for two

Dreams are sometimes picked up in group work situations in which two analysts are installed, establishing order, which is to say a system of rules of functioning.

(A)   Experience accumulated over a period of years with courses of psychodrama or discussion groups that assemble ten to twelve people around two psychoanalysts for a defined period indicates that under these circumstances, and with the theoretical frame of reference they have elaborated from them, the psychoanalysts can listen, elaborate, interpret and show themselves particularly sensitive to transferential, countertransferential and intertransferential movements (cf. D. Anzieu, R. Kaës, A. Missenard et al., 1972; 1982).

They can therefore linger over any dreams they have in such a situation, either while the course is running or even before it begins.

(B)   This is the case with the following dream. We had gathered before the first session. My colleague Yvonne Gutierrez shared with me a dream that she had just had:

'One cannot have two lovers at the same time. What are the theoretical, ideological, political or other grounds for such a rule, for such a prohibition?'

Between the two of us, this dream took its place amidst all the exchanges that we had had before this first session, and which bore essentially upon the group, which was going to gather four times a day for four days, and about which we had thought beforehand. It was supplementary material that added to what this project had already mobilized in us.

(C)   The dream cannot be separated either from something earlier that had preceded the formation of this group. In the institution within which these courses were organized—the

C.E.F.F.R.A.P.[7]—Y. Gutierrez and I had decided to contribute to a theoretical debate with a clinical contribution by exposing to our colleagues the development of one of the next courses, the modalities of our work and our elaborations. 'Not having two lovers at the same time' was certainly one way of affirming that the dreamer's essential preoccupation in the coming group would be the group and our work in common, and not the account that would have to be given to our colleagues in due course and later on.

It also affirmed that this group organized within the setting of the C.E.F.F.R.A.P. would above all be the two analysts' group, and they would lead and take responsiblity for it.

This interpretation was confirmed by the associations that I formulated after my colleague had described her dream: in the days that had preceded the course I had been thinking that our undertaking to give a report of our work should not take precedence over the work itself, and that in this group, above all, 'we should work for us'. Later on I even 'forgot' the undertaking in question.

(D) But this dream cannot be dissociated from the material brought by the participants in the first session and which contained an implicit question: what is the law, here, in this group? Is it an inhuman law, 'brute and vicious'? Or a law that is certainly human and contestable, but is also constant and sure? Were the monitoring analysts omnipotent, did they do what they wanted, did they have control and absolute power over the session, its timetable, and its setting, were they lords from whom anything—even the worst—could be expected, or were they, instead, themselves also subject to a law with which they had to contend, like the rest?

In the break that followed the first session the dream thus became, between us, the point of departure for another work of association on the theme of the law: Y. Gutierrez called to mind Antigone as the incarnation of the divine law, and I recalled the character of Creon as figure of the law of men and the necessities of life in the city. This elaboration took place in parallel to that of the actual material of the session, as schematized in the preceding paragraph.

This is not the place for a developed study of the transferential and countertransferential movements that must be identified for analytical work to be done on such a course.

The stress will instead be on the function of the signifier of the law, present first of all in the preliminary dream and then implicitly in the material of the first session. There, the question of the law proved to refer to different objects: it was in fact the law of the institution, the C.E.F.F.R.A.P., that had provided the setting necessary for the group to assemble, and which had a symbolic function. It was also the—occasionally omnipotent—law of the analyst–monitors and was then an imaginary formation. It was also the law that the participants phantasized imposing at their whim and to please themselves.

At this beginning of a course, the signifier of the law was what brought the participants as well as the analysts together. It was the common signifier that united members that had been scattered until then, unknown to one another, and were entering into the unknown universe of a group that was looking for itself, with the couple who had set it up and were taking on functions within it which they had already experienced.

This common signifier, already present in the preliminary dream, functioned from the very beginning as an anchor point for everyone. Starting from there, multiple versions of the law were gradually called to mind, and through transferences the objects from which it stemmed were distinguished from one another— C.E.F.F.R.A.P., the group, the analysts and the participants.

In fact, the diversity of the transferences and the spread of identificatory reference-points corresponds to the diversity of these objects. The common signifier under which all were subsumed at the beginning of the course in order to 'survive' or 'be born' gradually gave way to the multitude of exchanges and communications. Everyone there potentially had the alternating experience of his identifications and his radical differences (i.e. his counter-identifications). The dream had furnished the necessary 'material'.

(E) Where the analysts are concerned, the place and function of the dream should here first of all be defined negatively. What the dream of Y. Gutierrez did not in fact give rise to was analysis of its infantile source. Neither she nor I ventured to express anything at all in this direction. Work between two analysts 'in the field' does not aim at a sort of 'see-saw psychoanalysis', as R. Kaës humorously formulated it. It is only in so far as each respects a certain reserve and does not behave as an analyst towards the other that they can pursue their association to work as a couple: this is because the libido that links them can be displaced onto the object—the group—that they cathect in common, and in relationship to which, as things preceed, they will have to clarify their similarities and differences. It follows naturally that in this work, each is led to discover something of their own unconscious relationships with the group object—in particular—and to reveal them to their colleague's view.

In so far as during breaks and outside sessions they do this work on what unites and distinguishes them on the 'group' object, it is possible for the participants in turn to do it themselves. Y. Gutierrez's dream will have been the expression of the analysts' new and common position before it was an opening onto what separated them. Thus, by the same token, in starting from the law the participants will have been able to disentangle themselves from the confusion into which the group situation had put them and to acquire new possibilities of communication through revelation of unconscious determinants.

Since undertaking to report to our colleagues about the progress of this group, each of us had had an internal train of thought. Y. Gutierrez's dream conveyed the change that had taken place, confirmed by my own associations: this group was going to be our group, above all; and in the days that preceded the course I forgot the undertaking: 'one cannot have two lovers at the same time' conveyed that it was impossible for us to cathect at one and the same time the group of participants during the course and the group of our colleagues.

This change in our work project as a pair should also be related to what Y. Gutierrez and I already had in common between ourselves: for a long time we have been active in the C.E.F.F.R.A.P.—members of this association where the recruitment of new members is the fruit of a long period of 'trial' collaboration. Finally, Y. Gutierrez and I had together experienced a certain number of groups before this one. A common psychic fab-

ric and links existed between us, in which work at the
C.E.F.F.R.A.P. was the privileged site of exchanges; this fabric
was woven from the closeness of our theoretical conceptions, our
modes of functioning as a couple and in a group, and doubtless
other factors that are—deliberately—not verbalized. Thus, the
dream also had roots in these common zones of our psyches and in
the law to which we referred. But this dream was essentially the
elaboration of the day residue that for us had been the undertaking to expose our work later on to some 15 colleagues in the
imaginary position of supervisors, and the possibility of feeling
them present with us during the progress of the course. We certainly wanted nothing of that: the dream and my 'forgetting'
expressed this clearly. Y. Gutierrez had dreamed for both of us.

What, then, can we make of the dream's function in this context? For the dreamer, the dream had one function: it linked her
with her infantile history. It had a function for the analysts as a
pair in the group: like a dream of the second type, it directed the
two analysts on the one hand towards the work they would have
to do in this group, and on the other towards the unconscious
dynamic of their relationship, a dynamic to which each was sensitive, even if it was not to be verbalized, a precondition for mutual
cathexes partly to converge upon the common object of interest,
the group. Finally, the dream had a function for the group, whose
development was marked and organized from the very start by
what, between the analysts, was the field of the unspoken, if not
the forbidden, whose signifier is clear in the dream: 'One cannot
have. . . .'

The dream had a function as envelope for the dreamer as well
as for the two analysts: it would be necessary to break this envelope to discover what the dream hid and revealed at the same
time. It was up to the dreamer to do this on her own account if she
wanted to; and up to the two analysts to analyse its effects, and to
elaborate their personal position in relation to the law under
which they had gathered for this group that was to be worked on
in common.

The unconscious part of the dream, as well as the signifier that
corresponds to it, the law, became not an envelope for the group,
but the womb of its functioning, its organizing phantasy. Here
one could imagine not a common psyche, but psychic functioning
in common.

(3)   Dreams in a group, dreams of a group

In certain groups called formation or therapy groups, dreams are reported. Are they connected with shared phantasy activity, if indeed the latter is regarded as possible and identifiable?

The analyst's work in these groups aims to identify collective unconscious psychic formations (e.g. the 'group illusion' described by Didier Anzieu), underlying wishes that activate the common dynamic at a given moment, the forces that oppose them, the psychic organizations involved, and so on. The work depends upon the transferential, countertransferential and inter-transferential movements identified by the analysts. Work such as this, centred upon common psychic formations and shared among several people, can permit each to make a new differentiation of their own psychic dynamic, while some people can find a new standpoint by means of identifications and narcissism, in a situation that could be described as original.

Whether they be psychodrama or discussion groups, of short or long duration, whether they have no predetermined term, or else set themselves a therapeutic project, in all of them dreams are reported by participants. Admittedly, each of these dreams is primarily a personal dream, but it is also the dream of the someone who is making a narrative of it, addressed in this instance to the group members and the analysts.

The question arises of the function of these dreams in the group dynamic, relative to the processes that develop in the group and relative to the transferential movements that are revealed there.

The ideas that I will here propound enlarge and are inspired by those formulated not long ago by Pontalis (1972) and more recently by J. Villier (1982).

(A)   The dream, even formulated in a group, remains an individual psychic formation.

(B)   In a group session it is reported at privileged moments of the session and functions as an object (in the service of defence or of transference) between the dreamer, the analysts, the participants and the group as a whole.

(c)   The dream that is brought into the group also conveys the group dynamic and the phantasies being deployed.

Here is a dream reported by J. Villier: 'My mother wanted to make me a dress, something she never did in her life; she tried a lovely dress with flounces on me, but underneath it I was in a mess, and my mother did not do anything at all about that.'

This dream was taken up by the participants, who mostly identified with the dreamer. Besides representations of a broken-up body, associative work revealed a man–woman couple confounded into a terrifying imago, and the dreamer's anxious desire to take the place of one of the two analysts.

This material should certainly be heard as an expression of the dreamer's own dynamic, but also as an expression of the problematic of numerous participants, split between the anxiety of breaking into pieces that was mobilized by the plurality of persons, and the impulse to identify with the group taken as an imaginary object that would confer unity upon each of them.

(d)   Finally, dreams in a group are material that can be worked on in relation to the group dynamic. Some dreams, or some parts of a dream, can take on a particular density during the session for everyone: for through this material symbolization occurs that corresponds to what is actually going on in the group and in the transference. One dream about a participant's sick body became an opening in the session onto the problematic of 'badness' in the group, badness in infantile sexuality, badness inside—but which becomes visible—and badness outside that 'persecuted' the dreamer during the session. In this example, the signifier 'badness' was common to everyone at a moment in the group's history. Thus further connections are made between the individual (one person's body) and the groupal, and what only belongs to one and is then shared by the others. Given that later on the signifier 'badness' was to give rise to as many echoes and different associative threads as there were persons present, it served for a time as a common part, as a shared signifier. Dreams in a group are also sometimes dreams of the group.

(e)   Dreams are sometimes the outcome of the analysts' countertransference. This can be perceived unconsciously by the participants as soon as the analysts say something at the beginning of the course.

In one case, the course introduction mentioned an interest in the description during sessions of dreams that participants might have during the course. This proposition was experienced as seductive: a series of four dreams made by four participants was brought on the second day of the course:

'I was pursued by people who wanted to kill me; some helped me to escape, othes denounced me to my pursuers. I escaped them. Then I had a useless weapon, which was missing a piece.'

'I had forgotten my dentures in the bathroom; without them I could only feed on liquid.'

'I was drowning; but no-one came to support my head, I was alone. . . .'

'In a children's home, a nurse tossed a child in the air. The latter fell (I was very anxious) . . . onto a bed of skins, very supple. The child laughed.'

This series of dreams was perceived by the analysts as coherent in its sequence and content; like the adventure narrative of a single person in different guises, it was a narrative that took up the material of the day before, the persecution, the feeling of being disarmed in the group, and the (mortal) threat of losing something of the self there, preceding a happy birth despite the anxiety.

This series was a communal representation, a figuration of phantasies about the beginning of this group, made up of the 'participants and analysts' together. But it is also an echo of the unconscious inaugural seduction, which appeared as such to the analysts in a second phase. For several sessions it was to form the axis of functioning of this group and its transferential material.

In these groups there is psychic functioning in common; the group is an idealized object for everyone, organizing phantasies activate communal life, and transference impulses, identifications and counter-identifications are shared. But there is also a common psyche, especially identifiable between the two analysts. It undoubtedly emerges less easily between the group and the analysts than it did between Jennie and her patient. Nonetheless, clinical signs of it can be perceived: the analysts' transferential experience in sessions that reveals the effect of group material upon the unconscious of each of them; the affects provoked by the session (irritation, repressed aggression, lassitude, sleepiness, depression etc.) that shed light for the analysts upon the dynamic at work; group transformations that follow upon the analysts' elaboration (even ones not verbalized in the session); and the dreams the latter have while a course is running.

The functioning that the common psyche conveys can be referred back to the three concepts previously mentioned. *Primary narcissism* is here, too, conceived of as a 'dual unity' in which participants and analysts make up the two poles of the same initial ensemble. Its mark can be seen when the analysts' narcissism is found reflected in the functioning in common of the participants, who return to the analysts an unconscious image of themselves.

Primary seduction is a mode of functioning whose effects appear in the group dynamic: for instance when the analysts' first words to introduce the course, by means of their tone and timbre, accompanied by sign language, gestures and attitudes, are bearers of 'enigmatic signifiers' that are not initially identified as such by the analysts, return to them, and are discovered on analysis (cf. the seduction above).

Projective and introjective identification are to be understood here in the sense indicated above, as the effects on the psyche of projections it has received and which have modified it in its functioning according to the same modalities as in Jennie's dream. In groups, during sessions, 'reveries' and phantasies come to the analysts' minds and are the point of departure of their elaborations. The dreams the analysts have while courses are running have the same place and the same function. There are unconscious exchanges between group, participants and analysts: it is the latter's task to identify their traces, effects and outcome in order to get them to 'work'.

The common psyche is a phantasy that structures a functioning; these three concepts characterize it; 'reverie' is its most usual product, and dream is its most accomplished production.

In conclusion, these ideas tie in with recent more general scientific hypotheses on information theory: in addition to 'information-knowledge' (the content of a message), there exists 'information-organization' which modifies its recipient.

Dreams undoubtedly hold out a possibility of throwing a bridge towards those zones of the mind that are before language and onto which no direct view is therefore possible; on the retina, next to the *macula,* there exists another sensitive zone that allows night vision; does dream sometimes allow vision . . . in the night of time, shedding 'more light'?[8]

But dream is also an actualization of shared psychic functioning: the work that the analyst can do with it on himself then becomes a mode of self-knowledge for the other.

NOTES

1. Physiology attributes to the cell membrane the function of transforming elements that cross it, which themselves modify the structure of the wall as they pass through. This description will serve metaphorically for working on the notion of the dream envelope.
2. By contrast, the absence of dreams in psychosomatic patients with operatory thinking indicates that the dream is undoubtedly a 'psychosomatic organizer', as C. Dejours (1986) proposed.
3. This observation and these remarks tie in with the very interesting work of Cramer (1985), who also indicates that the 'baby's early psychic functioning takes place under the aegis of a fundamental absence of division from the mother's mind'.
4. Some shamans find means of therapy for a patient who consults them after having listened to the tale of his troubles, heard his names, forenames, and those of certain relatives, and after having seen the solution to the problem *in a dream.* The dream does not, however, only have this function, as T. Nathan (1986) indicates: it is also a 'logical organizer, mode of investigation, and unconscious guide in the therapist's training'.
5. In the practice of groups led within a psychoanalytic perspective, cultural isolation is often imposed.
6. The love relationship mobilizes this mode of mutual cathexis, 'in admiring one another they admire themselves' (D'Ormesson, *Mon dernier rêve sera pour vous,* J.-C. Lattès, 1982).
7. Cercle d'études français pour la formation et la recherche active en psycholgie.
8. Goethe's last words on his death-bed.

CHAPTER FOUR

The memory envelope
and its holes

M. Enriquez

(I) THE NEED FOR RECALL

E very human being who aspires to think of himself as a unique individual has in him a subjective organization that impels him towards memory and the investigation of the past. Wanting to know 'beginnings' and wanting to 'go back' to orient oneself in time, to find and master it, are coexistent with life itself.

Lying on his back in the dark, alone as only Samuel Beckett's characters can be, the hero of *Company* (1984) keeps himself company with his voice; he talks to himself and remembers:

> You saw the light on such and such a day and your mind never active at any time is now even less than ever so. [. . .] A small boy you come out of Connolly's Stores holding your mother by hand. You turn right and advance in silence southward along the highway. After some hundred paces you head inland and broach the long steep homeward. You make ground in silence hand in hand through the warm still summer air. It is late afternoon and after some hundred paces the sun appears above the crest of the rise. Looking up at the blue sky and then at

your mother's face you break the silence asking her if it is not in reality much more distant than it appears. The sky that is. The blue sky. Receiving no answer you mentally reframe your question and some hundred paces later look up at her face again and ask her if it does not appear much less distant than in reality it is. For some reason you could never fathom this question must have angered her exceedingly. For she shook off your little hand and made you a cutting retort *you have never forgotten*. [My italics]

It is significant to find throughout the ages and in diverse cultures a continuity of human behaviour where time is concerned. Mircea Eliade (1963) defined this behaviour as follows: '*to recover from* the work of time, one must go back and rejoin the beginning of the world' or, in other words, recover the past so as to know it and give it sense and thereby prevent it from breaking in on the present unless it be to signify that certain events not only happened, but helped to shape one's identity and being in the world. Insisting upon the importance of memory of what myth articulates for access to knowledge, Mircea Eliade also proposes that 'an individual existence becomes and remains a fully human, responsible, and meaningful existence in so far as it is inspired by its reservoirs of actions already accomplished and thoughts already formulated. Ignoring or forgetting the content of this collective memory formed by tradition amounts to a regression to the natural state (the acultural condition of the baby), a sin, or a disaster' (ibid., pp. 154–155).

One could not give a more eloquent description of the disastrous effects that memory disorders can have upon the human mind. Our clinical analytical work constantly reminds us of it every day, especially in the treatment of psychosis, which confronts us with the tragic consequences of ignorance of the past and lack of access to temporality.

Fanchon, a young schizophrenic girl, repeatedly said to me, 'I have no memory of life, I do not belong to the human race'. I have described observation of her in previous works,[1] and I have tried to show to what extraordinary lengths this young girl went to construct for herself a memory, a past and a history that would truly be hers, so as not to vanish into nothingness but instead feel entitled to belong to the human race. Her elaboration-creation of an envelope of suffering that was displayed to the view of others, attracting them in a movement of horror and fascination, had allowed her to detach herself from the clutches of her mother, the exclusive custodian of her body, her memory, her time and her history. In this way she was able to make herself an untouchable envelope, assuring herself of the feeling of basic security in her own skin. I shall not dwell here upon this observation that has been developed at length elsewhere, nor do I propose to tackle the pathology of memory and forgetting in psychosis. I simply mention it to show how the constitution of an 'ego-skin' in its function of inscribing traces and sensible qualities makes possible the representation that is indispensable for the maintenance of the mind and memory functioning.

Psychoanalysis works with words—words that function by a labour of memory, on memory, and through memory. The process of remembering that develops in treatment in 'the heat of the transference' allows active traces to be rediscovered, which, forgotten, distorted, and transformed by the effects of history, time, imagination and discourse, have made each of us into what we are. The analytic enterprise can be compared with historiographical recollection, which, in an effort to appropriate and interpret, re-weaves and remodels a particular envelope of memory that ensures the sense of continuity of the self over time, i.e. through difference, and thus allows it to be projected into the future.

Sometimes, working in concert, analysand and analyst succeed in approaching as close as possible to this ideal realization, after which there are no more than minor incidences of pathology in memory and forgetting. Ideal realization does not mean—quite the contrary—that in this instance treatment has brought about a restoration of all memory of the past. That would be yielding to a megalomaniac illusion. An excavated ruin is a ruin on its way towards obliteration, something Freud alluded to notably in his diary of the Rat Man's analysis. In the open air, having found its place in the sun, an excavated ruin crumbles and corrodes, though it does not disappear for all that. It then takes on another meaning and another topographical, temporal and psychic status. Only its representation and its committal to thought and memory bear witness to and recall what it has been.

The same goes for ruins excavated by analytic treatment. They crumble; memory of them changes, suffers the work of time and is forgotten to make way for other constructions and psychic realizations. They are wiped out of consciousness, to be preserved in other forms and in other places. The forgetting of 'analytic treatment' and the archaeological work that supported it is bearer of its memory.

(II)   OBSTACLES TO THE DISCOVERY OF HISTORICITY

Now, as I reflected upon what my clinical work with certain forms of pathology of memory and forgetting had given me to understand so far, I became aware that the observations that came to mind in the form of insistent memories concerned patients who had wanted to undertake a second analysis, citing in a painful way the 'memory wounds'[2] that a first analysis had left them with. These patients, who presented diverse psychic problematics, not psychotic, but all subject to the predominant influence of Thanatos, had behind them a long analytic experience that had marked them and left in them deep traces, happy or unhappy, but certainly ones that they, like the hero of *Company*, had never forgotten. The memory of their analysis and the relationship that they had lived through with their first analyst continued to be alive and at work in them, but more in the form of a thorn in their side than a force to stimulate the realization of their projects and the reappropriation of their history. The manifest complaint that justified their wish to undertake another analysis bore precisely upon the fact of feeling without projects and incapable of 'becoming'. What is more, they affirmed more or less clearly that their psychic suffering was located precisely in the region of a memory wounded by the analytic experience itself.

What therefore had the analysis awakened and hidden for its memory to be bearer of suffering and a standstill in their psychic activity and ability to cathect?

This finding has gone on raising questions for me. Although one could invoke the transferential sequelae that are inherent in any analysis and are admittedly most often negative, this did not in this instance seem sufficient to account for the symptomatology presented by these patients. I think we should instead formulate the question thus: what revelation of a past that could not be taken on board had the analytic work led to, for a neo-formation to be secreted that took the analyst and the analysis for its target? What transference, what repetition, what inelaborable conflict leading to denial, what psychic pain could the present relationship to the past analysis be indications of?

For the ancient Greeks, the greatest enemy of the goddess Mnemosyne, mother of the Muses, who 'knows all that has been, all that is, and all that will be' (Vernant, 1959), was the Fountain of Lethe—Forgetting—which was an integral part of death's domain. According to Plato, it was brim-full of malice, and the soul was forbidden to approach it. The soul had to follow the path that would lead it to the spring that flowed from the lake of Mnemosyne, whose fresh water assured mastery of time to anyone who drank deeply of it. What is more, Lethe had two redoubtable allies: Hypnos (Sleep) and Thanatos (Death), who were twin brothers.

In other words, *forgetting, obliterating traces and decathexis* as an expression both of dreamless sleep and of the destructive component of the death instinct are the worst enemies of the activity of remembering and linking. Seeking to wipe out traces, to decathect and to sleep in a dreamless sleep in which lethal passivity is engaged in at greatest depth tend towards psychic death and instinctual defusion. These different impulses also have their hidden face and are bearers of their opposite. Theory suggests this and observation demonstrates it. In fact, in order to try to survive psychically, subjects grappling with this general problematic of decathexis bring defences into play that present themselves in the form of turning the first instinctual impulses back in the opposite direction. It is in this sense that one can say that obliterating traces, dreamless sleep, and decathexis are always accompanied by the more or less open expression of their hidden face, namely:

- *a frantic refusal to forget,* playing on hate, resentment, and guilt;

- *an extreme vigilance* for anything that could turn out to be a cause of psychic suffering and the disappearance of identificatory reference points that had been costly to acquire;

- *a hypercathexis,* sometimes successful but always restrictive, of a narcissistic object that can never fail, over which the exercise of power and mastery is set up as though it knew no bounds.

These defences allow the realization of a paradoxical compromise in which, in a totally contradictory movement, the effort to obliterate traces is repudiated by the frantic refusal to negate their marks, and in which dreamless sleep and decathexis are held in check by the hypercathexis of vigilance and mastery. This is in reality an untenable compromise, because it aims at something and its opposite, simultaneously.

Lethe, Hypnos and Thanatos with their double face thus shatter the possibility of *discovering historicity*.

Discovering historicity—and here I refer to the definition proposed by Lore Schacht (1977)[3] in his very interesting study on this subject—is a necessary precondition for the experience of history. Discovering historicity only happens in a relationship and only goes on growing on the basis of an experience of shared and communicated remembering. If the effort to create history is to be sustained, it requires someone to participate in remembering; it is embodied in a game of memories, or more precisely in the lasting experience of the game of memories between the baby and his mother and later on between the subject and himself.

Thus the sense of history is acquired through an activity of remembering between baby and mother, experienced in the mode of an exchange of pleasure whose memory is preserved.

These various reflections upon the links that join memory and history lead me to formulate a first hypothesis, given the clinical field that I propose to tackle:

- *The phantasy of a common memory between analyst and analysand* is one of the conditions for fruitfulness in the work of remembering in treatment, and for access to the experience of history.

On the basis of what I have advanced in this introduction, a second hypothesis also suggests itself:

- *Denial of historical and psychic reality, and decathexis* (Lethe, Hypnos and Thanatos) are grave-diggers for the phantasy representation of a common memory.

I shall immediately put these hypotheses to the test of clinical material.

(III)   SARAH, OR THE DECOMPOSED PAST

Sarah presented herself to me smothered with resentment, both in the literal and the figurative sense. She was periodically asthmatic and allergic. She could not breathe in her family and social universe, whose most banal opinions she shared no more than their ideals. She was always on the verge of breaking with her milieu. Incapable of working except in a routine way and of fixing her attention, she could not sustain any project. Everywhere she felt like a fish out of water.

Sarah had previously had a long analysis, which, she said, had been a total failure. There had been no improvement in her symptoms and difficulties in living—rather, the opposite. She was riddled with a boundless resentment against her first analyst, with whom she seemed to have had a tumultuous and eminently disputatious relationship in which she had essentially taken both the analytic setting and the conditions of work that were imposed upon her as targets for her attacks. She warned me at the outset that this time she was not going to accept submission to the totally arbitrary rule that obliged her to pay for her absences whatever the reason, and to function at someone else's pace. This did not stop her from laying claim, in the same breath, to three sessions a week on the couch. She could not forget the failure of this first analysis and ruminated in an obsessive way over the extremely precise memories that she had retained of it. She remembered everything that was said or that happened in it. What is more, Sarah never forgot anything—the best or the worst. She was not like her analyst, who remembered nothing and never answered her questions. Sarah usually slept without dreaming. Sleep was her chosen defence whenever she had a problem. But when she did dream, she never forgot her dreams. She remembered even them with an extreme and meticulous precision. Her decision to undertake another analysis had moreover been determined by a dream that had greatly affected and disturbed her. Sarah gave me the following account of it at the second interview.

'She found herself at sunset in a historic and anachronistic ruin, rather like Pompeii—Roman—but more in the style of Piranesi's engravings. It was not very precise, as though remains of various epochs had been collected there without coherence. In the midst of these ruins there was a little cemetery such as one comes across in the French countryside, with crosses on the graves, which was very confusing in the context. She walked through these ruins with a great sense of sadness and nostalgia. The peace of all this, which was in some way immutable, was disturbed in her mind by a sense of anarchy and disorder, because to her great surprise she saw her first analyst standing at the edge of the remains of a temple that looked out over a ditch, apparently immersed in deep meditation. Sarah hesitated. Would she go to talk to her? Would her analyst recognize her? Had she forgotten her? Seized with an uncontrollable impulse, she approached her from behind and pushed her into the ditch. Her analyst disappeared. Was this a hallucination?'

The highly articulated construction of the dream narrative, its sophisticated cultural reference in which personal references and references alluding to Freudian themes (Rome, Pompeii, the ruins) were probably condensed, suggested that the secondary elaboration that the dream had produced had only allowed the violence of the affects and instinctual wishes that the dream contained to filter through in measured drips. On the other hand, it seemed to me that the text-recollection of the dream should be regarded as an authentic work of memory and an attempt at dramatized figuration of the patient's relationship with her history and infantile past, as well as with the analytic process in so far as it was doing the work of reinterpreting this history. Sarah had thought a great deal about the dream and had given it many interpretations, all relatively accurate.

The past (she had still not told me anything about her history) rose up in her throat (she choked). Vestiges of a past that was not her own—Pompeii, eighteenth-century Rome, a cemetery in the French countryside (whereas her parents were not born in France)—had a sorrowful attraction for her, but she did not find herself there. She also thought that this dream expressed her bitterness towards her first analyst, but there was a gap—a ditch—between that and wiping her off the map and afterwards doubting the reality of her murderous gesture. Something was eluding her. What sort of wiping-off was this? Wiping out of an experience, of an event that had or had not happened? Sarah rightly thought that this dream incorporated her fundamental existential problem.

The eldest daughter of Jewish parents who had escaped the Holocaust and the camps, and who rebuilt their life in France after the war in conditions that were good enough to allow them to 'forget' and to continue to live, Sarah herself struggled not to forget what she had not experienced and against the effort to wipe out the past to which her parents, accused by her of voluntary amnesia, devoted themselves. For this reason she felt the keenest resentment towards them. 'If I abandon this resentment, which I agree makes me ill', she said, 'I would no longer exist. I would no longer have roots. I cannot forgive or forget, like my parents.' But for all that, Sarah dared not ask her parents about the past, particularly her mother, whom she suspected, on the basis of various scraps of information gleaned here and there from conversations in Yiddish that she secretly overheard when she should have been asleep, of having superintended the rescue of part of the family.—How, at what price, and thanks to what compromise with the enemy?

The prohibition against questioning her parents presented itself to Sarah in two ways:

• She forbade herself to question them in order not to make them suffer, guilty by her questioning of reminding them of a tragedy, but guilty also of reminding them of their own guilt as survivors.

- She forbade herself to acquire any knowledge that could enlighten her about the history of a collective murder in which she thought, without being able to admit it to herself or anyone else, that her community of origin had been a consenting victim.

   Silence weighed on Sarah like lead. Her parents explained nothing, and she asked nothing. This silence *stifled her*. Various somatic symptoms, notably asthmatic attacks that had made her agoraphobic, had led her to her first analyst. Sarah had married very young, to escape her family. She married into a family whose traditions, ideals and mentality were in absolute contradiction with those of her original milieu, or at least that is how she described it. However, treatment was gradually to reveal that Sarah had set up her in-laws as a persecuting object, at the cost of a colossal denial of reality. Its various constituent members were like the characters in Jean Genet's *Balcon* (1960) ('policeman, priest, man of law'), erected as exemplary reminders of an oppressive persecuting power. Through the absurd war that Sarah daily waged upon them, she could remember, oppose, but also allow herself secretly to document what really happened in order to furnish them with proofs of their crime against humanity. At the same time she was making up her own version of her forebears' collective and unusual history.

   Sarah had, it seemed, engaged in the same battle with her first analyst:

- on the one hand, forcing her to make admissions, answer questions, and provide knowledge of things she did not know and could not find out about alone;

- on the other hand, avoiding at any cost acquiring knowledge that would allow her to discriminate, to construct a history for herself and bring her instinct for investigation into play.

   During her first analysis Sarah often had a dream that had as its theme the last session of her analysis, a last session during which the truth, hidden and revealed by her analyst before a witness, put Sarah in a great state and filled her with shame and guilt. Like every dream about a session,[4] its affective climate was very intense; it presented the analyst as organizing the transgression of the analytical rule and depicted (this was not systematic, but was nonetheless extremely frequent) three generations (parents, the patient and children of the analyst and/or patient).

On several occasions Sarah also had dreams on the same theme during her analysis with me. Among these, one turned out to be of decisive importance for the continuation of the treatment. Giving a prominent role to her first analyst, as in the dream that she had brought me before undertaking her analysis, it allowed Sarah to reinterpret her past analytical relationship in a new light.

She dreamed that 'she went to her first analyst for her last session. She was very anxious and wanted to act as usual. It was not her analyst who opened the door but the latter's mother, whom she thought she recognized from having glimpsed her once at the beginning of her analysis, and who she thought had since died. This woman led her to the analyst's room, who was waiting for her with an unknown young girl whom she introduced as her daughter. In fact, this young girl resembled a younger sister of her mother who had died in the camps and whom her mother never mentioned, but whose photograph was omnipresent in her parents' flat. Her analyst invited her to sit in the armchair facing her. There were little cakes on a plate, and refreshments. Sarah thought there had been a mistake, that the analyst's mother was mistaken, and that she should not be there. She wanted to leave, but the analyst held her very tightly by the arm and forced her to sit down. She looked her straight in the eyes with a penetrating and rather severe air, and said to her, 'Oh, yes, we are indeed in 45'.

This dream, this narrative, her analysis, and the *inscription-film* and *excitation-screen* (Didier Anzieu, 1985, *Le Moi-Peau*, Chapter 17) that they had brought into being, had allowed Sarah to free herself from a state of extreme anxiety with hypochondriacal overtones: she had something bad inside her, at the same time feeling physically threatened by the resurgence of childhood memories that *stifled her*. (She was then missing numerous sessions or arriving very late, and she had a tendency in general to stay shut up at home as much as possible, stuffing herself with televised images).

One memory, a characteristic screen memory, then returned insistently to her, accompanied by a sense of disquieting strangeness. 'She was about six years old. Lying in the dark, in the same bed as her four-year-old brother, she heard her parents talking to other people in the adjoining room in a foreign language (their native tongue, which she neither spoke nor understood at that time). She rubbed her eyes so as not to fall asleep and tried to understand the sense of what she heard and to identify the voices. She woke up her brother, who immediately fell asleep again. On the following day she questioned her parents, who told her that she must have been dreaming (cf. the inaugural dream: was this a hallucination?). Sarah still to this day felt quickened with a destructive rage towards those who had imposed this denial of her reality upon her. She had had this same feeling towards her first analyst, who would not answer her and denied her psychic reality. While this manifest confrontation with a denial coming from someone else took on this unforgettable, traumatic and even hateful character, it was equally obviously a reflection of other denials internal to the subject, about which she wanted to know nothing, and which she ceaselessly projected outwards. During this period that preceded the dream about the session, horrible, isolated images also came back to her just as she was falling asleep, ones that had assailed her in her childhood nocturnal terrors (a gouged-out eye that was watching her, a disembowelled doll, a stream of blood that flowed under a door . . .). What gave her the greatest anguish was remembering a bodily sensation of her boundaries dissolving, in which, changed into a small shapeless thing, she was swallowed up by the gaping maw of a lion. All these representations of terrifying things that were not connected with any meaning and had no means of being contained drove Sarah to *stay awake,* as she did in childhood, because she was afraid above all of their reappearing in her sleep. She tried to maintain her vigilance by forcing herself into voluntary movements of opening and closing her eyes, while also reciting addresses and telephone numbers . . . and other meaningless things that simply demanded an effort of operatory memory. The vigilance maintained by these stereo-typed gestures and forcing her memory spared Sarah suffering from the recall of particularly painful moments in her infantile past. *She forced forgetfulness on herself* and in a sense manu-factured an *envelope of wakefulness* for herself.

As I have indicated, the dream about the session that I reported above turned out to be of central importance in the development of Sarah's treatment. In addition to marking a con-siderable reduction of her anxieties, the principal reason for this was that it took Sarah back to the memory of the dream that had precipitated her demand for a second analysis. She immediately sensed the existence of a link between the two dreams. However, during the interval of about four years that separated them, Sarah had never returned to the first dream. I had not myself invited her to take it up or remember it, although the elements of the dream had often come back to me in the associations awakened in me by Sarah's statements. When she had recounted it to me in the preliminary interviews, I had given no special weight to any of the interpretations that she had given me of it, any more than I had suggested others to her. Later on I had intuitively felt, given the demanding context in which Sarah's second analysis was undertaken, that it was better to keep this dream in memory and latency, and to let its trace sink in, both in her and in me, without prematurely deconstructing and unpeel-ing it. It is also likely that the murder-obliteration of her first analyst in a field of ruins and the clues that that gave me about her past transferential relationship had prompted prudence in me. After all, she made out that she forgot nothing, and she did not like people reminding her of things.

It was precisely through associations about her analyst's murder in the first dream, which Sarah in fact remembered per-fectly well, that she introduced her reflection on the dream about the session, a dream that had troubled her dreadfully and made her feel guilty but had also comforted her. In this way Sarah could at last grasp that the obliteration-murder of her analyst that she had dramatized, while also contriving to doubt its reality (was this not only a dream within a dream, or was her analyst really present? Was it a hallucination?), was intended to destroy any participation by her analyst in the ordering of her past and its exhumation, and to fill in the gap/ditch (and the word ditch was justifiably loaded for her with unspeakable horror) between the generations. Sarah had always done the same thing with her parents, although she had always maintained the opposite. It remained true that her parents had certainly never explained anything, and that she herself, especially in adolescence, had scarcely questioned them, being afraid to revive wounds of memory in them and too great a suffering.[5] Here and there she had gleaned disparate scraps of information. She had used it above all to manufacture persecutors for herself, which she persecuted in her turn by projection, on account of their ignorance and forgetfulness of the past. But all the same, when her parents did sometimes mention their past in front of her, she admitted that she did not listen and did not remember anything that was said. Fundamentally, she had never wanted to know anything, having always lived in fear of the disclosure of a secret, of a revelation that she should not know about (the secret of her birth, evoking the secret of her parents' survival?).

In the grip of an insoluble psychic conflict between the contradictory demand to refer to a *necessary memory that forbade forgetting* and *a forbidden memory that necessitated forgetting*, Sarah could not have access to the dimension of historicity in the sense in which I defined it above and to the structuring phantasy that there existed a common, shareable memory.

Sarah's dream about the session seemed to me to reflect this attempt to initiate a process of communicable recollection. This interpretative hypothesis enabled her to return to the first dream and to view it as the opposite expression of the wishes and thoughts contained in the dream about the session.

Here I shall summarize the essential points that we sifted out from our work in comparing the two dreams.

In the first dream, *three epochs* were represented:

- Pompeii, so alive the day before, but inexorably frozen in a dreamless sleep from one day to the next by a cataclysm that was unforeseeable and radically murderous;

- eighteenth-century Rome, which hides behind its façades and in its cellars the ruins of ancient Rome that she exhumes and destroys in a single movement;

- a little contemporary French cemetery, the place of rest of ancestors that in no way belong to Sarah.

Sarah is alone in the half-light before the relics of the past. The analyst–witness is destroyed and disappears without trace, without a word, and even, one might suppose, without glimpsing the presence of Sarah, who in any case attacked her from the back.

In the dream about the session *three generations* of women are present together:

- the analyst's mother, whom Sarah believed to be dead, was there and very much alive (Sarah revives the dead);

- her first analyst, a figure to remind Sarah of her analytic past and a metaphor for a certain relationship that Sarah had to her past, is also alive and introduces herself face-to-face. In no way is she ready to let herself be pushed into the ditch. She invites Sarah to penetrate her interior, her intimacy. She feeds her, introduces her to her forebears and descendants and, to crown the transgression of the analytical rule, touches Sarah;

- the character of the analyst's daughter is condensed with that of the mother's younger sister, tragically pushed into the ditch, and whose memory had never ceased to haunt Sarah and doubtless also her mother, each in the anguished silence of their own night, but without anything at all about it ever being communicated by either of them. It then became possible to establish Sarah's identification with the dead child and with her place in her mother's wishes and past.

The scene took place in broad daylight; Sarah was closely surrounded, almost too much so.

Her analyst spoke firmly, giving a date ('we are in 45'), a period that signifies both the end of a nightmare and the prospect of a possible future.

At the same time as she was analysing and comparing the two dreams, Sarah set about digging not only into her psychic past, but also in her own and her parents' cupboards. She brought me document-witnesses of her childhood (photos, albums of drawings and notebooks), as well as some papers and objects of her parents' personal (and not collective) past (a pass that permitted a frontier to be crossed, photos of their native village before it was razed, little cult objects that had belonged to her grandparents . . .). She showed me all these objects so that I could get a real idea of her as a little girl, and of her family. She did not particularly want me to talk about them; I was simply to see these indications of the past before giving them back to her and then keeping them in memory.

The real objects that some patients show us, sometimes hand to us or want us to look after, have value as transitional objects, creating a space for exchanges and communication. But I also think that bringing proof and 'things' that relate to their past, something that necessarily registers in our material and psychic space, responds in them to a need for figurability, the same need that orders dream thoughts so as to weave their web, a web without which they could not secondarily be put into words.

I shall not take any further my account of this observation of Sarah's relationship with her memory and her past, examined through the experience and memory of a first analysis. In so doing I have of course left in the dark other essential aspects of her problematic, in particular everything in her that touched upon the unconscious equation that she had made between the fact of being Jewish and a woman, an *unforgettable* condition that for her meant inferiority and castration. With an unusual determination she sought unconsciously to wipe out its traces and destroy evidence for it, maintaining to the utmost her denial of reality by means of counter-cathexes and cultural and ideological hyper-cathexes.

Sarah had come to me complaining, amongst other woes, of the absence of a memory of her analyst, an absence that had wounded her in the same place as her own memory wounds. It was a repetition of her relationship to her parents, and above all to her mother, as she confirmed, but she unconsciously asked for it in her intimate conviction that no communication was possible and that she would never be able to find in another person the means of forming roots, a past and an identity. She could not find it in herself either.

Sarah's memory holes had developed at the level of her cultural history and her individual libidinal and instinctual history, with the two levels constantly reacting upon one another and being inseparable.

In fact, we know very well that the mechanisms of individual memory are in constant interaction with those of collective memory, without which they could not function. Conversely, the mechanisms of collective memory could not function either with individual memory being brought into play.

For Sarah, therefore, the break in memory that had separated her from her parents, themselves cut off from their roots, had confused for her the transmission of an individual myth about her origin. In parallel, reference in her collective history to a myth that defined the death of the community had prevented her, like many others of her generation, from sharing with her parents in a guiltless communal living memory, weaving a cultural memory envelope that could support validating identifications.

But these difficulties surrounding knowledge and the evocation of her past were also linked for Sarah with her encounter with excessive and premature suffering and psychic excitation (an over-protective mother who was not much available, a depressive and guilty father, and excessive proximity to the maternal body . . .) that had produced movements of hate and destructiveness in her, and decathexis of traces that were too pronounced. Unable to establish with another person a narcissistic relationship that was founded upon the exchange of pleasure and communications, thereby maintaining a 'good-enough' separation, she could not enter into positive communication with herself, nor with her memory. Every process of recall revived her wounds and swamped her in guilt, sometimes not without masochistic compliance and demandingness.

Sarah could no more write her own history and gain access to self-knowledge than she could locate herself within a genealogy and a community.

It is this that it seemed her first analyst had taught her and made her painfully relive. The work she did with the latter, and that she only completed with the dream about the session, by ceasing to denigrate, had also awakened in her the desire to recover her memory of it, even if she did not readily admit it.

These last remarks based upon observation of Sarah prompt me to take up several points of Freudian theory on memory and forgetting and the psychic processes that they bring into play.

(IV)   THEORETICAL PERSPECTIVES

In any analytical experience, we are dealing with two forms of memory and forgetting:

- a form of memory that is not memorable, is unchanging, repetitive and unalterable in time and presents itself in the form of *an unorganized, unconnected amnesia.*

- a form of forgetful memory, *an organized amnesia,*[6] that is incessantly being transformed so that it contradicts itself, is rewritten, is wiped out, surfaces again, is registered in temporality, and is worked on by phantasy, thought and interpretation.

The analyst's memories are cut from the same cloth as are the patient's. Memories of one will answer the other's memories in echo, will interpenetrate and weave a common web on which the analytic work unfolds in its uniqueness.

(1)   Memory that can neither be remembered nor forgotten

This memory, which could broadly be described as *prehistoric,* is not located within the field of the memorable. It resists the wear and tear of time as well as the temporal framework of the secondary process. It is made up of the indelible traces of *early impressions* left by real influences brought to bear upon instinctual and phantasy life. It lasts for the whole of life. This memory forms a disparate collection of inscriptions, *a reticulated network of con-tact barriers* or, more precisely in Didier Anzieu's words, an *'inscription surface, distinct from the excitation-screen* to which it is coupled for protection' (Anzieu, 1985, p. 79).

Freud always maintained that the impressions made or suf-fered by the child in an inaugural encounter between reality and his instincts have a decisive influence upon subsequent psychic activity. This reference to impression [*Eindruck*], in the strong sense of imprinting, is fundamental in the first Freudian con-ception of memory. It denotes the passive receptivity of the psy-chic and instinctual disposition towards infantile experience. In the 'Project' (1950a [1895]), where Freud states that memory is represented by differences in facilitations between the neurones, he defined memory as being the enduring power of an *Erlebnis,* a power that depends upon the intensity of the impression produced and the frequency of its repetition. However, this memory, erected upon impressions that are certainly susceptible to later elaborations, cannot be thought of in terms of 'past'. It *belongs* to the past and remains partly, if not wholly, unknowable as such. Only tokens (repetitions, unusual and insistent reminiscences, stereotyped gestures and reactions . . .) allow us to deduce its traces. In Maurice Dayan's words (1986, part 2, chapter 14), this memory is taken directly into the unconscious, whence its indel-ible character, its prehistoric dimension and its power. I feel that it is necessary to insist afresh upon the passivity that we display when faced with this active form of unorganized memory. In fact, it cannot be bound except by an excitation-screen that comes from someone else. Holding, according to Winnicott, Bion's alpha func-tion, the mother's capacity for reverie—and, I would add, for memory—her sensitivity to the baby's evident or supposed feel-ings, her potential for connectedness by means of touch and voice are so many sources of support for preserving his impressions in a containing bodily and psychic envelope. Neither connectedness nor mastery are within the scope of the subject on his own. This is why, as Jean Laplache (1984) stressed, the aim in treatment to reappropriate this sort of memory in the first person is illusory and boundless, if not megalomaniac. The analyst can only restore it to the patient by appeal to what I would like to call *deductive imagination.* It seems to me that this modality of approach is implicit in the epistemological perspective that Freud always maintained when he compared the activity of the prehistorian with that of the psychoanalyst. Prehistorian and psychoanalyst alike aim for a certain knowledge of the past; both believe in the initiating and determining function for the subsequent course of a history of processes and acts accomplished in the past. Deprived of the research materials, direct means of investigation and archival documents that are at the disposal of a historian or a biographer, the prehistorian and the psychoanalyst must restore the prehistoric past on the basis of traces inscribed unbeknownst and involuntarily in a place, a body or a mind.

To guide him in his prehistoric research, the analyst has the patient's discourse and all that it conveys, the transference in its different tonalities, but perhaps still more certain fleeting moments in treatment in which memory vanishes, images of indescribable things invade psychic space, and unformulable affects saturate the analytic field.

If we want to make interpretable what is going on in the patient at these times, we are led to resort to 'constructions in analysis'—as Freud (1937) described them—whose power comes from the content of *historical* truth that they tapped into in the repression of the forgotten original phases. When these constructions are pertinent and presented at the appropriate moment . . . they generally lead to awareness of significant memory traces to which there had never been access until that moment.

In my opinion, however, *constructions in analysis* owe their effectiveness to their *figurative potential*. I have already insisted above, in connection with the observation of Sarah, upon the importance of the imperative demand for figurability that asserts itself at certain moments in treatment, when words alone lose their credit and prove unfit for communication. I now come back to this again. In fact, I think that access to unrememberable memory comes about through giving figurative form to the impressions that compose it.

In treatment, the analyst's transformation of what he understands into visual evocations facilitates his recall. It also facilitates the patient's recall. However, under some circumstances, the bridges between words and things have been broken. This is

why it then seems that when we propose to the patient a construction–reconstruction of a moment in his prehistory that is
significant in our eyes, it is necessary to communicate how we
represent to ourselves visually something that he has explicitly
told us is incommunicable for him and constitutes a blank in his
history and his mind.

Thus, for example, when Sarah saw herself as having a sense
of disquieting strangeness, losing her boundaries, without identity, metamorphosed into a little shapeless thing swallowed up by
a lion's gaping maw, I said to her that I, myself, 'see in this
representation the image of a very little girl in distress, losing
her breath, without eyes, without a mouth, without ears, without
arms, without legs, who cannot either be aware of the external
world nor take anything from it . . . and that this image evokes
for me the painful absence for her of the gaze, mouth, breath,
ears, and arms of her mother, who during her early infancy was
too absorbed in her father's serious depression. . . .' With this I
suggested to her an image of her body that she could then see
from the outside, and which at the same time reflected to her the
difficult and scarcely containing relationship that she must have
had with her mother's body and mind.

I think that strength of conviction, upon which Freud insisted
so much, is to a great extent linked to the figurative[7] support that
provides the image of a body experience connected with an affect
upon which the analyst leans to propose his construction–reconstruction of a previously unknown past. All the same, infantile
amnesia is not entirely lifted, although part of the unknowable
that it conceals becomes imaginable, partially thinkable, and
interpretable within the mnesic system that obeys the secondary
processes. Through the slant of the construction, the subject gains
access to a part of himself from which he had until then been
separated.

(2) Forgetful and memorable memory

Forgetful and memorable memory is an *organized amnesia* that is
governed by the activity of the secondary processes. Its dynamic
and economy are determined by psychic conflict (conflict between
wishes and identifications, between organizations, between the

ego and reality . . .). It is by definition unfaithful. Always in transformation, it is written and rewritten in temporality, simultaneously giving a sense of continuity of the self and of difference from self to self over time.

Constantly undergoing processes of deformation, it works on traces and mnesic representations that are fundamentally connected with phantasy and ideational activities. Memories, phantasies and thoughts are not raw materials, but materials that have already been elaborated and composed and are of 'mixed race'.

Under the constraint of the rule of free association imposed upon the patient in treatment, they well up from apparently insignificant details, but ones that lead nonetheless to unconscious and preconscious associative chains that get going and set off a process of recall. But, and this is a fundamental point, this work of recall is a work of *transcription,* for all that every transcription *admits what it states while concealing it.* This evidence of the distortion that is inseparable from memory and memories prompts me to dwell briefly upon the importance of the memory-screen in the formation of a memory envelope, understood this time as a *surface of transcription.* The memory-screen, whose sensorial and perceptual liveliness is well known, serves as protective membrane for an unconscious and inadmissable memory that it nonetheless stirs up, and which seeks to return.

Recall is the outcome of an active psychic process that consists in working on the remains of a memory-screen or a phantasy of a dream . . . in such a way as to construct a new compromise between what they represent of the subject's eventful, libidinal and identificatory past, his current problem in relating to this past, what he will tolerate, and not knowing and knowing it.

In some sense the rememberable past, once remembered, is woven from the products of forgetting it, and the distortions and falsifications to which memory subjects the past bear witness to the effectiveness or non-effectiveness of its functioning.

Nonetheless, among the mechanisms that conspire to produce forgetfulness, only secondary repression (contrary to denial and foreclosure) leads to a form of constructive forgetting, because it allows the elements that went into its elaboration to be retained within the psyche. Only repression enables the past to be restored in the form of a historicizing memory. All the richness of the processes of distortion connected with repression is founded on a preserving forgetting that ensures the permanence in the psyche of lived experience.

Repression aims essentially at excluding from the field of conscious awareness those instinctual representations and desires that are incompatible with the unbreakable prohibitions upon murder and incest, whose internalization is indispensable for the construction of an identificatory scheme that is supported by the subject's own wishes while respecting cultural demands.

However, holes in memory that are consequent upon repression are not structuring unless they present a common thread (a common skin) with a repressing parental organization that has itself repressed the same wishes and the same instinctual and phantasy representations in the past. The baby's incestuous and murderous wishes produce echoes and reminiscence in the parents, thereby disturbing their own barrier of repression. This normally has the effect of stimulating their repressive forces, for they, too, must protect themselves from the return of what they themselves have repressed.

In reality, repression always errs on the side either of excess or of default. There is never a perfect accord between parental repression and infantile repression, but a compromise is always possible if the transmission from subject to subject of what is repressed remains assured.[8]

(3) Collective cultural memory

The repressive function plays a large part in the formation of an *envelope of organized amnesia* that is transmitted from generation to generation, maintains living links between them, allows access to collective cultural memory, brings the instinct for investigation into play and favours sublimations of instinctual impulses that have not been repressed.

But the contents of this envelope, preserved within it, remain peculiar to each individual. They are made from private memory, from the most secret phantasies, from the maddest desires, and from unique and indelible traces inscribed in a particular body and mind.

The restoration of the past through the filter of organized amnesia can be understood at one and the same time as *a failure and a success in forgetting*:

- *a failure*, which marks resistance by the unconscious to the wear and tear of time and the obliteration of traces and indicates the return of the repressed;

- a *success*, which, by contrast, marks the possibility for the mind of being transformed, of being changed by the effects of the work of time.

(4)   Attacks on memory

Unrememberable, unforgettable memory, forgetful memory that nonetheless remembers that it forgets, and cultural memory are in constant interaction, just as the different psychic organizations are, while each of them preserves its own respective area of activity. They are also in conflict and subject to the action of Lethe, Hypnos and Thanatos, which, in pursuing the obliteration of traces and decathexis, at the same time attack the subject's memory, that of others, and the representation of a possible communal memory, which goes hand-in-hand with a possible communal forgetting.

In fact, an ideal memory envelope cannot exist. That would presuppose that 'life's memory' could function in completed time, protected from all internal and external attack, could only know the structuring modalities of forgetting and could only come up against excitation-screens, and ones that were always sufficiently protective.

In any case, part of ourselves remains a stranger forever and is lost to recall. Work on the memory, through memory, which the analytic process aims towards, meets its ultimate limit there. What is more, the repressing organization is never without defects, any more than one could absolutely say that—as Freud maintained with well-known tenacity—every psychic trace is forever indestructible.

Clinical experience of psychosis demonstrates to what extent the repressing organization is defective there, devoid of any historicizing dimension, and does not respond to any imperative that transmits cultural prohibitions, but operates in an arbitrary fashion, tending basically to protect parents from the revelation of their infanticidal violence. We also know that in psychosis the attack on linking and the propensity for decathexis are such that they end up by destroying traces of what has happened and creating irreparable holes in representational activity (cf. Aulagnier, 1985). By the same token, psychic problematics organized around denial, by keeping what for them constitutes the unthinkable and the source of irreparable narcissistic wounds outside psychic topography and not merely out of awareness, are bearers of memory holes and decathexes that prove themselves far from being constructive. There, too, the repressing organization is especially deficient, to the extent to which, in order not to have to forbid the breaking of prohibitions, it aims to establish a disclaiming pact supported by a more or less perverse narcissistic contract.[9]

What is more, each one of us, at some moment or another, cherishes the impossible dream of waking up without memory, without past, relieved by a miracle of haunting memories, of alienating connections and of 'visitors to the ego' (cf. A. de Mijolla, 1981) that undermine our projects. Just as the ego-skin has a 'toxic' function (D. Anzieu, 1985) in the service of Thanatos, the memory envelope also has a toxic function, a poisoned, self-destructive tunic that instigates flight from all recall and encounter with memory, and memories of another person.

Letting myself to be guided in this work on the memory envelope by the preconscious and unconscious promptings of my own memory of an analyst, I have adopted a path that could look like a short-cut. I have, in fact, approached memory and its pathology from an individual slant, namely one that, in its manifest clinical form, turns back, on the wane of an analytic experience, past and present attacks suffered by the patient's memory as it complains about memory of the analyst and the work on memory intrinsic to the analytic process.

In fact, the singularity of the observation of Sarah's case allowed me to describe through the mangifying and distorting prism of the memory-screen of a past analysis, which had brought memory to life and led to a negative therapeutic reaction, what the psychic obstacles might be to the institution of a real and imaginary communal memory, without which no structuring memory envelope exists that can bear the power of transmission. In so doing, I have also indicated that patients who do violence to our memory, who fear it or refuse it, induce us more than others to canvass our colleagues' memory, and to want to leave some trace of the theorizations that they suggest to us, thus enlivened by the hope that they will come back to us in echo.

NOTES

1. Micheline Enriquez, Du corps en souffrance au corps de souffrance, part 2, chapter 4; L'ecriture représentative, part 3, chapter 1, *Aux carrefours de la haine* (1984).
2. *Blessures de mémoire*: title of a book by Michel Schneider, 1980.
3. Lore Schacht, La découverte de l'historicité, *Mémoires, N.R.P.* (1977), no. 15.
4. Cf. on this subject: Michel Neyraut, Les actes et les signes. *Le transfert*, part 4 (1973), p. 245; Micheline Enriquez, Harmonie et dysharmonie dans la cure. *Aux carrefours de la haine*, part 3, chapter 3 (1984).
5. Nadine Fresco has written an anguished text of truth on the psychic and identificatory drama lived through by the children of survivors of the Holocaust: La diaspora des cendres, N.R.P., No. 24. *L'emprise* (Paris: Gallimard, 1981).
6. The expression is by J. Rouart, Le souvenir comme amnésie organisée, *Revue Française de psychanalyse*, Mémoire et souvenir (July–August, 1979). Paris: P.U.F.
7. Piera Aulagnier has made an essential contribution on this subject, Du langage pictural au langage de l'interprète. *Topique, 26* (1980).
8. Piera Aulagnier has insisted at length on the importance for our psychic functioning of transmission of what is repressed from subject to subject. This allows the repressing function to be made into a cultural invariant. Cf. P. Aulagnier, Conclusion, Chapter 1: Orwell ou le mécanisme de la double pensée, in *L'Apprenti historien et le maître-sorcier* (1984), pp. 250–251.
9. On the 'disclaiming pact', I would refer the reader to the especially stimulating work on ideology of René Kaës, *L'idéologie: Études psychanalytiques* (Paris: Dunod, 1980).

CHAPTER FIVE

The hysterical envelope

A. Anzieu

One of the characteristics of hysteria is excitability, another being repression of the sexual instinct. This situation might seem contradictory, had Freud and his successors not given multiple explanations of it. The hysteric presents in some sense as an excitable surface whose contents do not respond to excitation. The hysterical adult's body functions like his psychic apparatus: communications between sensoriality and pleasure have been severed. Surface is separated from inside by the void created both by repression and by infantile amnesia. The baby, as we know, is caught up in his identifications with his mother, that is, in the dialectic of projection and internalization of objects.

My clinical experience has led me to think that when the mother is depressed, the character of the baby submitted to her projections is influenced in its structure by the mother's reactional stirrings towards her own depression. In particular, the form of the mother's defences against depression can induce in the baby an inordinate cathexis of sensory excitations that are confused with internal excitations, without the ego being able to integrate this overflow of excitation because of its insufficient maturity. In this case, the baby can make himself an envelope of excitation in which he gets enclosed and evolves separately. 'Fruitless excitations . . . produce a disposition towards anxiety' (Freud, 1926d, ch. IV).

(I)   THE HYSTERIC AND HIS MOTHER

(1)   Hysterical defences

During analytical treatment, when associations appear that reveal that an uncontrollable communication is taking place between body and mind, a communication that is often broken, inadequate, full of gaps and apparently illogical, it is then that it is possible to discern something of what hysterical defences are made up of. The work of reconstruction set in train by the first glimmerings of awareness, and then by the partial lifting of certain repressions, allows a glimpse of the dynamic structuring of hysterical defences out of their psychogenetic sources. What, or what anxiety, has the hysteric built his defences against? How can we organize an 'exploration of the mechanisms that produce the clinical phenomena' (Meltzer, 1980)?

On the subject of obsessional neurosis, Freud (1913i) considered how the ego's development seems to take the lead over libidinal development. Adopting this perspective, it seems to me, with S. Lebovici (1974), that in the hysteric it is possible to recognize an advance of libidinal development over that of ego mechanisms—an advance or even a prevalence, if one considers that genetically ancient processes (early identifications, primary narcissistic cathexes) have been resumed at the oedipal period and recathected afresh at puberty.

My curiosity and my wish to reconstruct, if not to repair, prompt me to look for what roots have become entangled in the foundations of the hysterical character and its suffering. Perhaps it is simply difficult to think that in the hysteric there is no psychic mediation between excitation and symptom. When Freud undertook to understand the sources of hysteria, he attached particular importance to anxiety. He established that the defence constructed by the hysteric was achieved in one of two ways:

anxiety was displaced either into the body, and that was conversion hysteria, or onto external objects, and that was phobia or anxiety hysteria.

The hysteric therefore presents as a person who is suffering from manifestations that betray a great anxiety whose source is repressed. Repression protects the ego from becoming aware of discontents or failures connected with the workings of the libido. The symptom deflects the libido and results in displeasure, which substitutes for and protects libidinal pleasure.

But it remains true that 'anxiety has an unmistakable relation to expectation: it is anxiety *about* something. It has a quality of indefiniteness and lack of object' (Freud, 1926d, Addenda). We can therefore attempt to identify more precisely the absent object and the forms that it takes in the hysteric, in order to approach the source of the repression and what has brought the symptom into play.

(2)   The case of Mrs G

Reference to clinical work often allows us to grasp certain initial moments in neurosis. Thus, Mrs G, who is under 30, is what would once have been called a grand hysteric. Nonetheless, I sometimes doubt this and catch myself thinking that she is psychotic. Her younger brother was not lucky enough to be able to avoid that risk. Filled with an infantile and mysterious charm, with a fringe over her eyes, very long hair, long skirts that clutch at her ankles and filmy capes and scarves, looking like a little girl, she declaimed in a rather shrill voice her somatic ills of every kind with a smile and an abundance of reproaches; after some time, she mainly spoke of the massive anxiety that gripped her at the idea of any and every contact.

As far as I could understand, her mother is manic-depressive, if not melancholic. Mrs G remembers her mother's gaze on her sick-bed: an empty gaze that did not fix on anything and was maddening for the child. Her father's principal characteristic was being absent and having other women. It is apparent from all her memories that from birth onwards she suffered both from her mother's deep depression and from her manic and erotic defences. From her tenderest years, she was

forced to sit unmoving by this mother. She was given to understand in violent terms that she was killing her mother. She
was accused of being born expressly to martyr her mother. Her
father's rare visits to the house did no more than stoke up the
internal fire that she had always felt was there. Nonetheless,
she was relieved of various excemas. Each time she came to see
me, she had 'her' colon trouble again, which she talked about
with an aggressive enjoyment. She was unemployed because
she was incapable of presenting herself for work. She was
never able to display self-confidence. Everything was difficult
and demanded a big effort from her; she often shook, her hands
would be paralysed, and she would drop things.

She was married, but she made out that her husband was
impotent most of the time. But she often contradicted herself
when she had enough critical spirit to recognize her own
refusal and frigidity. After a period of 'analysis' (I saw her face
to face), she was torn between the desire to change and be
active, and disgust or non-desire about committing herself to
anything at all. Nonetheless she was intelligent, refined and
cultivated, and she had qualifications, although she had not
been able to cope with the marked change that the end of her
studies and her marriage had made to her life. She could not
imagine having a baby, the object of many persecutory projections on her part. She was manifestly identified with the baby
who destroys the mother, with which her own mother, in her
own words, had 'inseminated' her. In her transferential
relatonship with me, the most obvious manifestation was the
massive anxiety that she experienced at every separation
(even in the interval between sessions), in dread of losing the
support that she was gradually internalizing. No less obvious
was her resumption of somatic experiences when she came
back to me, filled with more or less direct reproaches. There
also gradually appeared an unconscious dread of having to talk
to me about possible sexual enjoyment.

To return to Freudian nosology, Mrs G, presented symptoms
of a conversion hysteria. She expressed very well a certain
relationship between her bodily ills and the irrepressible feeling of anxiety that she very often felt, the little desire that she
had to go out, to eat certain things or to have sexual relations.

She was continuously preoccupied with her parents' lives and gradually connected moments of her anxiety to the worry that her mother had always represented for her. She sensed and expressed clearly how cruel and agonizing the repression of her childhood motility and the manifestations of her first desires had been.

She altogether corresponds with the way Eric Brenman (1985) described hysteria. Mrs G appeared 'extremely mad', 'malleable' and 'hysterical'. She herself described herself as having been a 'spongy' child.

(3)   Features of the hysterical character

I will note some features common to Mrs G and persons whose hysterical character is clearly marked:

- intense sensoriality and great affective sensitivity;

- recall during treatment of the more or less seriously depressive character of one or both parents, most often the mother, especially in the first months of the baby's life;

- the feeling that these persons have particular difficulty in handling quantities of instinct;

- finally, the early appearance of difficulties in the relationship between the subject and their maternal environment.

These difficulties reveal a certain global hyper-excitation, from which, in my opinion, oedipal cathexis will produce hysterical symptomatology.

The newborn baby who is received by a loving but depressed mother finds itself in a situation that has a direct effect upon the establishment and mode of its narcissism. It is therefore the mother's depressive stirrings at the time of the baby's birth that especially influence the formation of hysterical anxieties. These depressive stirrings adopt variable forms and intensities, depending upon the mother's psychic structure. In the differences of quality and intensity of this depression the baby's identificatory system may be pulled towards a hysterical character or neurosis.

In terms of the theories of the Kleinian school, one can think that projective, introjective and identificatory processes function from the first moments of life as an initial movement in the formation of the ego. The infant whose mother is depressed will find his reference points in the mirror provided—as Winnicott said (1971)—by his mother's eyes, but a mirror that is empty of desire when the mother is depressed. It is in this way that serious maternal depression can bring about infantile psychosis, and it is also this that I am sometimes afraid that I see appearing in Mrs G. By contrast, in cases of less severe maternal depression, compensated for by sufficient manic defences, certain newborns are perhaps predisposed to become hysterics.

(II)   MATERNAL DEPRESSION

The case of Céline

Céline is two and a half. She is pretty and curly-haired, and she talks well; she has a lively gaze. She has always been nervous and agitated and has a temper when people do not fit in with her. She has always slept little at night, something that was becoming a torment for her parents. For some time she had been screaming when put on the pot, explaining very well that she was frightened of the regular patterns of the floor-tiles, or else of drops of water on the ground. She was also frightened of puddles of water outside. She was afraid to go out. For some time she had also often been refusing to eat, particularly meat. The mother told me, blushing, how, having had a boy first, she had played dolls with baby Céline.

While telling me this, she took an enormous ham sandwich out of her bag and offered it to her daughter. The latter pushed it away, turning her head aside. Then, on second thoughts, Céline went to look for the sandwich and put it to my mouth. I bit into it. Céline, very surprised, gazed at me deeply. She then picked out two or three little bits of ham that she put between my lips in succession. All of a sudden she smiled, squatted on her feet against me as I sat, and ate all the rest of the sandwich, saying to me, 'It's nice, eh?' By all accounts, I was not a poisoner, and the sandwich was not deadly.

During this scene, as in each of our interviews, her mother revealed pathological anxiety. She wearied me with her complaints, her passivity, her absence of pleasure, her inhibition, and her multiple somatic concerns, especially gynaecological ones, that she would expound to a multiplicity of doctors. Céline's father had struck me on the first visit as having a rather effeminate and asthenic appearance. Over the period of Céline's psychotherapy he moved towards a sort of melancholia with mystic preoccupations and left his family for distant lands. The manner he had of caressing his little girl had seemed to me curiously 'out of place', without my being able to put my finger on what was inappropriate about it.

Freud would no doubt have talked about anxiety hysteria in connection with Céline. Nowadays, referring to the specificity of the symptom, we would speak of phobia.

When a child is afraid of the dark, is he not already somewhat hysterical? Céline did not sleep, and she disturbed her parents' sleep. Her phobic fears appeared crudely. It seemed, indeed, that the emergence of wishes and fears of an oedipal order were in process of installing symptoms on a particular ground of excitability, provoked by the relationship that had been established between the child, an overly tender father and a depressive mother. The latter was now becoming terrifying and could not serve her daughter either as excitation-screen or as container for a mental life that was emerging in the form of phantasms.

To some extent Céline seemed to me to be rather like one might imagine Mrs G to have been as a baby: submitted to the wishes of a mother who became depressed, the little girl was struggling with all her might against this submission. She demonstrated during her treatment how the solid part of her ego was shouldering her mother's weaknesses in the absence of her father, of whom she had internalized a sufficiently phallic image.

Maternal depression arises in many forms and with various characteristics. It is obvious that the couple who were Céline's parents and those of Mrs G did not both share an identical distribution of neurotic symptoms. Nevertheless, it remains true that the two mothers were depressed, Mrs G's mother even to the extent of needing several hospitalizations, and that Céline's father was to turn out to be melancholic.

Thinking about this led me towards a need to distinguish quantity and qualities of depression. Depression is usually described as deep or slight, thereby attributing a quantitative appearance to a psychic state that does not seem to me to be sufficiently defined in that way. If I try to systematize the observations that I have been able to draw from clinical work, maternal depression around the birth of a baby can be characterized by three degrees of intensity or seriousness, each with very different qualitative characteristics. These characteristics essentially depend upon the object relationship into which the newborn may find himself drawn by his mother.

(1) Psychotic depression

Anxiety seems to have completely invaded the woman's psychic space, not even leaving what is necessary for the expectation that Freud speaks of as the content of anxiety. No chink turns out to be free in the mother's psychic space for this object-to-be, the baby. The latter remains 'something' that is absent, at best included in a space whose representation persists in keeping it intra-uterine.

Depression in this sort of mother presents as an anaclitic depression. The baby remains included in the maternal self as a morsel, not differentiated from this self. But it is excluded as a differentiated object from representations of its mother's life and reality. The baby received by a mother in this situation is in danger of psychosis. It is faced with the necessity to detach itself from maternal identifications that make it into a false lost object, an object that is not one, and that finds itself at most identified with a morsel of a poorly defined and uncentred ego.

The baby will therefore have infinite difficulty in constructing an ego that will be its own, being gradually differentiated from this included part-object with which his mother permanently identifies him. As a result, his early defences will tend to be narcissistic or even psychotic, rather than hysterical.

Mrs G gave me cause to fear this difficulty when she wondered whether she did not sometimes hallucinate certain images of her father. Or again when she reported a very simple dream: she found herself inside an impervious ball. She left me thus in perplexity, reminding me of Bion's (1967, ch. 4) ideas about psychosis: splitting and projective fragmentation in identification, something irreparable for the ego. But undoubtedly Mrs G had also preserved elsewhere a non-psychotic part of her personality, which was able to take in and repair the sickest part. She 'suppressed a fragment of the id (instinctual life)', and this, according to Freud, distinguishes her from the psychotic (Freud 1924b).

If the mother is incapable of elaborating the bodily separation of a birth, identifying the baby with an irreplaceable content, without distance and without space for fitting together, the baby remains included in the same way as his own representations. Separation is denied. The psychotic infant has no psychic space of its own, because its mother has been unable to differentiate the object contained in her internal organic space from the external object that she has evacuated. Intra-uterine occupation has not been transformed into maternal preoccupation. A little girl of eight did, in fact, make this distinction during her therapy, and, when speaking of her mother's tummy, she called it a 'baby-box'; she used the term 'thought-box' for the head.

(2)   Narcissistic depression

The case of Mireille and little K

Mireille was under thirty years of age. A long history of anorexia, in which traces of a terror of abandonment were to be found, had left life with rather a bitter taste for her. Married, without pleasure, without much investment in her profession, she blamed on her permanent amenorrhoea the sterility that devalued her even further: her brothers and her sister all had children.

After several years of analysis, during a slow evolution towards more positive narcissistic feelings, Mireille became pregnant. She had great difficulty in believing it. So did I.

When little K was born, she was received by Mireille with an impassioned enthusiasm in which I thought I perceived that the young mother was completely identified with this baby girl whom she erotized in a manner that very quickly became excessive. After some while she confided to me the considerable depression in which she found herself because of the withdrawal of her husband as much from her as from little K. She was experiencing enormous difficulty in getting back her feminine identity, barely outlined previously, and she was lost for the present in the boundless primary love that she exchanged with K.

K became, and for long months remained, the only libidinal object in which Mireille was really interested.

For two years I had frequent opportunities to encounter K. In fact, for a long time Mireille imposed her presence on me during her sessions, on the pretext that she was feeding her and therefore could not be separated from her, 'given the times that I imposed on her for her sessions'. Then weaning was impossible—K refused any food other than her mother's breast. Finally K refused to be separated from her mother, or to walk in the latter's absence, as though she were dizzy. It took nearly two years to bring Mireille to distance herself a little from her daughter and to recathect her conjugal relationship.

During this time, when I encountered little K, she seemed to me through her smiles, the corners of her eyes, and her provocation towards me to be developing symptoms that suggested an early hysteria to me: refusal of food, vomiting, fear of her father and at the same time active searching for him, then repeated dizziness and ear infections, and libidinal pleasure became painful in her exchanges with her mother. Happily, the latter was able to emerge from her depression, which I shall call narcissistic.

In fact, I think that, thanks to Mireille's maternal achievement during her analysis with me, I have been able to characterize a sort of depression that occurs in a narcissistic woman at the birth of a baby. The fact that here the baby was a girl is undoubtedly not unimportant, but other similar cases have come along to support this observation.

In proportion to the fragility of her feminine narcissistic structure, the mother endures separation with more or less difficulty from a phallic object whose carnal possession she has cathected for months on end. It is not really surprising that this separation brings on a depression that could be described as reactional or even reactive—a pre-oedipal infantile depression accompanied by devaluing feelings of castration.

These elements of the depression have close links with aspects of the feminine Oedipus complex, already so much studied, and also with the distinction between feminine parts and maternal parts of the woman's personality and their harmonization. They induce in the mother a libidinal hyper-cathexis of the baby that is born under these circumstances, and a body-to-body relationship that seduces the baby inordinately.

Identifications with maternal projections can be perceived in the transference of hysterical patients, as well as in the content of their discourse. The patient's difficulty is one of differentiating herself from the maternal part-object with which she had been identified, while the ego seeks its autonomy in this differentiation.

Mrs G reported a memory from when she was five years old: her father had held down and hit her mother on the bed. The latter wanted to throw herself out of the window. The little girl cried hard, amidst the confusion of such a scene and what it evoked in her when she reported it. She turned and saw herself, crying, in the mirror. She then abruptly had the feeling of existing, but alone, for herself. Nowadays she often cries, so as not to feel 'transparent' any longer.

When she speaks of her transparency, Mrs G undoubtedly means the transparency of the libidinal part of her personality: her symptoms are there to annul the erogenous consistency of her body. The coquetry of a grown-up little girl that she flaunted validated the ambiguity of her character. Mrs G seemed to seek differentiation from her witch-mother—as she described her to me—in the fine delicacy of her appearance. But, conversely, she corresponded on this point with a maternal wish that she should not become a door-mat from whom men would 'profit' and whose longing for love they would betray by rejecting her.

Problems of identification appeared to Freud as an essential point for understanding hysterical neurosis. Like the Kleinians, I think that identification is a process that appears in the first days of life, linked with relationship to an object. Once the baby is deprived of the maternal envelope, anxiety from being alive induces it to find this envelope again around its own body. Seeking to do this will make construction of an independent psychic apparatus possible. The multiple facets of the baby's relationship to the maternal body and to what the mother feels in that relationship will shape the baby's identificatory possibilities and colour part-object relationships from the beginning of extra-uterine life.

In this context, a common feature may be noted in hysterical patients, as in the two cases cited here: the pathological sensitivity of these patients' mothers to an agitation in their babies, itself undoubtedly pathological. It is as though an anxiety were shared between mother and baby—an anxiety provoked by the baby in a mother who does not feel capable of containing either this baby's excitations, or those that he provokes in her. The libidinal mother–baby relationship functions in the mode of projective identification. Bion defined it in treatment thus: 'the patient splits off a part of his personality and projects it into the object where it becomes installed, sometimes as a persecutor, leaving the psyche, from which it has been split off, correspondingly impoverished' (Bion, 1967, ch. 5). Insufficient repression in the mother lets an anxiety connected with part-instincts and old phantasies that have been reactivated break into the ego. The mother senses her lack of capacity to gather her internal objects together in her ego and becomes depressed. She then puts a strain on her links with the baby, who in this situation represents a split-off part of herself. One could hypothesize that so-called post-partum depression shares in this reaction. The woman's emotional contact with an internal object that was imaginary for nine months and then suddenly became external and real brings back into play a multiplicity of libidinal conflicts whose solutions are bound not to have been securely and definitively established.

Without being pathological, the problem of mother–baby separation at a birth can, according to circumstances, reactivate archaic anxieties connected with object loss in the mother. This may be a part- or whole object, and variable according to the degree of integration of the mother's ego. But she is always identified with it in this unique situation. During pregnancy the baby occupies the internal space of the maternal body, and the mother dreams her baby as an object that occupies her psychic space. The thing and the internal object are identified; this thing is a part-ego.

If the woman–mother's ego does not present a solid enough narcissistic structure, the projective movement that begins at birth includes the baby in the vicious circle of depression.

(3)   Accidental depression

The case of Mrs A

This depressive separation relationship, often minimal, is commonplace or goes unnoticed most of the time in neonatal clinical practice and daily life. I think, however, that it is more or less explicitly recognized as prompting the multiple motives that underlie current perinatal research.

In fact the father's reaction, especially at the birth of a first baby, can produce stirrings of depression in the mother. The father has himself to adjust his psychic equilibrium by the play of new identificatory movements with the baby and the mother: feelings of abandonment, obsessional rejection, aggression and rivalry raise doubts about his love for this woman who has become a mother.

Mrs A had been talking to me about her young daughter of about sixteen: vomiting, sadness, refusal to go out, and disaffection with her school work. This mother told me straight away how she had felt devalued immediately after Colette's birth: her husband had started to go out frequently without her and had taken a mistress. It seemed to me that one could infer that she had been depressed for a while. Nonetheless, the couple seemed to function well, and the baby was very much wanted and well received. Mrs A 'fell back on' the pleasures of motherhood and 'found herself again' in her daughter. She did not truly find conjugal happiness again until several years and another baby later. But she had certainly overcome her accidental depression.

To be borne well, the situation of loss and separation in which the woman–mother finds herself requires her relationship to a whole object to be well enough established in her for her projections onto the baby not to be fragmenting. This loss should be able to be made good owing to the presence of the baby's father with the mother. This affective participating presence logically restores the balance: the representation of desired and loved object in which it sustains the woman compensates her for the change she is experiencing. A new affective equilibrium must be established that deeply affects object relationships between the partners of the couple. The presence with the mother of an affectionate father provides the baby with the possibility in due course of identifying through the mother with this stable phallic object. Thus the 'expectation' that Freud included in depression can be gratified, an expectation that, in my view, marks out the potentially active side of the life instinct in depression and the possibility of usable manic defences.

(4)   The aetiology of hysteria

Birth can, however, appear to be an irreparable mutilation, for the mother as well as for the baby. The suddenness of this separation therefore provokes an immediate search for indispensable defences against the anxiety that has thus been mobilized. The uterine void that is felt by the woman triggers the need for a completely new cathexis of an internal object, for whose representations the baby's father could be regarded as the most immediate support. He can act as intermediary for this object that is being constructed, which the thought of the baby and the baby itself is in the mother.

If immediate compensations do not function well, the loss of the identificatory object—the baby—that supports multiple cathexes brings about in the mother a depressive movement and feelings of intense devaluation. There is a risk that these will be imperceptibly communicated to the baby, either directly or in the form of a defensive anti-cathexis, whether loving or aggressive, or more often both at the same time. The baby, swept up in his mother's cathexes, reacts to them by identificatory processes that lay the foundations of his narcissism. The mother's depression, in so far as it does not let her express a sufficiently positive instinctual *quantum* towards the baby, can prevent the latter from having the experience of omnipotence that is necessary for mastery of the disorderly life instincts.

However, if the mother remains depressed, even if repression has allowed her to establish a free internal space for the baby, this space is in mourning—mourning for a phallic object about which the question of its equivalence to the man–father arises. The baby then finds in his mother's gaze the image of the lost object that he is for his mother, and that he introjects in return. The envelope of love is preserved for him, but it becomes itself the inaccessible object of maternal desire. In a text entitled 'The aetiology of hysteria' (1896c), Freud gave as the origin of hysteria an 'early sexual experience', which he thought was traumatic. I would at present say it was more an erotic experience, and initially an oral experience. It is in the dialectic of cathexes and anti-cathexes that we can identify what influences the construction of hysterical defences without the trauma being apparent. In fact, the malfunctioning of the process of introjection–identification constitutes a cumulative trauma. This dialectic imposes cathexes that are founded upon exchanges made through the hyper-excitability of the bodily and psychic surface. This system of exchanges is translated in the baby into a sort of reversibility in the symbolic system it constructs, a reversibility that gives the symbolic representative a libidinal charge that is equivalent to that of the object represented. The symbol becomes in a sense the envelope that contains the inaccessible object. It may be that in hysterical functioning words are envelopes detached from the object that suffice to evoke and recreate the excitation. This may also be one of the meanings of the phobic object. In the hysteric, representation may be no more than an envelope of sensory excitation detached from an object that it no longer contains, or against which it is hermetically sealed. The object is no more than an external representative of emotions and the symbolic (and not in the proper sense object-) target for loving and aggressive projections. It seems that we may find a displacement of this condensation of symbolic representations in the wealth of hysterics' dreams: repressed phantasies and curbed affects take shape on this side of neurotic censorship and amnesia.

G. Rosolato (1985, chapter entitled 'Le signifiant sans interdit',
p. 85) holds that: '. . . language is set apart to the benefit of
representations. . . . The hysterical metaphor has the task of real-
izing bodily substitution *while stressing the unknown* in two
directions at once: that of sex for the hysteric himself and the
unknown *relative to knowledge* for the observer. . . .'

The erotic charge provoked by the object and destined for the
object is displaced onto symbolic representations of the object. To
attain the object, the subject must confront a censure the effects of
which are manifested either through internal displacements into
his body in the form of somatic symptoms connected with phantasies of introjection, or through displacement onto external
objects, connected to phantasies of partial identifications in the
form of fears or phobias.

It is also this that has led J. McDougall (1986) to make the
hypothesis (as I also do) of an 'archaic hysteria' . . . 'that seeks to
draw attention more to the danger of psychic death than to that of
a phallic–oedipal castration'. This hypothesis J. McDougall herself supposes to be 'to a large extent the result of conflicts and
contradictions that inhabit the unconscious of both parents'.

(III)   THE EXCITATION ENVELOPE

(1)   Its contradictions

The inadequacy of certain of the mother's manic defences leads
her to cathect her baby in an exaggerated manner. Breast-feed-
ing, for example, becomes a mode of relationship whose erotic
intensity exceeds what the baby can integrate. Oral excitation by
the nipple, also felt by the mother, fixes cathexes on the oral zone
that will turn up again later in the form of symptoms. At this
level ambivalence mingles libidinal and destructive forces in the
first feelings of longing.

B. Grunberger has studied the hysteric's oral fixations in a
1953 article entitled 'Oral conflict and hysteria'. I quote him:
'What in my view explains this "marked tendency towards oral
aggression" (Freud) in hysteria is the fact that this neurosis is

based on *identification,* a process derived from *introjection,* that is from oral incorporation.'

If I do not agree with the quick connection that he makes between oral incorporation and introjection, I cannot but agree with his findings in the rest of the article on the subject of what Meltzer would call 'zonal confusions'. In fact it seems to me that one of the essential mechanisms of hysteria consists in the erogenous diffusion of a mode of oral excitation to other parts of the body, especially the skin surface and the sensory orifices.

I would connect with this remark what seems to me to be a peculiarity of feminine libidinal sensitivity, namely cathexis of the orifices of the body as erogenous place of *passage.* Persistence of the mouth–genital confusion is connected with this and determines the female perversions and sexual incapacities. In men it reveals a fixation to early feminine identifications and difficulties whose form makes one inevitably think of hysteria.

In her baby's body the depressed mother encounters an excitation surface and breast–mouth communication that substitutes for satisfactions that she has momentarily lost with the internal and phantasy object that the foetus had represented. This cathexis of the baby's body and the breast/mouth relationship is at least momentarily enormous, owing to everything the mother projects into it of a relationship that is at once infantile and feminine, and produces a hyper-excitation in the baby in the course of which the baby introjects part-objects that are sometimes too vividly charged with libido. It seems that the little baby's psychic apparatus is built up on the basis of this metaphorical breast/mouth representation. One could understand this process as a malfunctioning of 'original repression' that sets to work on the original seduction and the strangeness of 'enigmatic signifiers', as J. Laplanche (1985) described very clearly: 'The immature baby is confronted by messages loaded with meaning and desire, but to which he does not have the key'.

This ties in with one of Freud's ideas, which Mrs Klein also quoted when she considered that superego and inhibition could coincide with primary repression: '. . . it is highly probable that the immediate precipitating causes of primal repression are quantitative factors such as an excessive degree of excitation and

the breaking through of the protective shield against stimuli'
(Freud, 1926d). The baby who then runs the risk of hysteria is in
the paradoxical situation of constructing an excitation-screen out
of an over-exciting relationship and a bodily envelope of excitation. This situation could explain the 'archaic hysteria' whose
existence in certain psychosomatic patients J. McDougall (1986)
also stressed.

It is remarkable, however, that this envelope of excitation persists around an ego whose libidinal precocity has not prevented
its being consolidated, owing to the positive and validating identifications that it has been able to establish with the object of
maternal depression. The baby has precisely been very cathected
libidinally by his mother as a substitute for the paternal phallus,
as much in the relationship to her own father as to the baby's
father.

(2)   A reactive violence

This contradiction could undoubtedly account for certain persecutory reactions on the part of the hysteric who is submitted
defenceless to over-intense excitations. This would suggest to me
that a certain aggressiveness, if not violence, is secondary to
libidinal surcharges, since excitation can be felt as an intrusion.
These surcharges come together into the persecutory form taken
by relationships during the paranoid–schizoid period of early
infancy. In connection with his original idea of the creation of the
aesthetic object, Meltzer (1985) describes 'the paranoid–schizoid
position not as primitive, but as the position that is retreated to
for protection against the impact of the beauty of the object,
against emotionality, and against the problems and questions
that this impact poses. The paranoid–schizoid position is a
defensive position, and is always a defence against the pain
of the depressive position.'

In short, the hysteric would be dazzled by the excitation produced in him by the object of his desires. His regression to bodily
or phobic symptoms might therefore seem to be a regression to
the paranoid–schizoid position in preference to separating from
this object, which would be a fundamental loss for him. The hysteric never overcomes the depression caused by every separation

and remains partially identified with lost parts of the loved object, confused with parts of his own ego.

On the other hand, the object is never satisfying, because it is always an object of depression, an object lost 'beforehand' because it is emptied by the mother's depression—a breast that is never generous enough, good or available enough, whose oedipal cathexis imbues with guilt the desire that the hysteric feels for it. The hysteric never has satisfactory enjoyment of the object, as he has no access to it. The baby seems to have introjected his mother's unconscious censorship of oedipal wishes when he was born, together with this essentially fugitive object of desire.

In the chapter on the dream-work, Freud (1900a, p. 480) speaks of censorship being capable of producing 'not satisfaction, but the contrary affect', an idea that he took up again in 'A metapsychological supplement to the theory of dreams' (1917d), while making hypotheses about what the dream rescues of our narcissism: 'some amount of the expenditure on repression (anti-cathexis) would have to be maintained throughout the night, in order to meet the instinctual danger. . . .'

The censorship that forces the discovery of oedipal affects upon libidinal instincts therefore induces anti-cathexes. When a balance between the censorship and the ego cannot be established in the usual roundabout symbolic ways (play, for example), a tiny baby, like Céline, has no resort other than to let the instinct burst out into her body or her phobic delusion. In some children I have been able to establish that fits, apparently serious in their convulsive form, were triggered off by aggressive phantasies that covered up the unbearableness of oedipal non-satisfaction—the revolt of the being or the ego against the discovery of impotence and the psychic castration represented at this time of life by the necessity to abandon imaginary omnipotence over the libidinal object. In these children, affects connected with representations of castration and impotence are found expressed in anti-cathexis of sexual excitation and by an insuperable sensorial or aggressive excitation whose prompt eruption shows up in the form of acute epileptoid or phobic fits, as Freud already noted. In other cases, permanent motor agitation corresponds to what Freud supposed concerning the outcome of a sensoriality that cannot be mastered by an insufficiently constructed excitation-screen. Repression then produces unbearable suffering, and sensory data are represented poorly or not at all in phantasy formations. The ego lacks the links that attach instinctual motion to its active outcome, which would permit it to integrate this process. The system of discharge itself displaces the outcome of excitation: spasmophilia rather than orgasm.

These manifestations appear in the child as the pathological results of maintaining an excitation that overflows both in quantitative and qualitative ways. The direction taken by this excitation differs according to the child's age and sex, but it persists as a neurotic kernel that all the narcissistic and identificatory cathexes will have to take into account. The general meaning that it could be given corresponds more or less to this: 'I can only be unsatisfying, just as I cannot be satisfied. Something that is definitively lost remains inaccessible, both for me and in me. Desire has slipped away. There only persists in me this diffuse agitation that settles upon numerous objects, and whose acme is not tied to any particular object. My desire has been lost with the object of my desire.'

Representations connected with this non-satisfaction reveal an oral fixation: some of Dora and Anna O's symptoms involved speaking, the throat and the voice. The oral fixation that produces anorexic disgust and the incoercible greed of bulimia is closely connected with a compensatory excitation organized around unconscious oral representations.

(3)   The carry-over into sexuality

In adulthood these symptoms are carried over into sexuality. The enjoyment or the substitutive censorship persist in oral behaviour. One could also consider that a non-satisfaction of this sort, experienced at an age when orality alone serves as model for erotic cathexis, is liable to produce anorexia in the suckling baby, either by a movement of refusal that is assimilable to the consequences of what would be primary repression, or by the baby's identification with the breast that it incorporates together with all its non-satisfactions, and whose emptiness he feels by confusion between this breast and the whole mother, and also by confusion between himself and the breast.

This symptomatology is resumed in the oedipal phase, when the discovery of genital excitations prevails. It is then displaced and transposed into diffuse and varied somatic symptoms, or into inhibitions of every kind. This often appears more clearly in girls, for whom representations of internal bodily space are more directly linked to the sensation of excitations to representations of internal psychic space.

Non-differentiation of the erogenous zones and the body's internal spaces also reveals itself in the anal stage, particularly in symptoms of retention: the child preserves inside himself the thing/object of internal masturbatory pleasure that is undefined in the representations that he has of it. Anxiety is then centred upon the possible loss of the object and upon a solid part of the self that might escape from control. This anxiety can take the form of phobic obsession. Freud (1926d) was preoccupied with this process in studying obsessional neurosis, whose hysterical foundations he described.

(4) The death instinct

The symptomatology of hysteria seems to represent a confusion between the death instinct, the reality principle and the pleasure principle. When Mrs G spoke of the pleasures of love, she evoked the fear that the idea of possible orgasm aroused in her, which prevented her from reaching it. She talked about it as though it were a loss of herself and not a simple loss of consciousness, something that terrified her like death. For her, reality was hardly more than on the level of reverie, as Freud had already shown with others. It seems that non-integration into the ego of the qualitative differences of the erogenous zones, of mouth and genitals, together with non-differentiation of inside/surface and of container/contained, could be at the root of this confusion between dream and reality. Regression produced by the idea of penetration, which for Mrs G was always intrusive, triggered off early paranoid fears in her of being destroyed from the inside. Pleasure was assimilated to death. Early paranoid anxiety associated with internal excitations, then censorship by the superego of the Oedipus complex, filled the space between the excitable sensory envelope and the instinctual response to the internal encounter with the object of her desire.

The death instinct appears in the hysteric in the battles that he wages to reduce tensions produced by the hyper-excitation—libidinal or aggressive—that he feels; this aggression being a deflected part of the death instinct in conflict with Eros. The hysteric seeks a solution to the instinctual conflict in the decathexis of the self, in bodily devaluation and in the split between thought and emotion. Depressive stirrings are the expression of the death instinct; since the libido remains active, the hysteric is liable to turn to action in a disorganized fashion, by activity and symptoms, but does not commit suicide.

As defence against the anxiety aroused by excitation, hysterics make use of the fact that their body becomes an object of awareness first of all through pain. Feelings of need are painful and although pleasure comes from their satisfaction, it is secondary to them. Once satisfaction is attained and equilibrium re-established, tension is suppressed, and the absence of excitation is related to Nirvana, whose enjoyment Freud considered lethal.

It is only in the 'depressive' period that the baby gradually distinguishes his ego from the object and external excitations from internal needs. At this time the part-object of desire is bound up with the perturbation provoked by external excitations and the satisfaction of felt need. But the object is also connected with affects of non-satisfaction and therefore with the first destructive impulses towards this object. Here my ideas tie in with those of M. Klein about envy, as H. Segal (1986) understands them.

So far as the hysteric is concerned, he is maintained in the non-distinction between internal and external excitation by the fear of losing his close link with his mother. Relationship to the differential phallic object is split off, even in the approach to oedipal desires. This is undoubtedly the origin of certain forms of homosexuality.

(5)   Displacement inwards of excitation

As for cathexes, narcissistic non-differentiation displaces what is unbearable in the body's superficial excitation towards its organic and muscular inside. The uterine and vaginal space is not precisely determined by sensations. Its representation is transposed to the whole of the cavity delimited by the bodily envelope.

Sexual representations electively cathect the uterine envelope, which 'brings alive for the subject alternate experiences of identity and otherness'.[1]

As I understand it, everything happens as though sexual excitation found no container, either in sexual space or in the psyche. Excitement spreads out over the whole of the person's surface: the uterus is displaced onto the bodily and psychic surface. 'Its functioning as envelope of ambiguity ego/non-ego leaves a trace in the psyche' (T. Nathan, 1985). All the body content becomes a bearer of unconscious sexual representations. oedipal guilt cathects these confusions and transforms the outcome of excitation into a painful discharge, pleasure into pain, and the impossibility of enjoyment into castration. When hysterical patients, children or adults, can impart to the analyst representations connected with their symptoms, we can in fact see how much these evoke castration. The same is true in all the neuroses, but this is perhaps why one finds hysteria at the base of every neurosis, because it renders sensory excitation guilty. The term 'castration' is, however, loaded with a sexual genital meaning that does not sufficiently express the early libidinal non-differentiation to which I personally relate hysterical symptomatology.

(6)   The multiplicity of identifications

Let us now return to the hysteric's particular mode of identification. We may notice in the treatment of hysterics how oral fixation produces great malleability in the patient. This is undoubtedly linked with the acute sensitivity of these subjects, a sensitivity that oedipal censorship has not rigidified. If it achieves its aim with libidinal realization, the castrating superego founders on perceptual pleasure. Oral erotism is both the earliest erotism and the one most sublimated by the process of language. In fact, hysterics often suffer in their linguistic expression, and their thought slips away just as every libidinally cathected object escapes them.

This lability in cathecting leads the hysteric into a multiplicity of identifications that makes them into multiple characters, such as mediums and comedians who speak through someone else's discourse. In fact, no identification can be stable, because none is satisfying. None provides the subject with the omnipotent image he is seeking.

On this subject Brenman (1985) wrote: 'I believe that in these multiple identifications, a greedy dependency is practised with simultaneous identification with the breast as the source of wisdom, support and the victim of exploitation.' This expresses in another way that the excitation felt by the hysteric makes him identify himself with an omnipotent libidinal object. The subject repeats his primary relationship to the object/breast and masters enjoyment by making it impossible. The hysteric is locked into the negation of enjoyment, and this allows him to preserve his privileged relationship to the object of his desire—if not, or, perhaps, of his love.

A defined identity presupposes a limitation that the hysteric's unlimited excitation does not allow him. Although this limitation can indeed reduce his suffering in the direction of conscious enjoyment, it tends to make him run the risk of a loss, of surrendering a part of his self that is closely tied to the object of desire. The hysteric lives in depression. The impulses that he permanently feels to separate from the object of his desire are no more brought to fruition than his libidinal instincts attain satisfaction. These impulses that strike a balance between one representation of an exciting object and another of an inaccessible object are in fact intended to maintain the object's presence. To enjoy it greedily would be to destroy it and definitively lose it. Hysterics defend themselves and the object of their love against the destructive greed of their desire.

Identified with the object lost by their mother in the separation of birth, the hysteric cannot represent to himself the possession/enjoyment of the loved object except as the definitive outcome of a greedy oral desire that leaves nothing behind except internal emptiness and depression. He feels alive through his permanent struggle against desire, through the aggression that this struggle arouses and the non-satisfaction that it makes him project.

I do not think I have added anything new to the understanding of the hysterical phenomenon. My project was simply to approach a little closer to the roots of what it expresses, and thereby perhaps to help some patients to reconcile themselves with their imaginary mother, whose possession and loss they fear simultaneously, in their unstable equilibrium at the apex of ambivalence between pleasure and suffering.

NOTES

1. I am taking up Toby Nathan's (1986) ideas about uterine functioning represented in certain cultures as the functioning of an organ or even an animal that is autonomous in relation to the rest of the person. Instinct is then undoubtedly felt as being foreign to the ego.

The psychic envelopes of the psychoanalyst: some suggestions for applying the theory of psychic envelopes to the study of the psychoanalyst's functioning

J. Guillaumin

(I) GENERAL COMPETENCE OF THE ENVELOPES MODEL: PROBLEMATICS RETAINED HERE

Representation in psychoanalytic thinking of the *psychoanalyst's psychic functioning as such* raises some delicate problems. In clinical work, as in theory, it demands intensified listening to the patient where this has been lessened in current practice: an intensification that is not adequately described even by the notion, so complex and yet so necessary, of self-analysis.[1]

Reassure ourselves as we may on this score, it is in fact possible to observe that we all become somewhat confused as soon as there is a question of assessing our own 'share' of responsibility, notably countertransferential, in the work of treatment. This is no smaller than 'the patient's share', to extend to transference and countertransference relationships the comparison that Freud used in 'Constructions in analysis' (1937b), but it is doubtless illusory to suppose that it can be calculated accurately. Countertransference, in action, affect, and thought, whether conscious or unconscious—indeed even in theorizing elaboration—is surely nowadays[2] no longer regarded by anyone as the obtrusive residue or inevitable price to be paid for an analyst's want of equanimity, which should be teased out and eliminated at all costs to prevent the patient's process from suffering on account of it. On the contrary, it is emerging increasingly *in its fundamental reality as the habitual, indispensable, and even privileged instrument for understanding the patient's transference,* in the constant interaction of transference and countertransference. In so far as it always assumes—directly, as it were, and initially unbeknownst to the analyst—something of the *responses* that the patient's internal objects make to the entreaties of his own ego, it provides from the very outset a vital means of access to the confused exchanges that take place in his poorly developed psychic apparatus: a royal road perhaps, like that of the dream. But this road is more concealed, and one whose language, entered into and directly experienced, is not going to find a Champollion to decipher its lexicon and grammar. There will be no 24 July 1895 for the countertransference. Here theory cannot recover what practice is never completely master of and can use only by virtue of the way things actually happen.

Psychoanalytic knowledge, therefore, as we now realize more clearly, never escapes either before or after, nor indeed during treatment, from the epistemic position from which it springs, which is submerged, oscillating, cobbled together, and always compromised. In contrast with other cognitive approaches, described as positive, it espouses this and benefits from it. But it inevitably follows that the only useful theoretical 'models' that it can offer itself remain approximations. These make do with furnishing practice with mental operators that are *sufficiently* coherent and generalizable in given conditions and for given cases to permit felicitous transitions from one case to another, to encourage expectant thoughts,[3] and to regulate more or less lastingly the impact that the material makes on the practitioner, thereby responding indirectly to the patient's demand for an organizing framework.

Hence the interest in concepts such as those that D. Anzieu (1985) has developed and sought to systematize during the past ten or twelve years, beginning with his intuitions about the skin ego. It is doubtless a model, and one that alone in this system of ideas has the virtue—more so perhaps than one would think at first on close consideration of its systematic aspect—of *forbidding more effectively than others certain objectifying conclusions* that analysts too often crave.

(1)   In the first place, the constant reference that it makes to archaic bodily support leads on to the *limits of what can be analysed*: to the very place where the psyche has its subterranean springs or returns to plunge into the body, an obscure point in the self that cannot be named as such without having *already* left psychic space properly so called—as, indeed, Freud saw—and without calling to mind the unrepresentable and *im voraus* of every wish registered by the subjective ego.

(2)   In the second place, the problematic of envelopes inevitably brings the analyst's envelopes into contact with those of his patient and social partners involved in his work setting; further on I will specify in what way. In the patient's background and in that of figures in the analyst's professional or personal environment, further sources of support go on appearing both in bodily terms and in terms of institutions or groups, and this continues *ad infinitum*.

In either direction, therefore, *there is something unending*: sort of obscure boundaries of the psyche that are none the less necessary for the psyche itself and for thought, which they provide a basis for and in which they participate.[4] Might this then be the primal unconscious, bearer of the innate, the phylogenetic, or the biological, as well as the social? The 'bedrock' also, from which the movement of life must well up and spring without ever succeeding in dissolving or resolving it? The problematic of envelopes gives us a representable answer without forcing us into an alienating objectivization.

Nevertheless, in order to handle our particular subject, we must stop at more operable formulations, at the risk that being over-tidy may once again to some extent violate the complex reality. On the basis of D. Anzieu's work on the skin ego and my own observations, I shall therefore state three principles, which I shall use by way of postulates.

(A) *Envelopes only exist in the plural,* and we must conceive of psychic envelopes *as a sort of more or less homogeneous laminate.* Every issue concerning envelopes is therefore in essence intercapsular and brings into play relationships of space and time *between* envelopes. The two following principles could be regarded as corollaries of this first statement.

(B) Every specific envelope and every laminated system of envelopes has *fragile* and *reinforced zones,* which penetrate the laminate to a greater or lesser extent because of the effects of dislocations, slippages, shifts, detachments, fixations or adhesions that characterize relations between the envelopes. The topography and functional state of any particular system of envelopes result from the conjunction or disjunction, as well as the distribution, of these two types of zones or regions of envelopes. This includes the functions of filtering, protection, transmission, reflection, and so on noted by D. Anzieu, and which herein find an explanation. One can in fact always at least to some extent regard the irregularities, folds or cusps (in the sense of the modern physico-mathematical theory of envelopes[5]) that can be identified in the whole or at a given level of a system of envelopes, as the result of dissonances or entanglements between two or more of the envelopes of the system.

(C) Finally, and now clinically speaking, it will be held that *every enveloping psychic envelope is also itself enveloped,* and that it is in the nature of envelope systems thus to insert *each individual envelope between others* in a more or less concentric system of envelopes that *are virtually uncountable*—whether in the centripetal or centrifugal direction—and arranged more or less like Russian dolls. This clinical assertion is derived from the deeply seated effects of those types of identification with which very recent analytic research confronts us (I am thinking in particular of certain work by P. Bourdier, R. Kaës, E. Granjon, Ch.

Guérin, H. Faimberg, P. Aulagnier, J. Guyotat et al. and, finally, myself, which I will not cite in detail here).

This third assertion concretizes somewhat the epistemological area whose general outlines I have sketched above: in transference and countertransference the clinical observer *inevitably* encounters envelopes that are empirically speaking 'last' or 'first' within the limits of his means for exploring or investigating either himself or someone else. But these 'limits' themselves necessarily imply that there is something beyond or on this side (hyper-envelopes?) which corresponds to the *obscure presence in every identifiable 'layer' of the mind,* even its most remote, and on the side of the internal as well as the external world, of *nameless representatives of undifferentiable sources of support* that derive from the biological body and/or the social environment in question. A problematic such as this concerning boundaries is essential for psychoanalysis, as I already suggested in 1977,[6] and I still insist upon it. Intimately connected with the very nature of 'mind' as such (which is not thinkable except in relation to the 'nonmental') and with the presence of endlessness at the heart of the psychoanalytic *epistême,* this is what justifies hypothesizing a necessary 'negative operator' that is constantly at work both in the theory and practice of analysis.[7]

Having made these remarks that will serve as postulates, my reflections on the specific theme of *the psychoanalyst's envelopes* will be organized around three questions.

(1)   I shall first enquire into what has, since Robert Fliess,[8] come to be called the *metapsychology of the analyst.* I have already had the opportunity to discuss some of my views on this subject with various groups of colleagues. Study of the analyst's metapsychology (dynamic, topographical, economic and genetic) forces us into difficult choices related to the standpoint adopted for observation, according to whether one focuses upon:

(a)   the analyst's functioning in sessions;

(b)   the organization of the whole of the analyst's personality, insofar as it has been made capable of functioning analytically in his work as a result of his history and training;

(c)   the role of the support of family, friends and groups, and the 'external' institutional prop which this analyst has needed and goes on needing to secure his personality and analytical work.

It seems that careful application of the concept of 'envelope', in my sense, should allow the three points of view above to be better harmonized without undue artificiality or paradox.

(2) I shall then enquire more specifically into a problem of our own times that has been rather neglected, even magicked away, but about which Freud was very much concerned.[9] It involves what could be called the *'professional disorders' of psychoanalysts*. And I am naturally thinking less about the sluggish bowels or spinal weaknesses of people who spend too much time sitting than about the (psychic) changes that are brought about by traffic in unconscious thoughts, and other distortions of the backbone of analytic practice. These specific cases of dysfunction in the analyst's metapsychology will in my opinion also benefit from being viewed from the perspective of 'envelopes'. This is because on the one hand they have densely woven and multiple connections with variations in a practitioner's thresholds of sensitivity to internal and external messages of every kind and with his need for object- or erotic pleasure and narcissistic security during his work in sessions. And, on the other hand, they raise questions about the ambivalent (and usually idealized or anti-idealized) interchange of dependence/independence, love/hate, and identification/dis-identification that he can and quite often does engage in within himself and in social interactions with his teachers, superiors, colleagues or disciples, not to mention patients or former patients. Given the very implicating[10] character of such a subject (think, for example, of Freud and Ferenczi's rather passionate relationships), one rarely has the opportunity to express one's views on these matters in writing. The referent 'envelope' gives me the chance to do so in a manner that is sufficiently . . . containable so far as I am concerned.

(3)   Finally, I shall here take up again, but from a very specific angle, the difficult *psychoanalytic question of creativity*. I have already suggested that creative work belongs in an ambiguous or

paradoxical way to the creator's metapsychology and plays a very particular role in it in a sort of *topographical exterritoriality*.[11] My views on this matter seem to concur with those of Anzieu on the 'skin ego', as he himself points out in his book of that name. It seems timely to me to take them up again now in the light of the postulates set out above, and in connection with questions (2) and (1). This will tie in neatly and specifically with my concern today to connect the problem of creativity with the epistemological and clinical problem of the limits to what can be mobilized and represented within the analysable and more generally within mental functioning.

Of these three questions, the one that seems to me to be pivotal for my reflections is undoubtedly the second, whose line of attack—the chronicization of transference–countertransference difficulties—is, it seems, an *analyser of choice* for the functioning of the analyst's psychic envelopes.

Having outlined the themes of the enquiry, let us now tackle it in depth.

(II)   A METAPSYCHOLOGY OF THE ANALYST IN TERMS OF PSYCHIC ENVELOPES?

As we know, Freud distinguished three principal dimensions or perspectives in metapsychology—dynamic, topographical and economic. To this he added, less clearly formulated, a sort of diachronic axis that cuts across the perspectives first mentioned—the 'genetic' dimension. With its three principal dimensions, metapsychology is a 'witch' (Freud, *Analysis Terminable and Interminable,* 1937c), that brightly illuminates clinical facts but at the inevitable cost of conceptual straining and jumping to immediate conclusions, something that preserves a hint of the arbitrary and conventional, even of 'magic' in its very accuracy, since none of the three dimensions is in any case self-sufficient, but each bears a causal or co-operative relationship with the other two that is difficult to conceptualize exactly. This is an obvious case in point, which has original value in psychoanalysis, of the epistemological limits to models in this domain.

Only the 'impure' genetic dimension, which refers to a reality of becoming that cannot be skirted around and *can be sensed intuitively* on an existential plane (whether it is understood in terms of a succession of stages or, more rigorously, in terms of a dialectical temporality that is based upon the play of hindsight), escapes by this very token from an excessive measure of arbitrariness when problems as intricate as those that I am tackling here are at issue. I am therefore going to take as my starting-point in an empirical way this somewhat bastard metapsychology. My clinical observations in analytical practice with prospective analytical candidates or prospective analysts, and in the 're-analyses' that some call slabs of analysis, as well as in conducting supervisions, have in fact led to the discovery that analysts very often share a *common history in their early relationships with language*. To be more exact, one finds in almost all of them a complex and rather particular development of the first attempts to relate 'words' to 'things', in several stages, which when taken together amount to a post-traumatic reorganization.

(1) General schema

My hypothesis will be that the *development (disenvelopment?)*[12] of a *'psychic apparatus for analysing'* (which could be called 'an analyst's' if this apparatus is subsequently dedicated to, and kept in lasting order by, practice and an appropriate institution) probably implies at source an innate and/or acquired (with the degree of uncertainty between the two that Freud himself very clearly perceived) *infantile tendency to make a privileged investment in cathecting 'strangeness' in the relationship between words and things when listening to maternal*—or more broadly parental—*speech, perceived as the enveloping* ('sonorous envelope' in R. Gori and D. Anzieu's sense) but ambivalent *location* of a message that was at once excessively gratifying and irritating. What I mean here by the 'strangeness' of words (of which the 'disquieting strangeness' analysed by Freud in 1919 is no more than a late specific case) denotes a phenomenon of semantic ambiguity that is the result of a sort of condensation of differences that are at *once perceived and unrepresentable,* and therefore cannot be reconciled. It is like a very compacted block of schist whose laminate one can feel by touch, but without it being possible to identify and separate the layers. This sensory-motor metaphor borrowed from another perceptual register is, of course, very approximate, but appropriate here.

The various words and sounds of the baby's sonorous envelope at the beginning of life (an envelope formed by babble, lullabies, nursery rhymes and the mother's speech that resonate with the baby's own vocal output, whose phonetic range they orientate against the background of noises, sounds, and in due course words that derive more widely from the family and social environment) can in fact be seen as charged with ambiguity from the very first moment when they begin to function as meaningful messages and not simply as signs of situation. Enlisted in the construction of a *biface* (D. Anzieu) sonorous envelope shared by baby and mother by virtue of the very fact of being bi- or pluri-referential, these elements are vectors of *divergences, detachments, or mis-matches* between maternal transmitter and infantile receiver that the baby cannot sort out. To a certain extent his experience is shared by the mother herself.[13] But the means that the baby has at his disposal afford him no help in shaping or reducing on first principles the discordances that afflict the sounds and words that he hears (or picks up in a familiar sort of early mimicry), as his mother can because of other social messages that are coded and stored in her memory. He can only perceive these sounds and words as signifying a vague 'something' *between* outside and inside: sign of a reality that it pointed out to him or that he points to, *plus something else as well* that is added to it, that he cannot at present make out and which therefore cannot but *keep him in suspense or on the alert*.[14] This is a 'more' that presents itself to him as a 'less', something 'too much' or 'left over' that functions as a deficiency that he has to cope with. It is *this something else that is at once both 'too much' and 'lacking' that acts as vector of the strangeness of words*.

In terms of envelopes, therefore, we could consider the effect of the 'strangeness' of sounds and words, as here defined, as resulting from a confused feeling that collating meanings or cobbling them together conflates *several registers* or levels of envelope '*improperly*', and that 'something or other' is 'not working' in the interplay of these registers. The sense of security and narcissistic identification created by the sharing between transmitter and receiver *for part of the meaning* is disturbed and contradicted by the lack of concordance with and control over others that is *due to that part of the meaning which is not shared* by the baby and is dimly perceived by him as such.

Taken as a whole, it is in fact the work of identificatory and cognitive appropriation that the baby performs upon this resistant, exciting, and disquieting element by means of making differentiations and assimilative associations, that *supports and activates human mental development* as a vehicle for the problematic of desire, in a search for greater mastery of this 'other' that is always wanting in linguistic signs.

But in psychic development this quest is usually subordinated more or less swiftly to the installation of a conventional system of linguistic meanings that are practical and operative enough to serve everyday life. A consensual language, essential for schooling, takes shape in this way, one that makes the most economic use in a given situation of ambiguities of register, and which *joins* interlocutors *together narcissistically* in a sort of shared suspension or denial (a notion borrowed here from M. Fain),[15] by reducing to a minimum the metaphorical shifts that result from slippages or overlaps amongst the different inscription registers (mnesic envelopes) at their disposal. Only *specific areas or limited moments* are normally set aside for questioning these 'silent' conventions (in the sense in which J. Bleger[16] uses the term in connection with adhesive identification with the setting). Where psychogenesis is concerned, one could take the view that consensual operatory language is the developed heir of the baby's earliest narcissistic identifications with his mother, which, secondarily reconstituted by its use, fix or glue the individual's sonorous envelope onto that of his human environment.

A measure of tolerance towards self and others and 'being comfortable in one's own skin' depends upon a happy balance between this large 'solid' part of language and the shared narcissism that it contains and those limited moments of finding oneself unsupported by meaning that affects other things and gives rise to a problematic of identity crisis and desire. In fact the flaws in this libidinal/narcissistic economy play an important role in the aetiology of mental disturbance, which then appear to be due to an insufficiency or excess of 'holes' or lacunae between internal inscription planes or reference points on the one hand and the external envelopes provided by the environment on the other. These holes—or, conversely, points of adhesion or scarry bumps— could be conceived of as the more or less densely packed and repetitious sites where identificatory projection of unrepresentable endo-psychic experiences takes place. We may recall, in line with the remarks made above, that in every case, but here in a relationship of narcissistic confusion, there are *laminates* of envelopes that are undoubtedly analogous in their basic structure to the model of the 'magic block' simplified by Freud (1925a). Narcissistic supports, like their withdrawal, therefore depend simultaneously upon intra-psychic *and* inter-psychic adhesions and detachments.

Let us now return, on the basis of this general developmental schema, to the hypothesis stated above.

(2) Early cathexis of the relationship between verbal signifier and strangeness

In my view, the first necessary condition for future functioning as an analyst demands that *that part of the individual's relationship to the strangeness of verbal signifiers, which I shall describe as not joined up or not scarred over* and which is involved in the results of outside/inside relations between the envelopes, *must have been exceptionally important early on* and must for that reason have been the object of a *strong early libidinal cathexis.*[17]

The development of a predisposition such as this, which *conditions* later analytic listening, could obviously also be deflected outside analytic paths. Involving *words,* it is especially apt to develop under the impact of appropriate subsequent events in latency and after puberty—if it is not repressed or transformed into a reactive formation by intellectualization, or else put massively into operatory thought as a result of unbearable traumatic shocks—in the direction of narcissistic erotization, especially 'aesthetic' (literary or 'poetic'), of play upon relations between the different phonetic and semantic registers or envelopes of language. This undoubtedly accounts for the strange kinship between literature and psychoanalysis that both fascinated and irritated Freud, and which can each sometimes act as a defence or resistance towards the other. This observation will lead me later in this chapter to investigate the function of the surface or *skin* of words, their epidermic face, in relation to their *body,* or deep metaphorical layers, in the creation of written works and the self, and in moments of creativity such as in an analyst's practical and theoretical work.

All the same, if we stick strictly for the moment to the destiny of the future analyst, we must still wonder what series of psychic events the initial predisposition must *subsequently* encounter in order to reach the appropriate final result.

(3)   Complementary conditions

In the light of my own analytic and self-analytic experience and diverse other clinical information gleaned from professional relationships and writings that touch upon the training of analysts it seems to me that *we must presuppose, working outwards from the early situation* that has just been described:

(A)   *A subsequent or second failure in the latency and post-latency period of desexualizing environmental envelopes and their internalization,* envelopes that 'normally' curb or channel the cathexis of *verbal curiosity* by reinforcing manifest social codes. This involves narcissistic joins, adhesions or scars between the outside and inside of words that cannot be shifted, which implies a partial collapse in the laminate of the various envelopes to which they belong or refer, and a suspension or shared denial of plurivocality or the metaphorical power of language. This failure promotes a more or less massive *sublimatory displacement* of the identificatory work of differentiating between external and internal envelopes of the self, *towards verbal terrain, in so far as this is a privileged way into recognizing meaningful relationships* between outside and inside, with the various incription registers involved. A sublimatory orientation like this could then be the object of intense compensatory activity, giving rise to a particular skill both in keeping poorly differentiated and plurivocal signifiers within the purview of psychic attention, and in making use of them.

(B) *Narcissistic re-envelopment by a later, containing, environment,* in the course of which cathexis of the verbal biface—not only as analyser and organizer of rational intellectual life, but as metaphorical operator of changes in plane or level between manifest and latent within the laminate of discourse— will itself be *recognized, valued and reinforced by substitute persons who stand in for parents.* Among these, and the latest in the series (or one of the last), comes the analysand's counter-transferential-speaking-envelope–analyst,[18] which he can partially internalize during his one or more personal analyses. And in the background, in concentric supporting layers like Russian dolls or onion rings, come the institutional groups with which he is connected and, beyond them, 'relatives' in his personal analyst's lineage, not to speak of residual elements of his natural intimate lineage and that of the various persons thus 'involved'.

(C) To this I would add: *the use of analysis in the process of becoming an analyst probably sets a sort of limit to the analysis itself,* which is not recathected in 'normal' life except *under the specific 'condition' of continuing the process of disenvelopment/ re-envelopment of which the practitioner has himself been object* by reversing it towards his patients.

The fact that he is aware of this and has already examined it in his own analysis makes no difference at all, even if one thinks that this background awareness is *itself* necessary for an analyst's satisfactory functioning. It is as though for him the re-envelopment at issue in (B) became necessary not only to establish his identity as a professional analyst, but also for his own personal identity, at least to some extent. Herein lies the delicate problem of the distinction that has to be made between the amount of sublimation–creativity, and of hidden dependence and unfinished work that persists in psychoanalytic 'reproduction' or 'transmission'. We may note that the first and second conditions, like the general preliminary condition stated first of all, are probably common *both to future analysands* in general—at least for those whose resistance to a degree of contained hysteresis of thought is not excessive—*and to future 'analysts'.* But the third condition set out above is the specific foundation for an analyst's vocation. We shall return to this further on from the perspective of possible flaws in analytic functioning in relation to 'internal' and institutional 'external' situations.

All the conditions I have listed are necessary *together* for an analyst's professional work, because his work demands a very singular interaction between characteristics of envelopes that have been determined at a succession of inscription levels in the practitioner's personality. An analyst's work in fact essentially consists (as I tried to show in connection with the role of the preconscious in *interpretation*[19]) in disconnecting his listening and, by suspending all other relational activity, in connecting up, literally *mouth to mouth,* the weak or fragile zones of verbal messages to which attention has not been drawn or that have been covered up by a simple prosthesis, and that he receives from the patient *with his own zones of semantic ambiguity* that are maintained under tension due to uncertainty in his psychic apparatus, which has been trained to cathect and contain voids, hollows or contradictions as such.

From this *conjunction of 'holes' in the preconscious organizations of analyst and analysand* that belong to their respective sonorous envelopes and are signalled by defects in manifest verbal statements, *within the protective identificatory framework of a consensual analytic setting where basic narcissistic connections are nonetheless maintained* ('alliance', 'contact', 'good-will', 'fundamental countertransference' . . .[20]), what results is that *those word inscriptions, and those only, that have had their supporting underlay removed in this way descend to abyssal depth* and penetrate deeply. Torn up and isolated from their usual anchorage in the 'thick' or hardened regions of other people's speech and behaviour, they burrow into the patient's (and analyst's) psychic apparatus in quest of new supports in different levels, layers, or envelopes of the recording system of the memory. Thus the verbal biface roams in some way from skin to skin in quest of its lost face or counterpart. The analyst's associative process, whether internal or voiced, could therefore be described as a tour in light touch around the surface of consciousness (for Freud, the ego is a surface, as D. Anzieu reminds us), feeling out the abnormally sensitive or insensitive points of the patient's 'skin' by means of contact or 'tact',[21] skin to skin, or ear to chest, in which the organization of the analyst's psychic skin and its intermittent and partial capacity for disorganization plays a leading part.

There must be a confirmed and above all *sustained* solidity and plasticity in the overall stuff of the personal envelopes whose shortcomings, faults, rips or sensitive zones are brought into play by the analyst. And maintenance of this stuff depends upon the combination of the entire system of private *and* professional identifications at the professional's disposal, flexibly enclosed one within the other, that he sets working through his specific analytic activity of identification/disidentification.

This delicate and very 'engaged' activity entails dangers for the complex functional psychic apparatus that the analyst needs, whose topography and dynamic are thereby submitted to an intense interplay that is both highly exciting and testing, of being alternately supported and unsupported by patients' reality on the one hand and that of his professional and social environment on the other. It is for this very reason that his functioning is prone to suffer from envelopes that have seized up, stuck together, come unstuck, or been torn, on account of insufficient or excessive pressure and cohesion among endo-psychic inscriptions. These states truly become 'specific professional disorders' of the analyst as soon as they seriously and lastingly handicap him in his activity or in the related private comfort that this activity requires. I will now consider these 'disorders'.

(III) 'PROFESSIONAL DISORDERS' OF THE PSYCHOANALYST FROM THE POINT OF VIEW OF THE ENVELOPES

I propose to reserve the name of disorder in the broadest sense for *compulsive* functioning, in so far (and only in so far, since some measure of repetition is necessary for identity) as they prevent or greatly limit adaptation, in other words the putting back into free play of the transitory or relative fixations of energy that life demands. Skin disorders, for example—and this is not a random example in the envelopes model—alter, paralyse or jam up the constant conditions that enable the different layers of skin covering to perform their physiological functions, by repeatedly producing intrusive formations that incapacitate against mechanical impact or toxic effects and interfere with temperature control, etc.

By analogy, 'professional disorders of the analyst' are due to compulsions of narcissistic origin that fixate the analyst repetitively and encapsulate him in a countertransferential position that relates to a specific organization of the patient's and/or his own imagos, as well as the identificatory substitutes they have found in the course of his training and in his professional milieu. Such compulsions form symptoms and lastingly interfere with the function and interplay of his psychic envelopes in the intermittent work of treatment or the necessary balance of the practitioner's life as a whole. A rigorous definition of these 'disorders' as 'professional' must, however, also imply that they are recognized as products *solely of the practice of the profession,* under the impact of the specific stresses that it engenders. It is in fact very often difficult to distinguish causes of professional imbalance that stem from practice itself from those that arise from another source. This is partly because of the *continuous cooperation of the entire system of the analyst's envelopes in his work* and in his balance, and partly because of the onward march of life itself, which, facing everyone with inevitable changes, losses and bereavements, is constantly at particular moments more or less reshaping the *very conditions under which a young analyst has only recently integrated the practice of analysis into the economy of his existence.*

In spite of these inevitable overlaps and cross-effects, for the sake of the argument I shall list here *four sorts of disturbance*— called (A), (B), (C), and (D)—*under the generic term of 'professional disorders of the analyst'.*

I shall exclude from my categories the somatic disorders known as commonplace to which every office job exposes people, even though these disorders can also sometimes interfere *ad hoc* with the use of psychic envelopes, and although the unity of the psyche–soma economy is obvious, albeit still mysterious (not to mention the more or less temporary and mobilizable narcissistic or symbolic connections that can occur between a patient and his analyst, for instance on the occasion of a simple viral infection). But I shall, by contrast, include in these categories physical disorders that arise from 'somatization', however much that notion may also remain debatable. I shall not apply myself particularly to the study of this dimension or fate of the envelopes, which deserves separate investigation on its own in depth. But there is every reason to think that in somatizations and the psychosomatic economy, as it is conceived of notably by the school of P. Marty, adhesive attachments, stickings-together or fusions are very probably involved, as well as comings unstuck or tearings apart that are difficult to allocate as between truly psychic envelopes and the pre- or archaeo-psychic envelopes on which the first are necessarily overlaid. Finally, I shall distinguish:

(A) Problems or 'professional disorders' that seem to be caused primarily by the appearance at a given moment of *bad relationships among the analyst's psychic envelopes, inside his personality itself*. These often appear depressive, whether they result from circumstances that could be described as extra-analytical, or whether they have obviously been produced by the practitioner's professional activity, for example by his reactions to particular therapeutic setbacks or to the departure of some of his patients. They weigh upon professional work without necessarily interfering with it at depth.

(B) Problems whose dominant aspect seems due above all to the occurrence *in the analyst of abnormally difficult relations with the psychic envelopes of one or more of his patients.*

(C) Problems that are mainly centred upon a *disorder in relations between the analyst's personality and the envelopes of his training and professional 'environment'*, as defined above, and which have various repercussions in his conduct.

(D) Finally, problems produced by *a very close intertwining of all three types of disorders above*—(A) × (B) × (C)—which the nature of our postulates obliges us to admit are never totally independent, but which in certain cases form *veritable tangles*. Functioning in a paradoxical way, these tangles make one think of a sort of perverse untreatable moral masochism, resistant to efforts at aetio-pathogenic differentiation and classification both in self-analysis and in re-analysis.

I warn the reader that it is going to be very difficult, given the nature of the subject and the position of the observer, for me to give examples from clinical material that it would be pointless in this context to seek to disguise. Indirect allusions or time-honoured references should suffice if one bears in mind that something of each of the difficulties that I refer to here can be found—minimally or analogically—in every psychoanalytic practice. In principle, readers can be relied upon to produce their own topical associations, at least if they are analysts.

(A)   To start with I shall tackle the *first category*, which seems to be by far the most extensively studied, if not the only one in current writings, despite the intuitions of Freud (and Ferenczi) about the two following categories, (B) and (C). It is in fact only too obvious that traumatic or other circumstances can markedly lower, either temporarily or more lastingly (in the case of a more serious bout of anxiety or depression), an analyst's capacity to use his own frailties, momentary lapses of understanding, and diverse inhibitions and emotions in a profitable and flexible way in order to fasten them empathically onto his patients' symptomatic formations and let them work in these patients and himself without either regressing or becoming excessively disorganized. This is entirely banal and familiar. It was doubtless above all to alleviate such tiresome problems—prejudicial both to colleagues and patients—that Freud (1912e, 1937c) and Ferenczi (1928) recommended the periodic re-analysis of practitioners, 'for example every five years' (Freud, *Analysis Terminable and Interminable,* 1937c).

In terms of envelopes, this 'banal' and almost expected professional pathology amounts to an ageing or rigidification, which might be called natural, of the analyst's internal capacity for differentiation in the management of his identificatory positions where affect and representation are concerned. This is the cumulative outcome of life's losses, specific irritations, or particular reinforcements of open wounds or childhood identificatory scars. Quasi-sensorial (third eye!) 'pores' and 'information holes' seem to be invaded, blocked up, or, conversely, to be too enlarged or damaged by intrusive identificatory elements of an immediate and more or less 'extra-analytic' origin. And systems of associations—the lymphatic and vascular networks of the mind—clog or dry up locally, forming knots, inflammatory plaques, and various cysts, in what sometimes looks like a sort of ongoing inhibition neurosis in the practitioner. This gives rise to a need for new work to reinsert the phenomenon into a neurotic history that the practitioner has only recently worked upon in his own analysis, whose benefits and impact are gradually obliterated by the action of new concerns and need to be mobilized again, since they affect his practice more or less indirectly.

Referring back to my general reflections (II) on the analyst's metapsychology, I regard this type of problem as in some sense an endogenous affliction, due to the reappearance of old flaws. These tend specifically to confuse the economy and topography of internal depressive space organized within the analyst's self, an especially fragile area of the envelopes that is protected by flexible barriers and detached from sexualized relations with the superego to the benefit of the professional sublimations that are indispensable for identifications in work.[22] It seems to me that this type of disorder in the envelopes often remains benign unless, anti-cathected and strongly denied, it is complicated by other factors.

Within the framework of the four categories of problem that I have distinguished, I find the problems posed by the types of 'professional pathology' of the envelopes that I am now going to examine more noteworthy, more stimulating to curiosity, undoubtedly newer and more interesting for analytic research in general, but also *more serious*.

(B) In the second group, overshadowed by the question of the analyst's relationship with his patient's envelopes, come 'disorders' that mainly consist in a *lasting and precisely aimed capture of the countertransference by the transference*. Ordinarily, but not always, confined to the treatment of a certain number of patients endowed with kindred peculiarities of psychic functioning and personal history, they can therefore be regarded as the elective pathology of one or more determinate types of *transferential process* that are active at a vestigial blind spot in the analyst's psychic organization. Broadly speaking, this kind of problem could be defined in terms of situations in which the unconscious is blocked or its receptivity is shut down long and insistently enough for the patient's analyst to have great difficulty in using them profitably in interpretation and for him to tend to get bogged down damagingly by falling *time and again* into the same sort of trap. In these situations one will observe the practitioner *acting out unawares in the countertransference the imago position that his client assigns to him in the transference, without being able to withdraw,* and all the while *believing* that he is monitoring and analysing it. There are many cases to illustrate such a 'morbid' occurrence, and I have examined several elsewhere (Gillaumin, 1976, 1983).

In fact, one could take the view that everything suggests that *the analyst was hooking himself like a parasite into his patient's skin of phantasy,* without being able to differentiate himself from it (at some level or other of the superimposed identificatory coverings)[23] or was, if you like, beginning to *act the part of a masked character* (or sometimes one who has already been recognized, but only on an intellectual plane) *in his patient's fiction or primal scene,* whose cast-off identificatory garb he would therefore be donning. Here there is a sort of *uncontrollable neurotic inflation* in which the transference neurosis (which of its very nature extrudes the contents of the unconscious and distributes them about within the setting of the treatment) comes to merge osmotically or fuse with a 'countertransference neurosis' which sets about becoming an inseparable part of it. The analyst's internal 'frame' fixes itself irreversibly onto the canvas of the patient's internal objects, as a result of certain elective affinities inherent both in the cases in question and in the analyst.

When this happens, only the intervention of a third listening party can pull the two envelopes, or rather two collections of envelopes, apart from one another and restore a degree of free play to them, thereby, case by case, standing in for the alternating work of identification and dis-identification that is centred upon the symptomatic strangeness of the patient's words (see above). The most familiar, but not the only, paradigm for this kind of difficulty lies in the analyst's mothering response to the patient's suffering and call for help, insufficiently distinguished from his wish for archaic omnipotence, a response that conceals his participation in acting out, or in interpretative acting out, of some masochistic or perverse phantasy of this patient, that has become fascinating for . . . and untreatable by him.

But there are other circumstances under which this sort of blind 'pragmatic'[24] effect of the transference can affect the whole of his environment, if an analyst is lastingly contaminated, leading to rupture of the envelope of analytic confidentiality or the protective barrier afforded by the rule of abstinence. This can lead to sexual or other transgressions by the analyst, or to systematic counter-manipulation on his part, generally with the 'praiseworthy' conscious intention of helping the patient by the intervention of third parties. The properly psychoanalytic outcome is negative, *except in cases where the transference–countertransference seduction is taken up* (preferably rather promptly) *with the aid of a third listener, and before it turns into action, something that can transform negative into positive* and increase in hindsight the practitioner's capacity to contain and interpret the patient's symptoms. This is because the containing analytic envelope that has been stretched to breaking-point is able thereafter with its very wide mesh to put up a better resistance to the roughest assaults, thereby also securing the patient's ego.

But this is precisely not the case if the 'professional disorder' becomes chronic. Failing recovery by resort to a third listening party, it is uncertain whether *chaos can be averted even by stopping the analysis* under pressure from the patient or to relieve the analyst who is stuck in the transference–countertransference capsule. Stopping can, however, restore the reality principle by providing an answer in action, albeit very painful and burdensome, to the question of the limits of what can be analysed. It is therefore equivalent to a surgical operation that aims to separate, at whatever risk, two psychic processes that have become 'Siamese twins', boundlessly porous to one another and osmotically merged, and by any account each getting poisoned by the other. It then remains for the two partners, once surgically separated, to subsequently re-internalize, each on their own account, their mingled positions, with the help of self-analysis or another listener.

(c)   Perhaps one of the most astonishing of the professional pathologies of the analyst, and one of the most troublesome both

for him and for his patients—in so far as it never confines itself
to a single type of relationship and patient, and often lasts for a
very long time, sometimes for a whole career—is one that origi-
nates not on the patient's side, whom the practitioner contains or
envelops, but from the *institutional setting that contains and
envelops him himself.*

This type of professional disorder belongs to a very deceptive
'psychic dermatology' (I mean this to be taken with a pinch of
salt). For, inconspicuous in the manifest material of treatment,
and located at a deep countertransferential level, it lies eagerly in
wait for the most committed of analysts, and even those most
alert in their professon *and most careful to see to it that the indispensable representation of a third party intervenes inside themselves between them and their patients, and in these patients' own
material*—a third party in the shape of the local milieu, teachers,
colleagues, and the institution and its theoretical and practical
discourse, interwoven in a particular way. In short, in contrast
with what happens with problems of the last type, this in no way
spares, and perhaps especially threatens, both the most resolute
and the most prudent interpreters of the Oedipus and castration
complexes—those, therefore, whose psychic skins *would seem to
be* the most developed, but who prove to be fragile and poorly
detached from their collegiate and parental underlying support.

I shall define this deceptive pathology as an *anaclytic* addiction, or *idealization,* or anti-idealization or anti-addiction with
respect to representatives of the analyst's institutional setting
[the play on words—French *contre-addiction* with contradiction—
should perhaps not be brushed aside . . .]. Developed or resurgent
thanks to the very depth and quality of his analytic commitment,
which dredges him, so to speak, and strongly tests his capacity to
contain his own work identifications, it attaches itself adhesively
to representations of whatever is supposed to guarantee protection outside the internal setting of the analysis.[25]

The tendency to idealize, which was well studied from a more
general point of view by Janine Chasseguet-Smirgel (1972)[26] is
undoubtedly connected to a sort of 'internal anaclitic tendency'
(Guillaumin, 1976)[27] that is apt to be variously projected onto the
individual or collective sources of support that are available in
the environment. Due perhaps specifically to the 'incompleteness'

of the human being that is sometimes described as 'neotenic' (Bolk, taken up by Lacan[28]; R. Barande[29]), this is always at hand in each of us to compensate for the fragile part of our identificatory organization, which, on occasions when tolerance to ambivalence and to 'castration' by reality falters, cries out for a bandage, a plug, or a *narcissistic identificatory prosthesis*: a temporary emergency repair, an inevitably chronic and more or less localized scar upon hidden oedipal fragility. In his heart of hearts no analyst can believe himself to be definitively exempt from such fragility, even if others deny it in him, or he boasts a bit on the subject himself in his milieu. This belief in itself would in fact be a sign precisely of . . . idealization and attachment to a grandiose self-image. Routine analytic work does indeed consist to a large extent of keeping one's eye open for temptations to idealize in relation to *one's own person and objects of one's infantile history* that can be projected onto patients themselves and their objects. Strictly speaking, the problems encountered here could be reduced to the difficulties dealt with in the previous section.

But it will be noticed that category (c) *specifically* entails being watchful for improper, secret and even unconscious idealizations that have been *projected onto professional models* only recently received, models that should not be turned to without freedom of mind, attention and criticism all together, unless a fragile system of cast-off identificatory garb and internal dependencies is to be developed, of which the 'brilliant baby' is an example, which Ferenczi undoubtedly was himself (the inventor of the expression). In fact, the analyst's profession, and this is its major difficulty, specifically demands *resistance to the temptation to commit psychic incest with his patient*—cf. the 'disorder' examined in (B)—*by mobilizing internally, in a non-fusional and non-incestuous way, the theoretical and practical inheritance received from his kin-group of analytical 'relatives' and the 'tribe' whose language they speak*. The paradox is that this appeal to an internal prop for reality runs the risk of itself becoming confused to a degree that is in proportion to the cathexis of which it is object, with invocation of the analytic Ideal, an unattainable or miraculous resort. Good use of 'professional' models can only fundamentally be achieved at the cost of a delicate transference/countertransference reversal[30], *which implies that a subtle distinction is being maintained between the inside and outside of the psychic envelopes, as well as implying acknowledgement, ever labile and in need of restoration,* of the 'technical' operators of this positional distinction, based on the empathic links that the former patient, which the analyst is, has with his own patient. What has been demanded or taken from external envelopes must not be fused with internal envelopes at a fragile point. The trace of kinship and non-confusable reversal that it has implied must be preserved without running one generation into another. But *analytic zeal*—as will be seen above all in (D)—often tends to re-establish 'narcissistic lineages' (in the sense meant, for instance, by J. Guyotat in connection with kinship in psychosis, even though here we are dealing not with psychotics but only with *situations* that could in certain cases become quasi-psychotic).

As for their development and clinical form, and quite apart from the effects of human 'neoteny' in general, professional disorders of this group probably originate in a very specific way in *the part played by the incompleteness intrinsic to any analysis, and above all in the particular destiny, indicated above, that it has in future analysts,* who put it back to work, and, indeed, even project it in a more or less unworked-on state into their desire to analyse—a desire that certain candidates sometimes turn *violently* upon their institutions, seemingly out of a sort of urgent need for reparation, legitimate in their eyes, which is secretly meant to dress the ill-closed wound of the inevitable negative dimension of the transference–countertransference relationship, whose 'definitive' loss has not been well dealt with in a separation that purports to be 'good-bye' but contains a latent underlying 'see you later'. This avid desire can then come back at them from outside and/or from within as a denial of the *residual unthought element in their own analysis,* as much inherited from their training as concealed by it, and raises questions, whether unconsciously or not, about their *own analyst's kin-group* and the representation of his original relationships with is own analytical 'relatives'. This extends to three or even four generations the process that has to be represented. I have been able to demonstrate something of this sort (1985) in the link between the difficulties Ferenczi had with his patients and those that he had with Freud between 1918 and

1932.[31] I leave each reader the task of searching for examples or experiences that are closer to hand.

Clinically speaking, there are several possible fates in store for this 'residue' that has been thrown back so massively upon the 'relatives' to whom the analyst owes his choice of profession and success, without it being possible to 'work' upon it:

(a) *The first is direct idealization and psychic addiction to personalized or institutional theoretico-practical positions that are felt to be vital* and are, of course, those held by one or other more or less specific representative individuals, groups or sub-groups. The corresponding 'pathology' is then probably at once both *sado-masochistic and loving,* with a secret reproach but a zealous public cult and devotion towards representative individuals and organizations, whether personalized or not. The analyst suffers the pain of ambivalence and deception in his addictive love. And he can either pay the price for it unconsciously in rigidity or laxity (sometimes alternating) with his patients or colleagues, or by sinking himself in guilt-ridden depression, even if he later reproaches the institution with it (and demands reparation) for what it has cost him in his life, his person, his career and so forth. This is how I understand the *direct* form of what J. L. Donnet (1976) called 'transference to analysis', on the model of a veritable *skin-to-skin psychic clinging to the institutional envelope.*

I would willingly put forward the clinical suggestion (in line with my preceding thoughts about the arrangement of the analyst's professional topography) that, in this more or less personalized addictive zeal centred upon the group or extended and/or interconnected series of analytic 'relatives', the *solitary auto-erotic pleasure produced in treatment by the infinite interplay of work identifications is displaced* into a different arena in order to evade guilt.[32] This interplay in fact induces the analyst to penetrate into his patients' primal scenes and family scripts in an exciting and all too easily omnipotent manner, and in moments of anxiety he can try to exculpate himself by consciously or unconsciously bringing in the *substitute* scene and family script that are played out *for him* in his personal relationship to his own analyst and analytic practice, as objects of passionate appropriation connected with this particular parent analyst and the models that have been represented to him, and as presumptive material for 'transmission' in the desire to become an analyst.

(b) *The second fate in store for the residue that is left to be analysed in the analyst could, when reinvested in the institution, be described in virtually the same terms, apart from a reversal.* The (archaic) transference 'to the institution' and the clinging to it are dominated in this case by a *defence that is full of hatred* rather than lovingly reproachful, because of tegumentary attachment that is resented as being *too persecutory*. Here again, this position has its origin in an inextricable residual transference–countertransference element that derives from the analyst's own analysis. But narcissistic fury, in H. Kohut's sense, rages in a sadistic register, for reasons that can be due to the analyst's structure, or to the historical modalities according to which his one or more personal analyses were terminated, with or without mourning his analyst, who is subsequently found again 'out front' at a time when he has in a certain sense been left 'behind'. Something of this persecutory dimension (which involves the imaginary confusion of generations that I have called 'stolen countertransference'—Guillaumin, 1976) also appeared in the line of Fliess–Freud–Ferenczi–Ferenczi's patients. *In this specific case, aggressive–projective and reactive defence against an addictive transference to the institution and its representatives outweighs the desire to have his analyst inside his skin or be inside his analyst's skin,* as if struggling with an internal/external part of himself that necessitates violent rejection, unconditional condemnation, or manoeuvres to master or reverse received inheritances, whereby the practitioner has the ultimate unconscious aim of *'having' his own analyst's skin.* This 'analyst's disorder' is therefore a *disorder of transference love tangled up with counter-transference love, and turned inside-out in hatred,* that is sometimes extended to the whole institution. The person concerned becomes allergic to the latter: it gives him headaches, it suffocates him, and he cannot get rid of it.[33] And he attacks it while tearing himself apart, as from a damaged part of his intimate envelopes or the placenta of his birth, which would adhere to the body and be unable to find an opening for satisfactory evacuation of the negative part of the inheritance.

It can also happen that this paranoid hatred of the institution taints at source even the 'omnipotent' pleasure in analysing that is at stake, sterilizes professional desire, and in some cases leads the analyst to thoughts of suicide or some suicidal equivalent. It is as though the analyst's institutional envelope had closed up again over him, and the secondary exogenous masochism of the preceding case were transformed in some sense into primary masochism, unless he is induced to reverse received rules in an active but yet still megalomaniac way, by secretly identifying himself with the absolute creator of 'true' psychoanalysis, with an unconscious rage that is turned back upon his patients—a magical 'return' to Freud that also skips over any intermediate kindred relationships. In benign cases, something of this paranoid love–hate drama will simply be used in order to join or organize a form of more or less pertinent and useful 'dissent'; or else dissent will simply remain a tendency. In any case, the analyst gives himself a new 'external' envelope to regulate if possible the contentious problematic of internalizing the envelopes of his professional origin that replace those of his infantile history. This attempt at active self-healing has indeed curative and sometimes heuristic value, but it is difficult to evaluate its effects upon the analyst's patients.[34] The history of J. Lacan and 'Lacanism' afford some food for thought in this area.

(c) *The third fate in store for the analyst's transference–countertransference bonds with his institutional envelopes* will occupy little space here. In some sense it is 'normal'—which is to say obliged to keep itself in balance by frequent shifts back and forth to the limit, amidst the various pathological seductions of the profession. Here I again refer (see above) to the delicate interpretative work of suspending part of the unconscious that is as much transferential as countertransferential and guiding it in a negative direction, something that, by stressing lack of meaning, or 'excess' or 'insufficiency' in symptoms, cries out for a differentiation that must at all times constantly be made: the unlawfulness that is openly acknowledged, though without phobic retreat, of 'skin-to-skin' contact or seduction between the minds of analysand and analyst. *It is failure or breakdown* (by total adhesion or absence of contact) *in this work of differentiation within a state of empathy*, so essential for interpretation, that is ultimately found in *the two psychoanalytic pathologies B and C*.

I would stress, however, that on the whole disorders of type C are primarily distinguished from those of type B, which interfere with *the patient*, by their somewhat *parasitic* implantation *on or in the skin of the analytic institution of reference*. Perhaps they even form part (then in an attenuated and as it were vaccinal form) of the overall hygienic equilibrium of the institution, which 'needs' its disappointed lovers, its 'enemies' within, or its proselytizing fanatics, just as it needs opposable institutions, antigroups and enemy brethren!

(D)   *The fourth category of 'professional disorders' of the analyst* has the distinction of presenting itself as the *result of a sort of potentiation of all the aetiologies studied in the preceding categories*.

I know very well that in introducing this group of problems I am not exempt from the reproach of conceiving of it either as a purely residual category, destined to gather together all that the others were unable to contain, or else as the product of a general failure of my attempt at taxonomy. From this latter point of view, the group of problems described as type D would in a sense include all the psychoanalyst's 'professional disorders', in so far as there would not be any cases attributable to an unmixed 'aetiopathogenesis'. I declare myself incapable of totally eliminating these *two* reproaches, which each contain—and contradictorily—some element of the truth.

We know that in fact there is no 'typical treatment', nor are there any entirely pure pathological or character structures. Neither do there exist 'watertight' categories in the area that concerns us. All the same, category D probably qualifies as being the place for *the most severe* disturbances of the transference–countertransference process, which cannot be reduced to the preceding categories by the use of combined or isolated references. Its criterion—perhaps altogether provisional, and in any case altogether empirical—would be that of the *actual insolubility* of certain situations whose prototype (on the patient's side) would undoubtedly be what Freud called negative therapeutic reactions. In the same way there could in my view be 'negative reactions' *in the very process of the analyst's evolution,* which could then give rise to cases of negative therapeutic reactions in his patients. Freud's thinking about the negative therapeutic reaction certainly evolved, and he was able to remove a certain number of cases from the 'untreatable' category (see, for example, Freud, 1923b, *The Ego and the Id*). But he retained the notion, as in the very example of the limits of the analysable that are reached by an unexpected perverse turning against itself of the patient's analysis.

Discussion of the characteristics of category c has already led me to take account of certain aspects of the deep masochism that is apt to play a part in ambivalent attachment to institutions and formative objects. With some analysts a sort of 'narcissistic frenzy' (cf. H. Kohut) can settle in at this level, to destroy (themselves) or save (themselves) by means of maintaining a non-differentiation amongst envelopes that depend upon teachers who cannot be either expelled or internalized because of archaic idealizations, in a sort of exasperated, infinite and reproachful to-and-fro between what is given or due to patients and what the institution requires. Here I shall suggest that this evolution in an analyst should be understood *as a slow turning back* in treatment *like a flayed skin, of the 'inside' of envelopes that are engaged on the 'outside'.* As though, as I have already suggested in c, the deepening (in some sense subcutaneous or hypodermic) of the analyst's sensitivity in his work, as between patients before him and teachers behind him, *had stripped off alive and stuck onto his poorly introjected teachers all the subtlety of countertransferential perception that he had attained for dealing with the defences and identificatory trappings of his patients.* The narcissistic rage of one who has been flayed then hooks into the source of support while at the same time seeking both to tear it from *himself* and to tear himself from it. Here we have, all at once and indistinguishably, a patient's passion and impatience of any institutional suffering, whether due to excess and/or want of closeness, and confusion between active and passive in both directions, with all the envelopes crushed one against the other.

There are therefore good grounds for speaking of a sort of perforating activity that starts with an analyst/patient relationship that is more or less gradually reversed into a transfusion or *trans-*

fixion of the analyst by his source of support in the institutional kin-group (which at the same time pins him down to his patients' couch), and a real or imaginary transfixion of the institution by an analyst invaded by his patients' passion. When such a situation arises, in which the 'sick' analyst is undoubtedly the omnipotent/impotent 'hollow penis' (cf. the meaning of this hysterical perverse phantasy in Wisdom) of the institution/mother herself, it inevitably brings vertiginous defences into play which, through ever more refined interpretative work, affect his patients or his institution to a lesser degree, after or at the same time as the practitioner himself, since they are called upon unconsciously to play a real role in this inversion-confusion of psychic envelopes.

Some analysts actually go 'mad' (or even kill themselves) as a result of situations of this kind, which effectively gather together, agglutinate and mutually potentiate all the aetiopathogeneses already examined. This perhaps raises questions about the ends that Victor Tausk or Ferenczi met with.

What I am now going to say should not be taken as black humour: the statement you have just read is not in my view pessimistic. There are in fact reasons to think that the gravity of the developments that I have described is *connected with the inadequacy—still notable but temporary—of our efforts to achieve a true psychoanalytic understanding of what is going on.*

Here and there there are undoubtedly some poorly oriented analysts who did not have sufficient narcissistic solidity at the start to escape the vertigo of their own analytic development. And there are alas also some whose personal analysis or subsequent 'slabs' of analysis have occasionally contributed to the destabilization of the rather fragile but adequate order of their psychic envelopes, by failing to take account of certain points in their history and the imbalance between their narcissistic underlay and the interpretative interventions furnished by their analyst. But it seems certain to me that *in most cases* the elements for dealing with disturbances of the type described in D are, in a general way, within our scope—at least in principle.

Freud (1923b) noted—as I have mentioned—that *some* treatments that seemed to have nothing but a negative prognosis nonetheless succeeded if it was possible to identify a *hidden personalized model* of the patient's deep masochistic functioning and to work on this identification, which could be described as self-destructive. Now, as I see things, *there is always, in negative therapeutic reactions, an accurate hidden model* of the patient's deep masochistic conduct, and it is most often because of a sort of sloth on the analyst's part that adheres to the 'natural' unfolding of the treatment that this crucial identificatory model, held in denial by the patient, is not worked upon. Analyst and analysand are then associated in a sort of shared denial.

Of course the analyst's 'sloth' raises questions about a pocket of his own narcissistic identification with the patient, which he himself does not want to touch, and which he persuades himself has nothing to do with the matter. In order not to notice his patient's infantile identificatory alliances directed against oedipal awareness, he displaces his countertransference in favour of irritation, lassitude, theoretical speculations, and so on. In my opinion, however, all this can always change if a 'supervisor' gives sight back to this Oedipus who was in some sense electively blind, by helping him to interpret his affects and restore his sense of the place he occupies in the unconscious infantile scene he is playing in collusion with his patient, by idealizing the role conferred upon him. This favourable outcome of the patient's 'negative therapeutic reaction' will have come about through work upon the analyst's countertransference.

I believe that in the 'pathogenic' developments *in the analyst* that I connect with the fourth type (D), and which perhaps deserve to be called *'negative professional reactions'* in their own right, there is always a hidden identificatory model, experienced narcissistically but bound up with an unrecognized oedipal system that knits the whole situation together. But the true specificity of the structure of such cases, looped back upon itself, derives from the fact that *here the hidden model that handicaps the analyst cuts back and forth across at very least three generations,* or, if you like, *three sets of identificatory envelopes,* by fixing them to one another in a manner that is both undifferentiated and more or less reversible in phantasy. A passionate identificatory position that belongs to the family script or an archaic phantasy of the *analyst's analyst*—an identificatory position that eluded his own analysis—has been promptly reinvested by him in the reality of his practice and institutional ties, thanks to positional analogies between the significant characters of his training environment and those of his childhood. When the second-generation analyst, for personal reasons of the same kind, secretly makes a narcissistic identificatory bond and withdraws under cover of this relationship from psychoanalytic mourning, it is enough to make him find himself bearer of a sort of psychoanalytic 'mission'. He might, for example, feel moved to make an ideal repair to an old narcissistic injury of his 'parent' through his professional success, and work towards this end with his own patient–'children' in the third generation.

A secret mission such as this is like the one that Freud, according to M. Krull (1979), received unconsciously from his paternal line through the mediation of an unlucky father who had rather come down in the world, and was replaced by W. Fliess in a homosexual idealization; or, again, to what Ferenczi felt he had received in the capacity of 'secret grand vizier' to Freud himself, arising out of his mysterious self-analysis—cf. Ferenczi's *Clinical Journal* (1985); my work on Fliess–Freud–Ferenczi (Guillaumin, 1986a); and P. Sabourin's work on Ferenczi. This type of narcissistic inheritance provides the one who purports to have a mandate with considerable sublimatory energy, provided that its basis remains sufficiently concealed. If the energy in question is connected up in the third generation with some unconscious expectation in a patient, thereby joining forces with his own personal resistances against acknowledging oedipal configurations, *it obliges this patient to find confirmation in himself* (or, failing that because of ambivalence, anti-confirmation or disappointment) *of the 'hopes' that were narcissistically invested in him,* and this at the obvious expense of more advanced working through of his own personal neurosis, derived from his infantile history.

It all seems under these conditions as though the message transmitted across three (or four . . .) generations by the analysis contained a double and paradoxical injunction: to *become oneself,* and *remain conformist to another,* on pain of losing the love of the 'parent' charged with ensuring the 'child's' access to autonomy. The deep-seated contradiction in this position can lead either to an insurmountable and painful dependency, or to attempts at counter-control and unconscious narcissistic rivalry with the immediate parent analyst, in the quest for a direct identification with the parent of the first generation: to the detriment of all manner of work on the oedipal situation and acceptance of castration, as much in the analyst concerned in the second generation, as in his client at the end of the chain. On this path the analysis can become toxic and interminable, even disorganizing for the client (a negative therapeutic reaction properly so called). But this is the terminal effect of an identificatory obligation of which his analyst was the first victim *before him* in the collapse of the chain of idealizations and ambivalence.

In terms of envelopes, one could say that the psychic reality of these unrecognized concatenations is the very spot where both adhesion and ripping or reversal of identificatory envelopes takes place. It will be impossible to unravel the situation so long as the narcissistic identifications transmitted from generation to generation have not been identified, held in mind, and worked upon as being instrumental in the identificatory transfixion that skewers through the whole laminate of the psychic reality of the person concerned—flattened out at a given point—and pins it both onto that of his training analyst within the institution, and that of his client. And the analyst who is 'sick' in this paradoxical way (as carrier, perhaps 'healthy' in other respects, of a prognosis that frustrates the very ends of psychoanalysis) will to that extent gradually denude himself of the ability to restore his patients' envelopes.

(IV)   PSYCHOANALYSIS, ENVELOPES AND CREATIVITY

In this last section I shall repeat suggestions about creativity that I made not long ago (Guillaumin, 1980—D. Anzieu has considerably enriched and modulated these in *Le Corps de l'oeuvre,* 1981, and *Le Moi-Peau,* 1985), relating them to the analyst's functioning by means of the concept of envelopes.

(1)   The work of creation

It is easy to make the connection with the concept of envelope if one allows, as I do, that the object created is produced by an extension of the self or even of the organized ego, which at least during creative work takes the place of an *external adjunct to the psychic apparatus,* and that amidst temporary uncertainty about the boundaries of the self it can, in this way, substitutively reap the fruits of constructive work that has *topographical and economic value,* but from which the ego itself cannot benefit *directly.* In this case the ego or the self needs in some sense *to do focussed work, trained upon the object,* and on a determinate creative theme, in order thereby to weave, in mid-course and amidst ambiguity between outside and inside, an auxiliary system of envelopes that function at once as repository, prosthesis, and to a certain extent as stand-in and counterpart—envelopes capable of providing, by projective identification, scope for reinternalizing to some extent the psychic organizers that have eluded secondary identification.

But the creator's personality (arguably with some exceptions[35]) is not creative except along a particular axis and at particular moments. For the rest, it is, dare one say, commonplace, whatever its history may have been.

What then is the specific place that the created object on the one hand, and creative work on the other, occupy for the creator in the topography of his system of envelopes? Creative work is probably produced *at a flaw or a more or less broken fold* in a system of envelopes that include both the creator's intimate envelopes and those (interconnected with or disconnected from the former in ways already mentioned) that are managed by the external world by means of projective narcissistic communication with the reality of the body as the obscure place from which instincts spring, with the result that creative activity amounts to *a sort of work of reparation or scarring at these specific points.* This work is very often engaged in after particular shocks delivered by the external world have punctured the internal envelopes at a sensitive point that corresponds to a basic phantasy, often constant in the same author, and highly excitable. After a period of intense and complex experience of being under internal tension, which involves feeling a sort of narcissistic disidentification with the convenient and banal thinking of everyday life, and may go as far as becoming an experience of grave psychic illness with mixed depersonalization, excitation and inhibition, there suddenly emerges an urgent desire to gather all that together under the primacy of an energetic effort to *produce something actively that will re-establish outside and by outside means the order that had been lost within.* Creative work emerges, or is born, *out of this concerted topographical, dynamic and economic effort,* with the help of technical organizers of reality that are related to the laws of the external world (those of the peripheral envelopes) and are used to deal with the creator's intolerant phantasies. . . . This allows the work to take root and gain sufficient acceptance both in the environment so as not to be rejected as an incompatible allogenous graft, and in the creator's internal envelopes, together with the phantasies and memory traces with which it maintains an essential analogical and symbolic compatibility.

One could go so far as to say that the scar tissue or prosthesis with creative value is intended to repair the creator's external and internal envelopes *as a whole,* by 'creating', thanks to *aesthetic seduction,* and in a highly organized and stable way, *a pore, passage, or place for regulated switches and exchanges,* both channel and umbilicus between inside and outside for the author's ego. This is a function that can play an analogous role symbolically (and one that will persist later on, after the author's death) when turned around towards the public: between the work and the reader, spectator or listener.

(2)   Two types of relationship with creativity in the psychoanalyst

The psychoanalyst can have *two types of relationship* with creativity; or, rather, his relationship with creativity could be viewed equally in terms of either of the two principal directions with which we are familiar: one that leads towards practice with patients, and the other that leads towards institutional exchanges—especially towards writing and theorization, as the analyst's contribution to the construction or maintenance of the verbal and conceptual, even 'ideological' projection surface (the regulating 'ego-skin') of the shared institutional container. Let us examine, one after another, these two aspects, which also, of course, interact:

(1) In the direction of his practice in the consulting room—the first pole—the psychoanalyst seems to use transference–countertransference contact with his patient somewhat in the way in which the creative artist employs his creative activity in the service of his intimate envelopes at the same time as in that of the specific 'public' for his work. However, there are considerable differences. The patient already 'exists' in reality and is much more structured than the artist's piece of paper, canvas or marble block. And he is a living object, whose 'responses' will be very different from those of the work of art, which is itself infinitely more projective for the creator, even if, during creative work, the latter reinternalizes and deals afresh with the messages that the work sends back to him at every moment of its development. The analysand is both 'work' and 'public'. He creates himself, is created, more or less re-creates the author (the analyst) and remains interpreter and master of the ultimate fate of the 'creation' or psychoanalytic re-creation of which he has been object and . . . author. In short, this involves a sheath or auxiliary ego that is endowed with powers of self-regulation that the analytic regression temporarily reduces by supporting it on the analyst's envelopes but cannot subordinate to the creator.

But there are points in common, of which two at least are easy to identify: *appeal to the reality principle in analytic work at the very heart of a phantasy activity of identification and projection, and the problematic of the analyst's 'mourning' for the analysand* (the reciprocal of the analysand's mourning for the analyst, which is more often studied), which are homologues of the concern for realism connected with artistic technique, and of the fate of the artist's love relationship with his work.

All the same, the most remarkable analogical feature, from the point of view of envelopes, is in my view to be found in the direction of the use the analyst makes of the psychic 'zone of immaturity' that he preserves within himself, in line with the genetic and structural remarks and suggestions already set out above. This unstable zone, ready for hysterical identifications, but framed by the supple and solid teguments that the analyst is judged to have at his disposal elsewhere, is systematically matched up with his patient's fragilities by work of identification/dis-identification, owing to the psychoanalytic setting and rules.

Here the analyst's extreme and sustained proximity becomes a sort of skin-to-skin contact in which the sonorous verbal envelope is a privileged biface and bilocative envelope. Here the transference neurosis, with its counterpart in the countertransference, will conceive and temporarily develop a *hybrid umbilical formation*. I have stressed its anaclitic basis in other writings, and it has often been described as a more or less narcissistic sort of dyad or a 'chimera' (M. de M'uzan), ordained to evolve—after a functional reorganization of the different strata of the patient's personality, in critical interaction with those of the analyst's technically organized personality—towards a re-differentiation of the two phantasy systems that have been stuck together. This takes place through the patient's re-internalization of the imago projections, now improved, with which he had imbued his treatment. The boundaries and envelopes of analysand and analyst are then defined afresh, but *not without functional and controllable pathways remaining open in the patient towards other people,* whom he will be able to use for adaptive adjustments in his subsequent relational life. The analyst will in principle stand aside, leaving the field free for the recathexes consecutive upon psychoanalytic mourning at the end of treatment. This perhaps is the history in phantasy of the transference–countertransference hybrid that constitutes the *'creativity'* of analysis, temporary in this case, a biface, inter-skin [*entre-peau*] formation [*entrepôt?*] eventually destined to be reabsorbed in double mourning—outside and inside. Here we find the ultimate mourning that the artist, too, must go through for his work, abandoned as a temporary hybrid, or a past living part of himself, or a bandage, bud, 'crust' or chrysalis that has become inoperative and useless for him and fated to pursue its destiny elsewhere and otherwise at the hands of a public, who also consummate the author's own mourning (which the work robs him of) in the monument he has left them.

Our conception of the way a treatment develops seems to increase in meaning and truth within the framework of this comparison between creative artist and analyst. *Both set to work a measure of 'incompleteness' and an identificatory sensitivity that is sometimes unusual, and even experienced as disorganizing, with a view to producing change in 'external' reality* both for their own and others' benefit, instead of acting only upon their own psychic reality in a self-moulding way—to use Ferenczi's expression. External reality, which for the artist is, as I have said, inert at the beginning and symbolically figurative thereafter, is directly living and human for the analyst from the outset. But for both of them, right to the end, their work forms part of the 'skin' of the 'creator' *and* his object, until their inevitable separation for an autonomous future.

One would imagine that both cases essentially involve the realization or pursuit of a task of 'redifferentiating' the identificatory envelopes and putting them back in order, starting from the midst of an actual experience of *relative regressive un-differentiation or non-differentiation*. Lengthy work is needed here on a type of biface that is somewhat prone to denials (cf. Winnicott's notion of paradox) in order better to distinguish and articulate outside with inside, and, correlatively, the laminates of 'internal' and 'external' envelopes.

It is in the failure of this work in analytic practice that certain forms of what I have called 'professional disorders' of the psychoanalyst can be recognized. One would in fact also be justified in regarding these 'disorders' as *failures in the double creative function of the analyst's envelopes,* in as much as the psychic redifferentiation of the patient and/or analyst is not taking place satisfactorily, and the process is heading for chronicity.

(2) Let us now examine—second axis—the problematic of connections among envelopes as between the analyst and his environment, by giving special weight where communication with colleagues and the institutional setting is concerned, to *the phenomenon of theoretical elaboration viewed as an aspect of creative activity.*

(A) *First: the function of implicit and explicit theorization in analysis seems* par excellence *to constitute a meeting-point between*:

(a) its personal 'self-creating' creative activity, generating a sort of cocoon that protects thoughts that are linked by a systematic logic, in response to the destabilizing questions raised by clinical work, that are always in part unforeseeable;

(b)   the 'already created' of Freudian theory, rounded off by the activity *in statu nascendi* of theoretical thinking by colleagues and authors, and the analyst's professional knowledge;

(c)   the actual experience of the analyst's thought participating in theoretical thinking [*pensée*] in general—that is, ceaselessly rethought [*repensée*] and compensated for [*compensée*].

The conjunction of these three points expresses the analyst's active/passive presence at once inside, outside, and within the walls of the notional and institutional container of analysis, enclosing the analyst himself and his analysands; and the *immediate* cause of certain 'professional ailments' of the envelopes noted above can undoubtedly be seen in an imbalance between these joint positions.

(B)   *Second: there is in every case a see-saw movement, of compensation and work, between an analyst's creation of theory and collective thought, and his practical work with patients.* The mirror effects, helpful or hindering, that govern this sort of process have often been noted. I would suggest, in the spirit of my general views about the negative operator and the role of what is unrepresented in analysis, that *cooperation between the analyst's creative theoretical activity and his clinical work of 'creating' the patient is* governed by a law that I shall call 'the law of the absent third party', in which a central aspect of the practical and epistemological position of psychoanalysis is to be found.

It is only insofar as the work of theorization *propounded for the use of institutional colleagues* keeps an open window in sight, something unfinished that reflects that part of clinical reality that cannot be completely represented here and now, that this theory becomes 'good'—by the very admission that it makes of its systematic incompleteness. *Reciprocally, clinical work only improves in practice from maintaining under stress a theory that it is uneasy about not being faithful enough to,* knowing *nevertheless* that the said theory 'surely' applies to the case but *in ways that still themselves remain to be discovered,* or created, rather than recreated. This double game of returning to what cannot be completed in practical and theoretical thought is the very precondition for a fecund (creative) development of both in analysis, as perhaps in a general way in the movement of Life.

(c) *One last remark will serve me as a general conclusion*, by leading me back to my initial reflections: *the theory of envelopes is itself an envelope for psychoanalysis*. And the ease with which it seems to me that it allows some of its problems to be reformulated is due to the epistemological position that implicitly resides in it. There is no possible complete systematic description of the . . . 'system' of psychic envelopes, in their origin and functioning, that can adopt the positive viewpoint of an ethnologist, a sociologist, or a psycho-physiologist of psychoanalysis. The psychoanalyst writing and theorizing, like the practising psychoanalyst, is both subject and object of the experience of enveloping and being enveloped, as of being himself one envelope among others. In his practice, and in exercising his thought, he searches indissociably as he lives his life as a psychoanalyst, to connect up all the envelopes to which he belongs, where he is, according to the pattern of life, so that they may play, breathe, support one another, and become a continuous creation to their very utmost extent.

NOTES

1. Despite noteworthy examinations of this notion, particularly in the context of D. Anzieu's work on Freud's self analysis (1959, 1975).
2. Cf. my article: Contre-transferts (1976b), reprinted as chapter 12 of my book *Psyché* under the title: Contre-transferts ou Psyché et son miroir (1983).
3. In the sense in which Freud seems to have intended the notion of expectation, an idea that came to him at the outset of psychoanalysis.
4. It seems to me that my statement could be connected with the conception put forward by A. Green under the heading of theory of the double limit.
5. R. Thom, *Paraboles et catastrophes* (1983); J.-P. Duport-Rosan, Morphogénèse du symbole, régulation symbolique et formelle (1983), in J. Guillaumin (ed.), *Ordre et désordre de la parole* (1986b).
6. Cf. J. Guillaumin, La blessure des origines (1982); my book: *Psyché* (1983); see also note 7.

7. I refer in particular to my recent work: *Entre blessure et cicatrice, le destin du négatif dans la psychanalyse* (1987). I will not develop here the specific logic of this negative operator, noting only that it is not incompatible with the theory of envelopes.

8. R. Fliess, The metapsychology of the analyst (1942). The metapsychology of the analyst has given rise to various works with which I will not increase the already heavy load of references in this article.

9. Cf. especially: Wild psycho-analysis (1910k); Recommendations to physicians practising psycho-analysis (1912e); *Beyond the Pleasure Principle* (1920g); *The Ego and the Id* (1923b); Analysis terminable and interminable (1937c).

10. To implicate/imply, explicate, complicate, as also develop, deploy etc., are verbs that themselves . . . imply a latent problematic of envelopes, as their etymology suggests.

11. Cf. J. Guillaumin, La peau du Centaure, in the collection edited by the author: *Corps Création* (P.U.L., 1980). For D. Anzieu cf. also his book: *Le corps de l'oeuvre* (1981).

12. It would be interesting to work on the concept of psychogenetic *development* in the sense of differentiation of a sort of nucleus, *a primal condensation of non-actualized envelopes,* under the impact of the interplay of projections and introjections which the baby participates in from the start.

13. And the experience she has of it (and which acts in return upon the baby) has no little bearing on her ambiguous position as 'mother' and 'lover' in the sense intended by D. Braunschweig and M. Fain (1975). For a reminder of the guidance and interactional selection that the mother and the milieu make upon the baby's primary phonological and subsequently semantic stock, cf. J. Guillaumin (1976) on 'prelanguage'.

14. J. Piaget, in a non-analytic vein, defined what he called the schema of the 'living' or the 'animate', relative to 'disquieting' objects that are difficult to predict. The relationship that psychoanalysis has established between the development of psychic organization and the intrusion of the 'stranger' (Spitz's second organizer, at around 6–8 months) is also familiar. In both cases the sound of the voice and language in general play a part in the disquieting experience by introducing an unverified sonorous element into perceived messages.

15. M. Fain, in J. Bergeret (ed.), *Le psychoanalyste face à l'écoute du toxicomane* (1981).

16. J. Bleger, *Symbiose et ambiguité* (1967).

17. As I shall recall further on, this first condition which in this sense ties in with certain of M. Fain's hypotheses (1969), seems to me to be common to the potential destinies of 'analyst' and 'analysand', who

are, however, in my view, too easily assimilated to one another in analytic discourse simply on this basis; cf. J. Guillaumin, Transmettre la présence de l'absent, ou la part en tiers (1984); cf. also my work: *Psyché* (1983), last part; and my article: La curiosité pour l'inconscient, in the collection *La curiosité en psychanalyse* (1981).

18. Speaking . . . and silent. On this silence/speech relationship in the analyst, cf. A. Green, Le silence du psychanalyste (1979).

19. Le préconscient et le travail du négatif dans l'interprétation (1986); see also my article: Mots en souffrance et attitude d'écoute en psychopathologie clinique, in J. Guillaumin (ed.), *Ordre et désordre de la parole,* 1986 (previously published in *Psychiatrie Française,* May 1985).

20. Cf. my contribution: Prise en compte tardive du contre-transfert de fond dans la cure psychanalytique, in the collection, *Le psychanalyste et son patient* (1983).

21. Note the importance that many analysts, such as R. Greenson, D. W. Winnicott and W. R. Bion, have, under one name or another, accorded to 'tact', or to qualities that are necessary for it (cf. also the notion of 'empathy' in H. Kohut, 1971).

22. This involves work by the living preconscious, the turn-table of the analytical transference. Obviously, one could equally take up here the distinctions Freud made between insufficiently deep first analyses, analyses recently limited by the structure of the analysand, and analyses limited by the very nature of the power of the analytic process in general to penetrate deeply and bring about change. But these distinctions are better represented, it seems to me, if they are examined from the point of view of the future they allow for the dynamic preconscious which I have mentioned—at least where psychoanalysts are concerned.

23. Here I am thinking of interesting clinical observations by Joyce McDougall, *Les Théâtres du Je* (1982), or Micheline Enriquez, L'analysant parasite (1979), and *Aux carrefours de la haine* (1984), on certain difficult analyses, and also Michel Serres's essay on *Le Parasite* (1980). All this ties in, of course, with the views of D. Anzieu in *Le Moi-Peau* (1985).

24. The distinction between the semantic and the 'pragmatic' effect of the transference (insofar as it is 'action upon') has been indicated by Jacques Cosnier (notably in *Nouvelles Clés pour la Psychologie,* 2nd ed., 1981, for which I supplied a preface).

25. I would relate—no more—this practitioner's pathology to what J. L. Donnet (1976) called 'transference to analysis'. The exact meaning of his conception will not be discussed here. See below, where I again cite Donnet.

26. Cf. *L'Idéal du Moi* (1972), which develops a paper to the Congrès des Psychanalystes de Langues Romanes (1972).

27. L'energie et les structures dans l'expérience dépressive (1976), reprinted in Guillaumin, *Psyché* (1983), ch. 8.

28. J. Lacan, *Le stade du miroir* (1936).

29. R. Barande, *L'inachèvement de l'homme comme structure de son temps* (1975).

30. Cf. Guillaumin, Contre-transferts (1976), reprinted in Guillaumin, *Psyché* (1983), chapter 12.

31. Fliess, Freud, Ferenczi, création permise et création refusée, succès et échecs de la transmission dans l'appropriation identifiante du négatif, in *Bulletin du Groupe lyonnais de Psychanalyse.*

32. The very notion of transference to 'analysis' (i.e. to analytic work) also undoubtedly bears this important nuance, in which it involves analytic psychic functioning *first and foremost.*

33. Cf. F. Roustang, *Elle ne me lâche plus* (1980).

34. It will be noted that it tends in principle, even in commonplace cases, to stretch, change, or destroy something of the setting or envelope of the psychoanalytic approach itself, which is confused overall, so long as the passionate crusade persists, with incidental aspects that are unbearable for the practitioner at the time and which he cannot separate out from it.

35. Even a seriously unbalanced creator has a 'healthy' relationship to reality in the sector where he creates, and insofar as he creates. To create in the sense of the work of sublimation always presupposes, regardless of appearances, a realistic and coherent use of a technique.

CHAPTER SEVEN

Modifications of the psychic envelope in creative work

J. Doron

(I) INTRODUCTION

Among the different possible functions of the ego-skin, I shall give my attention to the way in which the subject relates its inside and outside and elaborates the self.

One can think a psychic fact in words, spoken or written, but also in shapes: 'psychic events are shapes, which is to say, organic units that are individualized and find their boundaries in the spatial and temporal field of perception or representation' (P. Guillaume, 1942). The self: for Pontalis (1975), psychology develops amidst the separation between the registers of the subjective self [*self*] and our objective self [*soi*]: 'the first conjures up a personal space or, better, the experience of this own psychic space . . . the second, an assemblage with a fixed reference point that is marked by dignity, or an inner tribunal/stronghold [*for(t) intérieur*]'. The self, or the intimate part of our person, is not perceived inside ourselves, but in the way in which visible parts of the self are deposited on an object, cultural or otherwise, that is external and is perceived as such. This gives its shape to the representation, which, in return, forms or deforms our psyche in its most intimate area.

Depending upon the subject's functioning and type of creativity, internal and external can be seen to alternate as categories of thoughts inside or outside the mind. This oscillation occurs around an axis, a psychic operator, or an object created by the subject or by others carrying projections. This object then puts the inside and outside into relationship.

How is the transition made from individual to object? How does the process of assembling the containers of thought unfold?

Following D. Anzieu's (1985) work on the ego-skin, I can postulate that the link between space and objects is a psychic envelope whose form can vary according to the subject's states.

Let us take a window pane as image. It is a transparent frontier on which reflections play. It cannot be seen, but one divines that it carries what one does see. Depending on the light, it functions as a mirror that allows one to catch one's own image and surrounding objects. In a more classic manner, as in a showcase, it allows objects inside to be seen from the other side of the glass. The glass (psychic skin) is the support for this optical play.

Internal or external objects, which give shape to our thoughts, appear as reflections on the glass, as 'interface' objects. Depending upon the light, one perceives internal or external reality, or both superimposed.

This reflection, differentiated from what carries it while at the same time revealing it, is a psychic operator that has its foundations on the psychic skin. This object can easily be confused with the envelope and thoughts, but must be distinguished from them. This is carried out in a work of creation, modifying the psychic envelopes, and this will be the subject of this chapter.

This psychic operator has its source in the primitive experience of skin-to-skin contact between mother and baby, a reassuring contact elaborated within a phantasy of a common skin (whose function is that of maintaining the ego-skin).

The transitional object was certainly the first psychic operator to be described. It permits a double differentiation, between internal and external realities, and between mother and baby, facilitating in the latter the discovery through play and symbolization of the paradox of the mother who is present although she is absent.

The creation of psychic operators develops in the subject a capacity to transform his envelopes, in three different dimensions:

- first of all, it makes distinctions which, resting on the skin, create a boundary between inside and outside;

- it then reinforces the psychic envelope by receiving internal projections (the mirror)

- finally, by reversing the psychic envelope, it allows new containers for thought to be created, while at the same time facilitating communication with the self.

This interface object can be captured in a double artistic and psychological description (Bateson, 1979).

Two examples will illustrate this. I shall then make a theoretical approach to the modifications of the psychic envelope in creative work, and finally I shall study the principal characteristics of psychic operators, particularly the psychic portrait.

(II) CLINICAL STUDIES

(1) Isabelle, aged six, and her family made contact for the third time for a child psychiatry consultation. She was a charming but unstable child, most particularly with her preparatory school teacher, a rigid character. Mother worked in a children's hospital.

Isabelle was two years old when her mother, pregnant, contracted toxoplasmosis. The family's distress was then very acute, and the mother was depressed. She took medication during the last six months of her pregnancy. She gave birth to a completely normal boy. Shortly afterwards, Isabelle swallowed her mother's medicines. She was hospitalized under intensive care and had to have her stomach washed twice.

This incident had never been mentioned in the preceding consultations. Sensing a family confronted with a traumatic neurosis whose only solution was action, I chose to talk at this first interview. I told Isabelle and her mother that moving, talking and fidgeting are undoubtedly ways of feeling very much alive, in contrast with the situation of immobility in special care. Isabelle, attentive to my words, expressed her despair for the first time:

'I had tubes coming out of my body, and injections everywhere.'

I suggested she should draw this memory (her mother remained present during this interview). She took a piece of paper and drew the outline of a little girl with big hands covered with pimples. She gave back the paper and said:

'I was little, and I cried.'

She drew a hospital bed; the child lying there had a big head. She added the eyes, the mouth, the feet and then the tubes and the needles that penetrated her abdomen. On either side of the bed, which massively occupied the centre of the drawing, she added two shelves and said, while drawing some gift parcels:

'No one offered me anything.'

The mother smiled. Isabelle added huge hands:

'Her finger is swollen, and there are holes in her hands.'

ME: 'I see that you can draw and put words to very unpleasant memories.'

Astonished, Isabelle took another piece of paper.

'This is Mummy with measles.'

She gave this drawing to her mother and gave me 'the intensive care ward'.

'The nice one is for Mummy, the nasty one is for you', she said to me.

For the first time Isabelle and her parents could talk, without too much anxiety, about this traumatizing memory. This encounter altered the family equilibrium.

Isabelle had created a psychic operator. The drawing had installed communication between herself and her family on the one hand, and her internal world, her mother, and me on the other.

It is interesting to note that the stuff of this operator is the envelope, the surface of the ego-skin.

The trauma connected with intensive care and the stomach being pumped was transposed into holes in a skin that was otherwise solid. In a less distressing way these were replaced by pimples, leaving marks on the ego-skin but not wounding it.

Thus the psychic operator only takes shape on an expanse, the psychic envelope of the ego-skin.

(2)   Let us now study the transformations of the ego-skin in the course of a work of artistic creation.

Completing a picture is always a surprise. Besides the necessary technical mastery, it depends upon successive modifications of the ego-skin, reversal of which is most perilous of all.

Port de Goulée

I wanted to paint, but I had to go at the beginning of April to spend several days with my family. It was a contradictory need, for the place I wanted to paint was far from the one where we had to go. I therefore chose not to accompany my family and found myself in a first situation of rupture with everyday life.

I therefore set off alone, on a day with a strong, cold northeasterly wind that was driving the clouds. The countryside was still wintry, grey-brown, with a cold blue-and-white sky. Port de Goulée is a frontier port on the map. It is on the shoreline, but also at the edge of the truly maritime part of the Gironde estuary. On my arrival I was startled by the cold. The water, at low tide, began to rise, so much so that there was no reflection. Everything was brown, grey and black. The port was dissymmetrical; to the left, as you face the opening, were the fishermen's huts, mostly in ruins. Facing them, on the same side, were the landing-stages, in more or less good condition, some grounded boats, two little fishing boats, and several *piballous* very low on the water, allowing little eels to be caught in the shallows. Nothing moved at low tide, and there was no sound of hulls knocking together. Only gusts of wind resounded in the huts and ruffled the grass that pushed up to the limit where the water met the earth.

I had already done several paintings at Port de Goulée, and I had also had failures. I felt, internally, that in this known spot I needed to make a change in my way of painting. I walked along the whole front with my materials, trying to find a satisfactory viewpoint, and I made several sketches; they came to nothing. For, taking the landscape and its organization into account, I could only capture great expanses of grass or of hulls, whereas I wanted to capture the port as a whole, and above all the clouds.

I had either to change the port—and there were, in fact, ports at Richard or Saint-Vivien, but because of the low tide I would not be able to use wide perspectives there either; or I could wait for the high tide and try to find a favourable spot later on. What was needed at the level of the organization of the landscape was plenty of space, a very dissymmetrical arrangement, a low horizon line in order to paint the sky, and also some luck in order to succeed in what I had been seeking for in vain for a long time.

I then decided to cross a boundary, to go to the other side of the port to a place opposite the huts and boats. This is a marsh on which lay wrecks of punts and oyster-fishing boats. After several false starts, picking my way from wreck to wreck to avoid—what is more, without success—getting my feet wet. I reached the other side of the port with all my materials. It was a place where I did not feel threatened while painting in the gaze of others; I could contain or avoid the aggressive or destructive impulses that I was going to project outside myself.

For some time I looked for the right distance and opening of the landscape that would permit the whole to be captured with the sky. Finding a place where one feels good, and not threatened, is an important part of the work, which allows the being to concentrate and project itself onto the objects that captivated me.

I began with a rough outline, stressing the symmetrical effect of the sky and the water, and notably the line of clouds, which should be found echoed in the water. The masts of the boats and their reflection gave rhythm to the general organization of the landscape. Finally, the horizon line closed off the bottom of the port, but not excessively, so as not to block the movement suggested by these different lines.

Then came the moment for putting paint on the canvas. In front of me I arranged the palette, the sketch, the water under my eye, while taking care that nothing blew away.

I placed the first lines—boats and masts low down on the right—which would serve as measure for all the lines. My perception of the port changed radically. I was no longer someone looking at this or that part—I was a noise, a balance, painting. The feeling of being a whole being disappeared. I was projected into things: the weight, the rhythm of the colours, and their shape were inside me and acted on the painting that was coming into existence. This state of openness, of reversal of the psychic envelope of the ego, lasted for the time it took to paint most of the landscape. Then came a delicate moment: stopping.

By working too long one destroys the general harmony; by stopping too soon, one has the impression that something is missing. To add or subtract a major element later on means irremediably destroying the whole.

This moment is difficult to determine. In the end the attention slackens, and one feels painful sensations in the body; to stay without moving for about an hour results in cramped muscles. Everything one adds to the canvas becomes dissonant and must be quickly removed. I resumed contact with reality amidst a shock of sensations, a series of impressions that I did not understand. Internal and external bodily perceptions, unrelated to the picture, gradually invaded body and mind. The state of projection, openness, and of turning inside outwards became blurred, and it was time to stop.

I then arranged the materials and looked from a distance at the picture and the landscape. I was not looking for verisimilitude but for the general balance. It was all finished, it was time to go home, I was freezing because the wind was very cold, and a few words ran through my mind, which I snatched as they flew by:

Empty
Hull is knocking
In my body
Water thrusts, bearing
Clouds
Empty
Of any company

These words recalled sounds, the only sensations that made the body's boundaries palpable.

Commentary

We shall try to specify the moments at which modifications of the ego-skin seem to be determinant.

As in the psychotherapeutic situation, there are two preoccupations: First of all to create a framework that permits entry into and exit from the experience of symbolization and, finally, inside, the creative process.

At the level of the setting, one sees the desire for a break with everyday life, then the crossing of a frontier. To paint clouds or reflections, one must not let oneself be imprisoned by the perception of objects close at hand. For me, crossing to the other side of the port was to cross an internal frontier and distance myself from objects in order to capture the landscape as a whole. I then needed to determine, with the help of several preliminary attempts, the spot that felt right and from which the whole of the landscape could be seen. There is only one such spot, which varies according to one's internal state.

Once situated in relation to these spatial and internal boundaries, it becomes a case of starting the picture. It is in the first lines that the general balance and proportions play a part. These first spontaneous, vital strokes are the ones that get the whole work and the modification of psychic boundaries going. The latter are no longer the body and what surrounds it nearby, but the objects and rhythms perceived in the act of painting. It is at this point that one could say that one is throwing or projecting outside oneself what is inside, or reversing the psychic envelope by putting the inside outside. One then has the experience of the boundaries of the ego dissolving in the external world. It is important to note that the perception of reality at this point has nothing to do with the habitual view of things. The only awareness one can have of reality comes from sounds, sensations that are auditory and in some respects corporeal. They are like a feeble light in the darkness, the means by which one preserves a luminous awareness and a feeling that the ego is unified.

These sensations are fairly often perceived as painful, threatening and even persecuting. It is important to be aware of the aggression, the wish to destroy, that one must contain or deflect in order to complete the painting without damage.

Auditory and body sensations gradually creep into the awareness. During the last moments of creative work, when one might unbalance everything with a maladroit line, one's attention oscillates between the picture and internal sensations, boundaries of the psychic envelope that is on the way to being reconstituted.

When everything is finished, certain mistakes have been removed, the ego-frontier is filtering sensations, and one discovers habitual perceptions again, one has emerged from this experience of symbolization.

Modifications of the ego-skin can only occur within a context that it is advisable to set up. This work on the 'setting', in Winnicott's sense, is made by breaking with ordinary life and crossing an internal frontier, often concretized by actually crossing space. This experience continues in the search for a spot, for a viewpoint that will allow what one perceives outside to be transposed onto the delimited projective space of a canvas. This transition, the entry into and exit from the experience of symbolization, presupposes projection of internal sensations and the reversal of the psychic envelope. The bodily frontiers are perceived in peripheral auditory sensations. When the work is finished, they invade awareness and fill the subject's internal emptiness from the outside inwards.

(III)   MODIFICATIONS OF THE EGO-SKIN
IN CREATIVE WORK

Two processes are juxtaposed in time. One involves projecting shapes, gestures, or invented words onto the internal part of the interface: one is not imitating reality but creating objects, psychic operators, that reinforce the boundaries of the ego-skin. The other process consists in reversing the envelope and making the external world enter oneself, on the canvas. Drawing and precise writing give a convincing representation of reality.

If the work is done inside oneself, internal sensations are projected onto the internal surface of the interface. If it is done outside, the envelope is reversed, and reality is inscribed on the external face of the ego-skin. In the former process one is reconstructing the boundaries of the ego; in the latter, one loses the boundaries but finds the self, both organized and not organized.

Communication with the self presupposes a destruction of the habitual boundaries of the ego. Painting consists in representing internal psychic space by reinforcing the envelope of the ego, or by reversal in representing the indeterminate self in the form of a landscape without precise boundaries: water, light or clouds. The self is perceived in the rupture and reconstruction of the ego-skin.

This boundary is perceived as a lack of balance. If the tension slackens, one is at risk of being precipitated into psychic chaos, or else into destroying the canvas. At what point should one stop painting? Too soon, and the whole is incomplete; too late, and it is disfigured. This experience allows the boundaries of the self to be elaborated, but not the self itself.

These two psychic functionings are not similar to one another. For one, internal reality is made and felt to be inside oneself; for the other, external reality unfurls inside the ego and gives it shape, makes it function as container. This psychic fulcrum that bears the marks of creative work, this space of indefiniteness, would be the impression of Winnicott's potential space on the psychic envelope. This space would be the battleground where internal and external perceptions of the self confront one another on the psychic envelope, which either resists or not.

Creating, from the individual's point of view, consists in giving a double description of the self. Representing his psychological life on the internal interface means using the work as container for his emotions. Allowing the envelope and the space of indefiniteness to be crossed by sensations perceived on the outside means captivating the internal part of the self and turning inside out, breaking and reconstructing his identity through light, water, objects and faces. Painting or writing under these conditions means skirting a precipice, walking on a crest where the least false movement could destroy the person or the work. It is a representation of the self—the calm in the eye of the storm. We discover two conjoint processes, which must not be mixed together but interpenetrate.

In spatial terms the model of the 'fold catastrophe' can be used to represent them. (Thom, 1983, suggests comparison with the bottom of a snuff box—concave or convex.) By projection onto the internal interface, everything is drawn back to the bottom of the same attractor hollow. When reversed on the psychic envelope, the created object can at the least false movement race down and destroy itself or destroy the subject from one direction or the other.

Let us now try to find a model that permits representation of the modification of the psychic envelope in creative work.

One might, first of all, think in terms of depth and extent, by rigorously separating the levels of logical functioning. This method has the disadvantage of lacking flexibility. It describes one state or another, but not the intermediate states. It has the advantage of being clear, at the expense of lacking nuances. Transition from one state to another by means of a qualitative leap or reframing can be represented by the fold catastrophe. It is a functioning in all or nothing. This description in successive planes avoids confusion and describes a psychological fact outside the psychologist. However, it lacks effectiveness if the fact happens inside, outside or on the boundary itself.

With phenomena of inscription on the psychic envelope, the indefiniteness of discontinuous phenomena is of prime importance. The scientific metaphor of the cusp catastrophe seems more fruitful to me, and gives a more refined description of these internal transformations (Thom, 1983).[1]

It involves describing two transformations: on the one hand, that of the psychic envelope reversed or reinforced and, on the

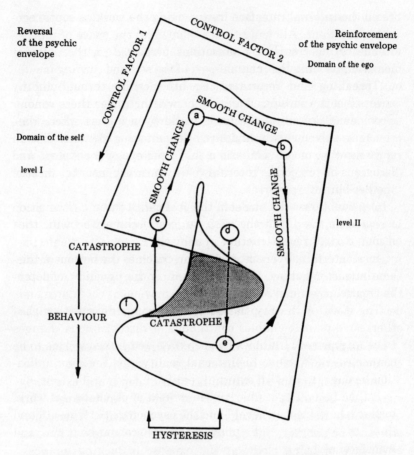

FIGURE 1.   *Continuous and discontinuous change seen as paths on the graph of the cusp catastrophe* (general diagram from A. Woodcock and M. Davis, 1984).

other hand, the concomitant inscription of reality on the internal and external sheet of the ego-skin (cf. D. Anzieu, 1985). One might describe the work in progress in terms of a 'discontinuous' or 'smooth' movement. One is based upon communication with the self by reversal and loss of the habitual boundaries of the ego; the other reinforces them by projecting the internal world. This oscillation allows transition from a rigid ego-shell to a supple ego-skin.

The plane or surface represents the ego-skin, tactile support for all the subsequent changes.

Transition from one state to the other can be 'catastrophic' by reversal of the psychic envelope, or 'smooth' by its reinforcement. From direction d inscription is made by a 'catastrophic' leap, reversal of the envelope and incription onto the external sheet. In b we have a 'smooth' transition that reinforces the envelope and functions by projecting internal reality onto the internal sheet of the ego-skin.

One functions with the self, the other with the ego. Transition is made on the lip of the cusp by loss of the ego's boundaries from b to d, or reconstruction from d to b.

In a determinate space, transition becomes continuous or discontinuous. This spot is the inscription, on the envelope, of potential space and transitional phenomena.

The model of the cusp catastrophe, in comparison with that of successive planes, enables continuous or discontinuous changes to be interpreted. It allows two separate and linked worlds to be connected: the subject, his internal reality, and the communication he engages in with external reality.

It then becomes possible, in the context of psychological work, to place the subject at Level I and the psychologist at Level II, and thus to interpret the phenomena of communication and transference.

This model could appear abstract. Here is a more concrete metaphor for it.

Let us take waves that break on the beach. The ego-skin would be the surface of the water; the psychic operator, the beach; the inscription—the marks left on the sand—would correspond to the deposited objects.

If one watches a wave as it approaches, it rises, then at a given moment one part unfurls, and the other rises up before breaking. On one side it unfurls in the subject on the psychic fulcrum by reversing the envelope. The other side represents the subject braced to contain internal reality, which makes the wave-envelope rise. The extremely unstable transition from one to the other is made on a crest line: this is the image of creative work. The water that breaks imprints a mark on the sand, brings objects forward, then turns back towards other waves. This movement illustrates the modifications of a creative subject's psychic envelope. The objects produced permit relations between self and ego, internal and external, to be rethought through the hard or supple filter of the ego-skin.

(IV)   THE CREATION OF PSYCHIC OPERATORS

(1)   Thinking by means of shapes

The clinician's principal difficulty consists in not confusing interpretations of one person's psychic functioning with psychological theories. In the first instance one's thoughts turn to the complexity of clinical reality, in the second, to methodological reflection.

For Bateson (1979), a psychological fact can be approached from a local point of view (study of an individual, or of a group in a given situation) or a global one: using certain general points of knowledge to understand some particular behaviour (for example using a theory, or development of understanding and psychometric data). This opposition (local or global) is complementary and must be used in a conjoint but differentiated way. Thus there is a margin between the development of a baby as an ideal and necessarily harmonious statistic, and that of a real baby, which is always irregular.

The other axis is the opposition extent—depth. A fact, a psychological change, can be understood either by attending to the subject's internal psychic functioning, by stressing development and regression, or by replacing the subject in his family and social group, in the register of extent.

Most of the time clinical material is obtained by words (written and spoken), but it can also come through drawings. We must ultimately situate clinical experience by distinguishing it from the theoretical axes and registers of symbolization that are used. The whole must take a simple figurative shape, accessible both to the eye and to the mind.

After several sketches, I think the cruciform flower is a particularly suitable model. The two theoretical axes—local/global, and extent/depth—are represented by separate petals of convex shape. These petals, as in nature, are carried by sepals, representing the registers of symbolization (writing, speech, drawing and projective construction). I place clinical reality and concrete work at the centre where the viewpoints meet, while remaining differentiated. It is at this spot that the work of symbolization and interpretation is done. If one moves off, one is taken along a single axis, local, global, extent or depth. At a certain moment the petal bends, instead of being constantly pulled back by its slope towards clinical experience and its complexity: one finds oneself in a single viewpoint, separated from reality. This space, the petal's extremity, is in some respects a refuge for the psychologist, but it is also a spot that allows the fact to be grasped from a particular angle.

(2)   The psychic portrait
(Doron, 1984)

In the examples quoted above, the created objects (drawings or paintings) could in fact be self-portraits.

One (the hospital bed) done in someone's presence and the other realized alone (the Port de Goulée).

These works do not aim to represent the mind: they involve symbolizing a traumatizing event, or playing with water and light. It is possible to imagine an explicit way of painting the psyche, in a relationship in which a psychic operator is represented for the other in the form of objects: the portrait. This work that is centred here upon the individual can be used for groups.

It involves creating an interface object, the portrait, a frontier or psychic skin between the individual's internal and external reality. I determine the variants of psychic life as well as the potential for changes, internal and external rearrangements, aiming at once to reinforce and transform the psychic envelope.

This operator is created in two phases.

A psychological investigation, for a determinate period and in a determinate rhythm, aims to reveal the subject's capacities for symbolization in his relationship to the psychologist. This work is done through speech, drawing and projective construction.

After having analysed and interpreted this material, I try to create the portrait in a second phase: I draw and paint the different functions of the psychic apparatus, focussing myself on each individual's unique disposition. It is a work of artistic creation that aims to collect the personality traits into an aesthetic whole. Starting from theoretical models of the ego-skin, I mainly study the transformations of the psychic skin during a work of creation, differentiating the subject from others and reinforcing and transforming the psychic envelope.

In this way two essential moments can be noticed: psychological investigation and interpretation, and then the creation of the portrait.

One could represent the different places of communication of the psychic apparatus in the form of an intersection between two closed ensembles. One, *vertical,* represents interiority; the other, *horizontal,* communication. The two forms represent a simple arrangement of the ego-skin, the envelope separating its inside from its outside.

The intersection between interiority and communication could represent potential space, the place where transitional objects and psychic operators are created.

Depending upon the individual's functioning, one attends to the containing function, communication, or transition between these two dimensions.

These two complementary functions could be represented with the aid of three styles.

(A) *The differentiator*

This is the stroke, the mark, the rhythm, the non-figurative that delimits conjoint spaces on a picture. The accent is on the filtering function. This first model delimits psychic places; those that follow delimit functions.

(B) *Reinforcement of the ego-skin*

There is projection from the inside of psychic life onto a space, and the portrait functions as container. We are still in the domain of the interiority of the ego, the style is figurative, and it is found in the drawings of children. This creation demands a very precise adjustment of the symbolic function. What is essential is the spontaneous stroke that reproduces and represents the internal world and reinforces the ego-skin.

(c) *Reversal of the ego-skin*

Both of the preceding functions aim to create internal and external boundaries, which are necessary for the subject but can imprison him in a repetitive functioning.

Reversal of the psychic envelope permits a double differentiation: communication between the ego and the self, and ability to dip into the archaic, the instinctual, the non-organized part of the self, to transform it into an operator that modifies the habitual limits of the ego.

The self at its deepest level within us is never perceived inside, but in the way in which one lives with objects (myths, furniture, cars, clothes . . .), and these, in return, form the self. The self is the reality that pours into us. The difficulty is to pass without too much damage through this essential moment in which one transforms the boundaries of the mind by modifying the containers of thought.

The psychological and artistic creation of a portrait aims to collect together in a given space the particular arrangement in each individual of these operations of differentiation, reinforcement and reversal of the psychic envelope.

CONCLUSION

It is possible to describe the work of symbolization by situating the processes of thought in relation to the ego-skin; they can serve to differentiate, reinforce and reverse the psychic envelope that functions above all as boundary between inside and outside. We become aware of these models in the way in which we cathect objects in the external world and the space that links them. In the creative process, all of these modifications are organized through an object, the psychic operator, which lets the subject make the link between inside and outside. It makes psychological operations possible, notably establishing communication between the shape given by objects external to our thinking and our emotions. It thus becomes a psychic container, whose modification provokes an internal rearrangement in return.

The ego-skin seems to be the support for all these transformations. It remained to find a simple model to represent these psychic transformations in a synthesizing way. The use of shapes seemed necessary to me. It is necessary to take account of two types of changes, continuous and discontinuous, inscribed on the surface of the psychic skin, without forgetting the spatio-temporal dimensions of the interrelationship between the subject and the psychologist.

These shapes must be used as poetic or scientific metaphors for change. To take account of all these data, I propose to use the model of the cusp catastrophe (Thom, 1983).[1]

It helps to situate in a single place the modifications of the psychic envelope of a subject confronted with a work of symbolization, and therefore with transformation of the ego-skin by reversal or reinforcement.

This model, non-temporal on the whole, situates both differentiated psychic states and the place of creation of a psychic operator that allows transition from one to the other (the lip of the cusp, the crest of the wave). By using these thought processes that are linked to the creation of objects in a reasoned manner, one can imagine a new type of psychological investigation, which seeks to represent the psychic functioning of a given individual.

Psychological interpretation is not only formulated in words, but by creating objects (psychic operators) whose form is a container of thought that varies from person to person. This psychic portrait is elaborated by using in conjunction the continuous and discontinuous changes that occur in the subject in his relationship with the psychologist.

The global, metaphorical interpretation then becomes an arrangement of shapes, a portrait of the individual's mind. It is an object perceived outside the self, a filter that contains the chaos of internal perceptions of the self, while at the same time rearranging the boundaries of the ego-skin.

NOTE

1. On catastrophe theory, the works to consult are: A. Woodcock & M. Davis, *Catastrophe Theory* (1980); R. Thom, *Paraboles et catastrophes* (1980).

Let us look first of all at a definition.

'Catastrophe theory is a controversial new way of thinking about change—change in a course of events, change in an object's shape, change in a system's behaviour, change in ideas themselves. Its name suggests disaster, and indeed the theory can be applied to literal catastrophes such as the collapse of a bridge or the downfall of an empire. But it also deals with changes as quiet as the dancing of sunlight on the bottom of a pool of water and as subtle as the transition from waking to sleep' (Woodcock and Davis, 1980, p. 9). There are several types of catastrophes: the fold, the cusp, the swallowtail and the butterfly.

I shall only present the cusp catastrophe. It is useful to refer to the diagram reproduced in Figure 1.

'But the cusp catastrophe graph also suggests the possibility of *discontinuous* changes, those that occur when a point moving to the left or right reaches the lip of the pleat. [Figure 1] shows the situation: the system can pass smoothly from *a* to *c* and back, *a* to *b* and back, *b* to *e* and back. But if the system is at *c* and control factor 2 is increased, the point reaches *d* . . . and there isn't anywhere else to go. What was a stable minimum has turned into a point of inflection, and any further increase in control factor 2 obliges the system to "jump" to the only stable minimum left, the one at *e*. It passes as quickly as possible through the non-equilibrium states; the transition is a catastrophe. A similar jump occurs if a system at *e* is altered by a decrease in control factor 2: it moves to *f*, then has to jump catastrophically to *c*' (ibid., p. 57).

The figure 'shows that it is possible to get from *c* to *e*, for example, either smoothly or via a catastrophe. Which will occur in any particular case depends on the sequence and the degree of the changes in the control factors. In an experiment, we would need to have both factors subject to our control in order to have a choice between continuous and discontinuous paths. If a system is at a point *c* and control factor 2 alternately increases and decreases by a suitable amount, the result is a cycle of behaviour with two smooth portions linked by catastrophes. Such a cycle is called *hysteresis,* and is found in many dynamic systems, from electrical circuits to manic-depressive psychoses' (ibid., pp. 57–59).

CHAPTER EIGHT

The musical envelope

E. Lecourt

(I) THE PROBLEMATIC OF SONORITY
AND THE NOTION OF ENVELOPE

The problematic of sonority is characterized by a certain number of parameters, of which I shall only mention the principal ones: first of all, *the absence of boundaries.*

Absence of boundaries in space: sound reaches us from everywhere, it surrounds us, goes through us, and, in addition to our voluntary sonorous productions, sounds even escape surreptitiously from our own bodies.

Absence of boundaries in time: there is no respite for sonorous perception, which is active day and night and only stops with death or total deafness.

Sonority is also characterized by *the lack of concreteness.* Sound can never be grasped; only its sonorous source can be identified (not always), modulated or even manufactured. The sound-object is an acoustician's construct, not a fact of experience.

Finally, sonorous experience is one of *omnipresent simultaneity.*

It is clear from these few lines that we are not here concerned with sonorous perception from the 'point of view' of experimentalists—attempts are in fact made to master sonority by using vision—or with sound as analysed by acousticians, but more precisely with the 'point of hearing' of the clinician investigating *sonorous experience itself*. By that I mean everything that goes to produce everyday sonorous experience in which sensation, perception, emotion, interpretation and imagination mingle in connection with stimuli made up of sounds and silences, in a density that cannot always find appropriate words to describe it (poverty in this respect of language, and French most particularly). I shall nonetheless use words to try to give an account of some aspects of this sonorous experience.

The notion of *envelope* contrasts, in the clarity of its delimitations, its reference to a precise visual representation, its concreteness and its function as container, to the experience of sonority as I have just described it: furthermore, if one thinks of the sensation of envelopment, it is the tactile dimension that is then resorted to, which is still not the sonorous experience itself.

The concept of 'sonorous envelope' proposed by D. Anzieu (1976) seems to me to include several phenomena that I prefer to distinguish, in so far as they seem to me neither to be equivalent nor to be contemporaneous in their elaborations. I shall therefore propose that in order for there to be a sonorous 'envelope' it is necessary that sonorous experience should have been able to find underlying support, on the one hand in tactile and visual experience, and on the other hand in a mental elaboration of sonorous experience based on the ego-skin (D. Anzieu, 1985), leading to the notion of envelope.

The problematic of sonorous experience in fact poses very sharply the need for mentalization and its difficulties. The pathology connected with it illustrates this abundantly by its diversity, its complexity and sometimes its gravity.

In this sense the 'sonorous envelope', characterized by the absence of physical support, is the very type of psychic construction.

(II)   THE SONOROUS BATH

The notion of sonorous bath, also employed by D. Anzieu (1976), seems to me to account well for a certain number of characteristics of sonorous experience that have already been mentioned. All the same, this term lays stress upon four particular points, as follows:

- a relationship of surface to volume;
- the quality of caring;
- the experience of weightlessness, and of being carried;
- the function of surrounding.

It leaves out of account sonorous aggression—trauma, violent intrusion—and sonorous production—expression, excretion, outburst.

The notion of sonorous bath introduces something that is not proper to sonority, but rather to the coenaesthesia, the weightlessness, that I for my part associate with music. In a text not yet published, I develop in fact this particularity that musical movement has of leading us into weightlessness. One then feels borne, transported, lulled or dancing, in a movement that has no grip on reality, is 'for free' and for pleasure, which I relate to the gesticulations of a baby being carried, and the qualities of 'holding' (Winnicott, 1971).

I also proposed elsewhere (E. Lecourt, 1985) the concept of 'original-music-group', the precursor of the group illusion (Anzieu, 1971, taken up in Anzieu, *Le groupe et l'inconscient*, 1975), as it appears in musical improvisation groups, that is, in the form of 'group-music'. By this I mean the musical quality of the harmony of the group and, in the first case, of the family group, around the baby, for the baby who gives and takes his note amidst a sharing of sounds (noises, music, words), vibrations and silences: a fusional experience of omnipotence. Relational sonorous qualities that touch, caress, envelop, protect from intrusions and receive excretions and sonorous expulsions, a group formation produced as protective barrier and receptacle for sounds, a veritable acoustic womb. At this stage, the mother's 'sonorous envelope', namely her capacity to mentalize her sonorous experience (in verbal and musical forms), forms a first excitation-screen for the baby.

(III)   THE FIRST HUMAN EXCHANGE

Sonorous vocal exchanges, simultaneous, successive (Stern, 1975), in counterpoint or in echo, are superimposed upon material transactions (food, excrements) that are strictly dependent upon needs and go in a single direction (from mother to baby, or from baby to mother) in successive moments, and upon visual attention and clinging. Thus the early beginnings of human communication and significant exchange make themselves understood.

Certain zones of the sonorous bath become differentiated: the mother's voice, identified very early on, qualities of vocalization, and times for sonorous exchanges come to organize relational spaces and times within a common zone, which will subsequently exist on its own, without the body contact that accompanies it, becoming a communication over distance and even in absence. This bilateral exchange, this sonorous feedback (Anzieu, 1976), are actors in and evidence for a mental organization, with the active use of memory, which no human sonorous expression can do without.

(IV)   THE SONOROUS CAVITY

In 1959 René Spitz forged the concept of *primitive cavity* or 'oral cavity' to designate the experience of the inside of the mouth as it related to the breast, a global experience in which touch, taste, smell, pain and temperature were not yet distinguished, any more than were the active–passive behaviours of absorption, containment, excretion and rejection. The author also made it 'the cradle of all external perception and its fundamental model' (p. 231), the first bridge between internal receptivity and external perception. He went on to say, 'Subsequent intra-uterine phantasies are based upon imagery of the early intra-oral experience' (p. 221). It is interesting to note that sonority is conspicuously absent from this fundamental article about early sensory-perceptual experience. We should not be exceptionally surprised, given the difficulty psychicists have in approaching this domain.

In the article already cited, D. Anzieu (1976) speaks of the 'bucco-pharyngeal cavity'. I shall propose not to dissociate the three cavities involved in this fundamental global experience, and to speak instead of the 'bucco-rhino-auricular cavity' (designating by buccal the opening that leads to pharynx and larynx). This primary non-distinction places the accent squarely upon the notion of cavity—a hole or orifice through which sensations, perceptions, actions, substances, objects and . . . sounds pass.

In this connection it is interesting to remember that the auditory function of the ear was not discovered, which is to say differentiated from this ensemble, until a very late date.

One can see that this non-distinction has a particular imaginary force. The difficulties that psychicists have in theorizing sonorous experience are perhaps no more than an echo of those that anatomists and physiologists had until the last century in determining the processes of hearing.

In fact, until the end of the seventeenth and the beginning of the eighteenth centuries, the organ of sonorous perception remained diffuse and of confused localization. The development of autopsies allowed it to be pinpointed, although for a long time to come the idea that the inner ear contained air—'innate' air, vehicle of the soul—was to remain strongly rooted. This aerial conception had its converse in excretions from the ear (or its disorders), that were then interpreted as excrements or faeces (and purging was recommended). It was indeed the cavity as such, its function as container, and the definition of its contents, which preoccupied the ancients.

Even before the buccal experiences of suckling, the first cry, at birth, starts up *the internal/external relationship of all sonorous vocal production*: the sound that is emitted is simultaneously heard—albeit differently—both in its internal, bucco-pharyngeal production, and in its external (aerial) repercussions: first distancing.

From these first moments—and perhaps even before, during foetal life—the sonorous cavity is the site of a rich sensory experience in which *the association between touch and hearing* has, for our purposes, a particular importance. It is in fact through the presence or absence of motor and tactile participation that sounds produced are differentiated from sounds external to the self: first fundamental advance on the sonorous plane in the establishment of the boundaries of the self (E. Lecourt, 1983).

In other respects buccal tactile exploration is enriched by multiple sonorous sensations and perceptions that will be identified and refined by means of the repetition and precision acquired in these internal contacts: relations of resonance between full and empty, hard percussions (of the palate or teeth), soft percussions (of the lips and tongue), etc.

This audio–tactile relationship of the buccal experience has a particular development in speech, in the direction of pronunciation and the articulation of phonemes. The sounds thus produced are certainly the result of these internal contacts (lips, tongue, teeth, palate, glotta), more or less sonorous and more or less differentiated. One notices, for example, people who speak 'as though without touching themselves', no more than hinting at the touch of articulation (as when one tries to speak with a full mouth or with something too hot in it), and, at the opposite end of the scale, those who produce a verbal porridge, thereby maintaining a permanent and undifferentiated contact.

It also so happens that religion, as in India, characterizes divine sound by the particularity of not originating in a contact, an 'untouched' sound, which gets its purity from this dissociation. One could also wonder whether the prohibition in Judaism upon pronouncing the name of God derives not only from the value of the name, but also from this requirement for purity.

In these situations of speaking without articulating and producing an 'untouched' sound, the dissociation of the auditory–tactile complex in favour of sonority could be connected with the prohibition on touching analysed by D. Anzieu (1984).

In contrast with speech, vocal music privileges properly sonorous, vibratory qualities that do not necessitate body-to-body contact (part of the body to part of the body), sometimes in defiance, precisely, of the articulation of the words when it accompanies a text.

The sonorous cavity therefore constitutes an altogether privileged zone within the sonorous bath, a zone that has the advantage of offering a pre-form for sonorous experience, which will subsequently become a basis for the elaboration of the corresponding psychic container.

To these theoretical considerations I will add three arguments of very different origin—they are taken, one from mythology, the second from musical practice and the third from clinical work.

(1) Mythology

The sonorous cavity is represented in mythology by the cavern, a resonant place with multiple echoes, domain of the god Pan.

In a preceding text, I showed that the myth of Pan is the most illustrative of the problematic of sonority. This 'noisy' god—for such, indeed, was his description among the gods—was not offered a temple, but a cave. This resounded and echoed, two qualities that located it at the boundaries of interiority and exteriority.

But the cave is also anteriority, reminder of origins, in this case those of a god abandoned by his mother at birth in an arid and isolated place, just like Apollo. Pan, in his cavern, creates the sonorous illusion that produces panic in a group and a panic attack in an individual. And in both cases, sonorous perception of language and music is disjointed, giving way to an immense confusion, with loss of identity and invasion by persecutory noise.

It is as if it were an illustration of what the sonorous cavity could represent without the experience of the sonorous bath.

(2) Music

Here I am tempted to suggest that musical instruments came into being from the sonorous cavity as it has just been defined.

Wind instruments, strings (plucked, scraped, struck), and skin instruments—does this classical classification not in itself point to this bucco-rhino-auricular origin, a respiratory, vocal and audio-tactile origin? To give only one example, think of the Jew's harp, that little instrument present in most folk music, which, by using the buccal cavity itself as resonator, gives the necessary volume of sound to the metallic vibration, while the articulatory and vocal positions of the mouth modulate its expression. The sounding box, amplifier for any instrument, is a direct use of the pre-form offered by the sonorous cavity.

(3) Clinical work

The demand of some patients for music therapy is good evidence at the clinical level for this combination of sonorous bath and sonorous cavity. One of the most frequent demands is, in fact, for continuous musical listening, which the music therapist would propose, and not require a verbal account of it in return. The behaviour of these patients in the situation of musical listening seems to be a combination of a search for envelopment, support, consumption and absorption, which are little differentiated (absorption behaviour will be found characterized in my article on depression, 1974), a situation that leads us to the borderline of need.

The sonorous bath and sonorous cavity, in fact, allow aspects of the foetal experience of the uterine cavity to be revivified, figured and represented, as Spitz stressed. However, like every cavity, the sonorous cavity poses the problem of control of entries and exits, and of its closure. The auricular part of this cavity illustrates this point most particularly by its wide openness.

(V)   SOUNDS OF THE FRONT, SOUNDS OF THE BEHIND

I have deliberately retained this elementary formulation, which is closest to the problematic with which it overlaps.

The problem of representing and receiving sound arises first and foremost in connection with bodily sonorous losses. Here I shall present an observation that illustrates several points of this problematic.

David was four years old when I met him for the first time. He was presented to me as an autistic child. He was not clean, he could not speak, and he was regarded as something of an automaton, but he showed a quite selective interest in music and hummed in tune.

On first contact I was immediately dumbfounded by the intrusive violence of the gaze of the woman who accompanied him (a person who had been in charge of him in his mother's house since he was six months old). While we talked about him, David ran frenetically around the table, round and round, without stopping, until the end of the meeting. I perceived this *encirclement* as a veritable *visual barrier,* a barrier against which his escort battled, for she did not let him out of her sight, while at the same time trying to keep me also under her control—a veritable feat. . . . It is in fact impossible to meet David's eyes, which display an asymmetry on account of his anxiety.

Afterwards I saw him alone, and here I shall summarize several observations. During the first months he always displayed a major expenditure of motor activity, essentially directed towards the opening of the room, doors, windows and cupboards. Several times in each session he escaped by the door. David is hyperactive, does not sit down and gave evidence for a veritable tactile cuirass; I sensed the necessity to remain at a distance and to avoid too much physical proximity.

On the sonorous plane, he invested everything in the piano and found himself 'transported'—excitation, pleasure, omnipotence—by a single sound: a low one, G in the second octave. He shielded himself from sonorous intrusions and/or invited them by *putting his hands over his ears* and taking refuge at the other end of the room. This skin supplement also sometimes allowed him to hear better, in complete protection.

David retained nothing of things and persons other than their sound, which he reproduced perfectly and which he used to make them present by magic. It is thus that he soon began to 'call me' by means of the buccal reproduction of a fart. The first time he hid under the table to do it. I answered, playfully, with another fart, and this game became a sign of recognition between us. I understood this fart as my designation as a living being, but also as a reference to the toilet training to which he was subjected (he was put on the pot every half hour!). David showed that he was very surprised by and interested in my response; I realized that for him this was far more than a game. Then, in the same session, he made farts and his preferred sounds, pretty crystalline sounds on the sonorous blocks, alternating repetitively. These were the first sonorous reference-points between us: body noises and 'pretty music', instrumental (good and bad sonorous objects[1]). There followed a period during which, having produced sounds on the piano, he would rush towards the mirror and check his face in it.

It seems to me that recognition of this creation—the fart—made sensory experience proceed to the arena of sound as psychic content. M. Milner (1969) showed herself to be very sensitive to these aspects of sonority in her analysis of Susan, a schizophrenic for whom music was no more than clattering sounds, as witness numerous passages in which the functions that distinguish buccal and anal perceptions are differentiated; I shall only quote this one: 'This theme of music being introduced into the drawing in conjunction with what looks like a shouting mouth also suggested the aspect of music which is to do with the need to impose an order on frightening or disorderly noise, whether it is the noise from a screaming mouth shouting for a mother who has gone out, or the forbidden noise of bursting flatus' (p. 124).

David communicated his first preoccupations on the basis of the latter. He showed a particular interest in all my sonorous productions with my mouth and in my play with wind instruments or toys. Sometimes he came very close, as though to monitor their functioning, himself introduced and removed the instrument from my mouth and observed my breathing. As for himself, he refused all buccal contact with these objects.

David's mouth was an opening that did not seem to belong to him. He had no control over it and continually let saliva dribble down his body. He had, moreover, major difficulties in feeding.

During one session I took the liberty—and I was surprised at myself—of giving him a little pat on the back while congratulating him on having discovered a sound: I had brought a new key-ring, which answered to its master's whistle, and I blew my lungs out demonstrating it (since the key-ring did not respond!), when he immediately made the appropriate sound. I was perplexed when during this same session, and also in following ones, he asked me to repeat this gesture. I sensed that he was nervous and agitated, jostling me as he passed by, and I realized that in this way he was seeking for more physical contact. Finally, when we listened again together on the tape recorder to the sounds produced during the session, I understood why he always passed in front of me, from one side to the other of the machine, while turning the buttons—buttons to which he had perfect access without moving: he was seeking *back contact.*[2] *David needed protection behind while he pro-*

duced sounds in front. My response to this demand—by a more sustained presence—brought about an initial relaxation, followed by a veritable 'caress': David, laying his back against my chest, let his head rest on my shoulder, against my cheek, and tried to meet my eyes. He asked me afterwards to support him in the same way while he played the piano. I had already noticed that his predilection for this instrument related, of course, to the richness and quality of the sounds it made, but also to the mirror provided by its varnish: *David could produce sounds while checking and monitoring his image in the piano. But he still lacked this protection behind, and a whole face of his body was vulnerable,* precisely the face whose sounds—farts—remained uncontrollable (inpromptu noises, obligatory silence). This development quickly led to the beginning of buccal mastery by means of being able himself to blow on instruments: David took pleasure in putting all the sonorous instruments and toys in his mouth. It was then that speech developed, and a little later mastery of saliva production. From then on his mouth opened and closed voluntarily, to produce sounds or words.

I had never proposed that he should listen to music, but I know from his mother that David, like many autistic children, demands it and then seems totally absent. The sonorous bath that is involved is, as it were, disconnected from the experiences of feedback and the sonorous cavity. It does not even carry him, and the child does not relax with it. Is it perhaps pure aesthesia?—an experience that he seemed to find again by producing that deep sound himself on the piano. It is possible to imagine an inanimate sonorous bath, frozen in rapture or glaciation—whence also the importance of the fart, as animate sonorous substance.

One can see from this example at what point the sonorous orifices, which produce and/or receive sounds—mouth, ear, anus, urethra (and one should also add the vulva for girls)—raise the problem of the sonorous container and flaws in the skin. Sounds behind elude control more than all others.[3] David's ability to recreate the fart with his mouth, which meant making it move from the uncontrollable behind to the front, to mentalize it and repeat it, and my remembering it—opened the way for the beginning of control and auditory–visual coordination (the mirror). This transfer from behind to the front also raises the notions of surface, volume and interiority. I am thinking here of the myth of Marsyas analysed by D. Anzieu (1985, pp. 47–48). I will risk offering a purely personal interpretation of this.

Athena's horror at the grotesque sight of her face blowing the flute, reflected in water, seems to me to be more connected with David's experience than with horror of the penis (which could be a second phase). His insistence upon monitoring the production of sound behind/in front, and upon monitoring the continuity of his being—upon my person, and by means of the mirror—make one think of the search for a sonorous envelope. It is interesting to note that Apollo's challenge to Marsyas bore precisely upon this point: *taking the reverse for the right side up*. Apollo, in fact, asks him to play his instrument—the double flute—reversed (namely through the hole opposite the 'embouchure'), as he himself could do with his lyre. This meant posing *the enigma of the source of musical sound and its mode of production* (by reversal, or transposition)—perhaps a Sphinx-like question? But Marsyas did not use language to reply, he did the thing . . . and only produced a body noise, of blowing, or wind. He lost his skin for this (he was hung and flayed) and was found again in a cavern, a return to the sonorous cavity, its resonances, noises and music.

David used me as prosthesis for the parts of his body that were not connected together (E. Bick, 1968) by an auditory–phonic containing skin (D. Anzieu, 1976). The sounds he produced could be reused and monitored by him with the help of a tape recorder and thanks to the sounds in my mouth, the sounds of my mouth and my breathing he could explore the sonorous cavity, whereas my skin served to protect the parts of him that remained naked. At this point David let his tactile cuirass drop.

In the following sessions, once sufficiently assured of these acquisitions, David drew me away from the piano while he played on it, and at this point I no longer felt it was a rejection, as in the first sessions—when he was anxious about any proximity—but, instead, an invitation to support him from a distance and watch, which I did by sitting for the first time at my table, watching him and listening to him play (and verbalizing to him). Our eyes met, and it seemed that we understood one another—David knew he was being watched and hammed it up. A few minutes later he came right up to me to play with the sonorous objects on the table. Tactile-sonorous-visual coordination was established, which allowed him to stay in contact close to as at a distance, without his cuirass.

I shall recall in this connection that Orpheus' weakness was precisely non-integration or a flaw behind: forbidden to use speech, touch and sight, Orpheus, just like Marsyas, was put to a musical challenge and succumbed: he could not bear, musician that he was, having as his sole sense that of his art, hearing, and at the sound of his loved one's footsteps *behind* him, he turned around to verify her presence, broke the pact and lost her life. Did not Condillac in 1754, in his research into sensoriality, imagine a statue that had nothing but hearing?

Here one can observe that musical space is organized as a frontal space (certain types of present-day experimental music put this appearance back into question), where musicians and audience face one another. The use of computer screens now fixes the visualization of sonority.

(VI)   THE SONOROUS
MUSICO–VERBAL ENVELOPE

To speak of a sonorous envelope is certainly to arrive at a level of mentalization within sonorous experience that ensures surface, continuity and containment without necessarily resorting to the other senses. I think this level is only truly attained with the codes of verbal language and music—different interweavings of sounds and silences.

These codes are characterized and differentiated on the sonorous plane by:

* delimitation of privileged zones within sonorous experience, made up of totally familiar, masterable, reproduceable sounds, sounds that can be associated and dissociated at will (notably in music), token of suppleness and solidarity;

- different modes of selecting sounds; those of speech being a sub-group of musical sounds;

- the use of sonorous characteristics: amplification of the intensity and accentuation of the timbres in music (perhaps in the sense of hysteresis, as J. Guillaumin suggested to me);

- particular structurings and types of combination: monodic for speech, polyphonic in music;

- the integration of silence, 'heard' silence, in common and different forms: breathing, punctuation (the word, the song, instrumental play), extending to rhythm and counting in music (a minim, crotchet or quaver rest, for example), thereby reducing it to its duration and its temporal function.

If therefore silence is well grasped in 'quantity', duration and even biological necessity, its qualities still elude these constructions, even if one speaks of 'musical silence' or yet again of a silence 'that one would call long'.

Work of theoretical elaboration remains to be made on this point, and D. Anzieu reminds me of this lacuna.

But what is essential here is that *the combined integration of sound and silence, realized by verbal and musical codes, forms a protection that is generally effective against their traumatic (intrusion, hole and rupture for sound, and hole, rupture and gape for silence) and persecutory dimensions.*

We have already seen the first stages of this work of mental elaboration of sonorous experience: the sonorous bath, bilateral exchanges, the sonorous cavity, integration of the rear face of sonorous experience, stages during which tactile, visual and sonorous sensory links are made and sustained.

The quality of envelope cannot be envisaged, properly speaking, unless it is overlaid upon the experience of the ego-skin. I subscribe on this point to what D. Anzieu has indicated:

the ego-skin is a psychic surface that interconnects sensations of diverse natures and makes them stand out as figures upon the original ground provided by the tactile envelope: it is the ego-skin's function of *inter-sensoriality* that results in the construction of 'common sense' (the *sensorium commune* of Mediaeval philosophy), whose basic reference is always to touch.

Lack of this function is responded to with the anxiety of bodily fragmentation, and more precisely of dismantlement (Meltzer, 1975), which is to say an independent, anarchic functioning of the various sense organs. [Anzieu, 1985, p. 103]

I propose to consider the sonorous envelope from the perspective of its two faces: *a verbal face and a musical face*. I shall put forward the hypothesis that what holds them together is, on the one hand, the sonorous sensory material and group structure from which they came and, on the other hand, the intensity of mastery that sonorous experience requires. I consider in fact that levels of differentiation and articulation extend from one to the other. The verbal face, more linear (in time), univocal and a visible thread in the texture, is turned towards the outside. The musical face, in thickness, woven of voices (in space as in time), and plurivocal, is turned more towards the inside.

Their modes of contact are very different: one sounds, sings, vibrates and resonates—as in the sonorous bath—the other is articulatory and more abstract. One is 'us', the other is 'I', recalling the group bases of their structurings, one more turned towards the internal group and its cohesion, the other towards the external group and differentiation.

But both are indissociable and complementary, as I argued in an analysis of the motet (1985), a Mediaeval musical genre in which these two faces of human communication—speech and music—were combined, mingled and composed in every way.

At this point in my reflections, Jean Guillaumin's text in the present book prompts me to clarify the relations between the two faces of the sonorous envelope. Here I am particularly referring to the pages the author devotes to the 'separations', 'unstickings' and 'ambiguities' of the envelopes, of which this is an extract:

It is this something else that is at once both 'too much' and 'lacking' that acts as vector of the strangeness of words. . . . The sense of security and narcissistic identification created by the sharing between transmitter and receiver *for part of the meaning* is disturbed and contradicted by the lack of concordance with and control over others that is *due to that part of the meaning which is not shared* by the baby and is dimly perceived by him as such.

Taken as a whole, it is in fact the work of identificatory and cognitive appropriation that the baby performs upon this resistant, exciting and disquieting element by means of making differentiations and assimilative associations, that supports and activates human mental development as a vehicle for the problematic of desire, in search for a greater mastery of this 'other' that is always wanting in linguistic signs.

To return to David's case, I shall propose that a sonorous hyper-excitability, even a self-sustaining excitation towards strangeness and towards the interstices of the tactile–musical–verbal envelopes in particular, an excitation that produces an outburst in the form of absence of mind or trance, produces a sort of verbal deafness. I shall illustrate this hypothesis with two examples that seem to show that David used *repetition* to attempt precisely to 'grasp something'.

In the first situation, David asked me to repeat an action: pushing the 'stop' button of the tape recorder. This lasted for a moment (because each time he made it go again), and I understood nothing of this, especially since he knew perfectly well how to do it himself. After a few minutes I heard him say 'Top' and then realized that I had very often associated 'Stop'—or, by abbreviation, 'Top'—with the action he requested. Was David's quest not to appropriate the word (specifically a word of mastery) by means of differentiation within the global excitation?

The second situation related to the recording of the session and its use by David. On this day, when David wanted to take the tape recorder, which was on the piano, I intervened—in view of the roughness of his gesture (he was still in omnipotence)—by snatching the machine, while commenting on this action by saying something like 'you have to hold the tape recorder properly to put it on the table'. Since David was still very impatient, he could not wait for the tape to be rewound, and we have therefore never had the chance to hear a beginning of a session—it is always the last minutes (of the recording, not the session) that are replayed. This time, therefore, my injunction was among them. It was repeated five or six times in a row, to suit David's manipulations. In the next session, after a moment, David stopped his piano playing, looked around, and found that the corner was filled up with the piano cover, put on a pile of chairs. I wondered what he was looking for, when I saw him go into the room and return with a chair that he brought me so that I could put the tape recorder on it. The usual table was not, in fact, there. It was the first time that David had taken such an initiative.

The tape recorder offered David the possibility of finding the sonorous situation again and repeating it as many times as necessary to master its degree of excitation and to differentiate its elements.[4]

The appropriation of words and of meaning necessitates this work of differentiation and a neutralization of sensory excitation. It is by means of this elaboration that the musico-verbal envelope is woven.

(VII)   THE CONTEMPORARY MUSICAL ENVELOPE

Contemporary music leads us into sonorous experience in a different way. Two phenomena of this present-day reality seem to me to relate precisely to the question of the sonorous envelope:

• First, there is the importance attributed in contemporary musical experience to the first stage, of the sonorous bath and the search for sutures, that is, repetitive, hovering music, the use made of the synthesizer—in the sense of a continuous flux, a sonorous binding that is difficult to realize with classical instruments—and the place accorded to certain types of mystical music, meditation and the commercialization of relaxation music. The sonorous intensity and rigorous repetition in rock music constitute another, more strenuous, form of this same searching for suture. Finally, the quantity of these types of music diffused on radio, television, in everyday life, in the street and in all public places—in shops, the Underground, airports, lifts, and so on—and the almost permanent use of background sound by our contemporaries, to the point of R. Murray Schafer's (1979) warning cry about pollution of the 'sonorous landscape', or architectural utopias, soniferous projects (houses, gardens)—all these manifestations surely mark a specific cultural quest.

• *Testing limits* is the second point that I would like to raise here. Limits of intensity, or of sonorous volume, for example, is our everyday lot.

Musical research during these last fifty years has constantly modified and pushed back the boundaries between noise/silence/music by introducing more and more noises into music: the development of percussion in the classical orchestra, works such as those of Pierre Henry (*Les variations pour une porte et un soupir*, 1963, and all that followed), or J. Cage (starting with his *piano préparé*, 1938), and many others, are illustrative.

This may be a way of seeking to reinforce and stretch this sonorous envelope. Musical sound itself is decomposed and recomposed (this is the sound-envelope of the work of Marietan: *Musique d'été 2*, 1982, or else again the work of Grisey: *Modulations*), as are the voice and instruments (Bério, V. Globokar, for example). Disarticulated musical harmony attempts recompositions based on 'agglomerations' and 'aggregates', included in the ever more complex web of musical writing: an attempt at stitching up these holes and knots. Finally, the sonorous limits of speech and the explosion of words are explored afresh (as they were already in the period of the motet).

The dispersal in space of the group of musicians and the individualization and particularization in musical writing that has once more become closer to the pictogram is associated with this disarticulation of classical material and rules.

It should be noted that this movement is contemporary with a general preoccupation with the body in our culture (gymnastics, bio-energy, relaxation, sexology), with the implication that it corresponds to a weakness or flaws in the ego-skin, as though the sonorous bath and sonorous cavity had to be explored in a completely new way, in order to recompose a musical envelope that has been burst by distension and asphyxia and holed by a sonorous experience that exceeded the habitual possibilities of mastery.

The work of Stockhausen is one of the most contained of these experimentations, and classical harmony, refined, serves as container for an exploration of breath, words and sound, as in *Stim-mung*. Here, the exploration is located more on the inside of the sonorous cavity, in its volume, whereas with others, such as Pierre Henry, it takes place on its periphery.

(VIII) PATHOLOGIES OF THE MUSICAL ENVELOPE

A certain number of pathologies of sonorous experience relate more precisely to the difficulties or flaws in this mental elaboration in the shape of an envelope. We have already encountered in the observation of David the relationship of the *cuirass* (or the second skin of E. Bick, 1968) to the lack of sonorous skin and protection).

In contrast, D. Anzieu describes pathological envelopes 'composed of a barrier of incoherent noises and motor agitation, which ensure not the controlled discharge of impulse, but the organism's adaptation for survival' (1985, p. 112).

The same author puts forward the hypothesis that ' . . . an insufficiency of echo-tactile experience produces an insufficient cathexis of sight, hearing, gesture, and posture as instruments of communication'[5]—a hypothesis that could perhaps apply to the case of Paul (but biographical elements are lacking here), a very heavy narcissistic pathology, presenting as psychic deafness to all noise and all music, but not to speech (case presented in my thesis, 1985). At fifteen years of age, Paul literally 'woke up' to the sonorous world, to the extent of taking a real pleasure in it.

This leads us to the concept of '*sonorous wall*' proposed by R. Gori (1978), which seems to me to be the counterpart on the sonorous plane of the cuirass on the tactile lane: 'the overflow-of-signs or overflow-of-sounds construct a false skin, a sonorous culvert, a pneumatic cushion, which—like walls—protect the self from communication that is perceived as an intrusion threatening the boundaries of the ego' (p. 117). Here I see two aspects of the pathologies encountered: total obstruction on the one hand, and the reverberant surface on the other. It is the first that the author is alluding to. For my part, I also think of those echolalias in which it is the patient's sonorous environment that returns physically, acoustically, as an echo. This was the case with

Damien, for example, the psychotic child (Gossein, 1986) whose psychic skin was all in holes, searching for physical containers (a corner of the room, a cupboard, the foot of the tree), a child who made himself a *reverberant surface* from his sonorous environment. Damien had experienced neo-natal suffering and respiratory trauma at the age of two. His attitude of prostration and isolation in a 'bubble' was accompanied for several years by a bulimia of musical listening, then a systematic echolalia. Through this constant need for a musical bath that was both bath and filling, Damien seems to have been searching for a volume of existence (here there may be yet another particularity of the possibilities afforded by sonority), whose other face, defensive, turned outwards, the verbal face, turned out to be a surface that was totally smooth and reverberant. At the same time, Damien lived with a pressing need, at every change of place, to find himself a physical prosthesis for this psychic skin that was all holes, and one day he was found after several hours, shut in a cupboard.

The invention of the Walkman has highlighted certain of these *frontier behaviours* (Bettelheim), here the ambivalent search for stimulation, enclosure and protection, which I could compare with David's behaviour when he put his hands over his ears, seemingly to protect himself. But I then discovered that for him it was at the same time a sign of calling for noise, and for listening without risk, by creating a listening space under his control, by means of a skin supplement—his hands.

In this one could also read, following Meltzer (1975), a disconnection between sight and hearing. In fact, lack of coordination and avoidance of eye contact corresponded at the beginning to the hypersensitivity and vigilant listening that David displayed.

There are several ways of 'treating' harm to the sonorous envelope: *the wall* is certainly the most massive, but *sutures* are also possible—while remaining on the periphery—and so even is *filling*.

Here I will draw on examples from clinical work with sonorous improvisation groups. In groups the sonorous suture is heard essentially in the form of a very restrictive use of beat and tempo (without rhythmic organization), a veritable physical grip (almost biological), a sonorous chain. The insistence, repetition and rigidity of these rhythmic sequences, sometimes veritable hammerings, and the impossibility of 'getting out of it' that participants feel, are hallmarks of this framework barrier. However, some groups are unable to use such defences and seem to lack an envelope in another way. This is conveyed by their inability to function and structure themselves musically.

First of all, I shall cite a very brief experience of sonorous improvisation, conducted in a college, with a first-year and a fourth-year class, under identical conditions. I was struck by the behaviour of the first-year students, who, in contrast to their elders, did not seek to organize themselves within sounds (by using sonorous reference-points, rhythmic, melodic, etc.). During three consecutive sessions, the first two of which were carried out in sub-groups, they 'formed a group' by means of the sonorous volume produced that filled the group space, then by creating a very particular acoustic effect: arranged in a circle, eyes closed and backs turned to one another (this was part of the assignment), they produced an acoustic beat by means of revolving cries on two shrill frequencies, very close together. I then entered the inside of the circle in an attempt to define this experience and found myself seized and encircled by this very particular revolving vibration (the teachers present put their hands over their ears!).

Deprived of their visual, verbal and tactile reference-points, these children created a physical, acoustic and vibratory link among themselves from which it would have been very difficult to escape.

A group of adults, psychiatric nurses in hospital service, with whom I worked, did something similar. In this case, too, musical structuring could not become operative, and a sonorous 'jamming' was produced in its place (by shaking bells and maracas), this time also founded upon an acoustic sensation, a veritable skin-to-skin vibration that linked all the members of the group together.

The last example concerns a group that I had in music therapy training, for seven stages spread over two years. During the seven sessions of sonorous improvisation, one at the beginning of each stage, I felt the difficulties pile up without understanding what made this group, unlike the others, unable to structure its sonorous experience. Nevertheless, the group was 'forward' in organizing itself in the first moments around a sustained pulsation. This was repeated at the second stage, and again at the third. A richer sonorous exploration was carried out at that point (noises, voices), an exploration that bore notably upon the inside/outside boundaries of the group (noises from outside the room were integrated, and noises from inside the mouth, and splitting the group). This same theme recurred at the fourth stage, which began with throat noises but ended this time with an outburst of sonorous volume, a veritable din and, overstepping the bounds of the assignment by resorting to the visual, to scenic play. In the following stage the theme of a festival was then developed, still on the basis of buccal exploration, ending up with the group illusion and attempts at rhythm and harmony. But the different musical attempts scattered through the sessions did not take shape.

It was only with the last session that the group realized a communal production that was satisfying for the group: it was a veritable sonorous envelope, verbalized as such by the participants and shared by the leader. On the background of a pulsation still maintained so strongly, there emerged a chorus of a floating harmony on a continuous drone, a communicative bath made up by vibration and sonorous volume. This sequence ended in relaxation and self-satisfaction, mouth noises and yawns. . . .

The difficulties encountered with this group guided me on the way towards the hypothesis of a lack of envelope, and led me to question Madeleine Fajon, who was responsible, in these same stages, for leading work with the body. I then learned that she was confronted with a systematic evasion of this work and very heavy absenteeism. She also observed that it was a group that 'did not touch itself', and she found it impossible to carry out the usual programme of her sessions. She had the very unpleasant impression of work 'broken into bits' and wore herself out trying to reconstitute its unity.

In these three examples, we observe a reinforcement of vibration and coenaesthetic acoustic effects (beats, for example) in the

sonorous output, sensations that came to the rescue of the difficulties in organizing the experience of sonority. They lead me
here to draw a parallel between defects in the ego-skin, an experience of a fragmented body at the group level, and difficulty in
forming a musical envelope, precondition for moving on to structuring and creation of the group (such as I was able to analyse in
1985). Pulsation, a quasi-biological sonorous production, the
search for boundaries between inside and outside, exploration of
the sonorous cavity, an appeal to the visual for help in mastering
sonorous outbursts and, finally, the creation of a common and
harmonious sonorous and vibratory volume were in this last case
the stages of treatment internal to the group for this specific
difficulty.

I would further like to mention two reflections in connection
with pathologies; one provides an additional argument for the
importance of the sonorous bath for psychic functioning, the other
a working hypothesis.

The synthesis achieved by H. Hecaen and R. Robert (1963)
concerning the hallucinoses—hallucinations that do not carry
belief—that accompany certain deafnesses and ear disorders
allow a regularity to be identified in the development over time of
hallucinated sonorous contents, proportionate to the aggravation
of the deafness:

> This work of progressive elaboration of the hallucinosis had
> already been indicated in several cases by Régis, who wrote,
> 'Subjective ear noises follow an ascending scale, from simple
> droning to songs and clearly articulated words, passing
> through the series of differentiated noises. The voices thus pro-
> duced are absolutely bound up with the previous droning. They
> are superimposed upon it and formed from it like a sort of
> transformation or perfection.' Our observations [. . .] clearly
> show that this work of progressive enrichment of hallucinosis is
> not a simple 'mechanical' evolution: it brings personal factors
> to bear, elements of character and background, temperament,
> tonality of mood, mode of reacting to the pathological situation,
> and affective dispositions proper to the subject [p. 314].

We thereby establish the psychic necessity, in certain cases of
deafness, to re-create a sonorous bath. We find that Régis's

patients reported on a number of occasions their observation of 'a distant choir, distinct but light, and an isolated voice singing various songs, well articulated' (ibid., p. 279), a reference to the two faces of the musico-verbal envelope—for this 'preparation' of apparent sounds heard internally in fact leads to music and speech. And if verbal hallucinations often look persecutory—which authors attribute to the depressive component in these patients—'in certain cases of musical hallucinoses [. . .] the subjects' affective state leads them to get veritable hedonistic satisfaction from them' (ibid., p. 318).

Finally, I would propose the hypothesis of a possible dissociation in certain pathologies of these two faces, musical and verbal, of the envelope. In David, for example, only the musical face was cathected, speech remaining the face of the Other, as speaking subject and subject inciting speech. G. Haag (1984) has associated this split[6] in certain psychotics with the predominance of one hemisphere over the other, the left hemisphere being the one for music. We know that recent research has tended rather to consider different listening strategies (Lechevalier et al., 1985), for example, giving the experienced musician possibilities of more numerous trajectories in either hemisphere.

This dissociation could also be supported by and originate in the first auditory–tactile coordination that is indispensable for the elaboration of this envelope; we have in fact already noted how the cathexis of touch is different in speech and in music. This hypothesis would relate to the sensory dissociations that Meltzer describes.

The sonorous bath is surely a fundamental element in introducing the young baby to his human environment: its qualities of containment, its harmony and continuity (or its chaos and ruptures) go on evoking fusional intra-uterine experience. But at the same time it inaugurates, by means of the bilateral exchanges that it promotes, relational activity with his milieu on the baby's part and thereby lays down the first beginnings of the self. Exploration of the sonorous cavity condenses several of these aspects.

Indispensable for development, the sonorous bath is not, however, enough to ensure the elaboration of a musico-verbal envelope. This takes place by means of mentalization of sonorous experience overlaid upon tactile and visual experiences. Inside this envelope sonority is differentiated and articulated by internalizing the group structure of family exchanges, a structure that is normally implicit in the sonorous bath. Attempts at musical and verbal codes then begin. The enlargement of the environment to the societal group will complete their development and ensure that they are given shape. The complexity of the mental elaboration of sonorous experience on the one hand, and the importance of its investment in relationships on the other, account for the fragility of this psychic construction and the frequency and diversity of pathologies encountered at this level.

NOTES

1. The first 'signifier of demarcation' (cf. Rosolato, 1985) of a series that were to organize our relationship.
2. Cf. Grotstein's concept of 'background object' (1981), cited by D. Anzieu, 1985, pp. 98–100.
3. Rosolato (1977) already noted this.
4. I shall take up in a later text some of the meanings condensed in this manipulation of the tape recorder.
5. 'Le double interdit du toucher': from a conference paper given by D. Anzieu, passage not retained in the published article.
6. A bad 'weld' between body and self, which, 'separated from the object, does not feel that it is more than half of itself' (p. 353).

CHAPTER NINE

Two dream representations of the ego-skin

T. Nathan

(I) SKIN AND ANGER

Anger is a mood that is seldom described in psychoanalytic conceptualization, despite the fact that it is frequently used in psychoanalysts' interpretations ('You are angry with me and you are unable to tell me so!'). Yet this lack of theorization about a very common affect is surprising. Undoubtedly it stems from the difficulty in distinguishing clearly between the affect, the impulse and the object of the impulse. Is it a question of aggression, or rather of a generalized discharge of all the impulses? In moments of anger the object is always present, at least at the onset of the state—anger remains a violent discontent all the same—but the storm develops in its own way and blurs the distinctions between subject and object, between sexual and aggressive impulses, and also (perhaps above all) between inside and outside. Bile [*Khôle,* in Greek] is no longer contained and is discharged without reserve into the body of the patient and his environment: we speak of crises, of fits of temper; the angry person chokes, shakes, prances with rage; he feels his anger rise, attempts to hold it in and then abandons himself to it, allowing it to explode; finally he loses his temper and discharges his bile. This quite naturally puts me in mind of the story of Achilles.

This hero actually possessed every virtue, but he had one major defect: it was not easy to dispel his anger. Now, Achilles had an unusual history with envelopes. When the Trojans began to burn their boats, the Achaeans, retreating before the enemy, were on the brink of losing the war. Achilles, still under the sway of his anger with Agamemnon, refused to take part in the battle. Patroclus, his friend and double, perched on a boat, despaired of the outcome of the battle and begged Achilles to lend him his armour. The latter consented, on condition that Patroclus did not use his appearance except to make the enemy retreat, and asked him to promise not to make a more forward engagement in the combat. In the heat of the battle, heady with the victory that he felt was imminent, Patroclus pursued the Trojans. Hector then noticed that it was a trick, and that inside the famous armour, the invincible envelope, a usurper was fighting. He turned, killed Patroclus, and seized Achilles' armour, which he donned. Rent with grief by the death of his dearest friend, Achilles finally decided to return to the fighting. He asked his mother Thetis for a new suit of armour, which Hephaistos fashioned in a single night. Achilles was to fight in his new armour against his own likeness: Hector wearing the first suit of armour. It is hardly surprising that although he won, he died, on account of that bit of flesh that could not be protected when, as a suckling baby, his mother had wanted to make him invulnerable to the blows of mortals by transforming his skin into a sort of armour, hardened like steel in the fire.

Killing his envelope (his double) inevitably led to his own death; a theme which many nineteenth-century novels took up again under the pens of the most prestigious authors (Dostoevsky, Poe, Wilde, etc.).

Anger, death, detachable envelope, double: these are the ideas that I want to consider. Thus far, certainly, they are not psychoanalytic concepts; but what does that mean? Can it be that, in the concept of the *ego-skin,* psychoanalysis has produced a new instrument with which to probe the surprising allegory of the *Iliad* in an original way? And might this allegory have some clinical extension? I have noticed that certain patients, fundamentally activated by impulses of *anger,* readily conjure up images of *envelope* and *double.* Sometimes we also fear for their lives. I would not be surprised if the allegory of the *Iliad* contained a profound psychological truth.

(II)   THE SKIN, AN 'AS-IF':
THE CASE OF 'PATROCLUS'

Patroclus is a tall young man, 34 years of age, of pleasant appearance. He presented as a relaxed and well-mannered lad, making easy contact, talking willingly, with precision and intelligence, telling me with feeling about his life and his plans. I thought, "Why the devil does he need me?' Something nonetheless caught my attention—his bearing, sagging, as though he had no spinal column; his skin seemed like a bag, a sort of military hold-all containing his organs pell-mell. What gave me this idea?

'I am *in-between*', he announced straight away. 'First, two boys were born, my elder brothers, then two girls after me. I always wonder whether I belong to the group of boys—the older ones—or the group of girls—the younger ones.' Large or small, boy or girl? This was the first double question that Patroclus posed me.

From a very early age he decided to lead a life *identical* to that of his father, a dynamic businessman who had been very successful in a small provincial capital. 'When I was nine or ten years old, I was reading economic reviews, I knew the stock exchange quotations by heart, and I dreamt of flying to far-away countries to present the products of the business, whose managing director I was.' But an indescribable anxiety—'madness'—had dogged him longer still. He remembers lengthy episodes of banging his head against the wall at the age of six, and even later. Perhaps this was only a whim, to get the adults to give in to his demands. He admits that there is something intransigent in him. When he was seven, the headmaster, whom he otherwise liked very much, punished a pupil. He thought that the same could just as well have happened to him, and he ran away into the woods for the whole day. His teacher and parents found him. He did not want to return. His mother usually took his side and always defended him; but he found it so difficult to talk about his father, such a complex figure, who wanted to monopolize everything, possess everything. Born into an aristocratic family, his father had had a gilded childhood, until his own father went bankrupt. He subsequently built up his fortune with his own hands. During his childhood, Patroclus viewed him as a god. Even now, he is unable to resist his father's injunctions. If they dine together at a restaurant, his father's advice affects him like a command. 'You should order sole', and he feels obliged to eat sole, although he has no desire for it. When he was around ten, his father decided to send him to spend several months at an English school in order to learn the language and 'good manners'. Terrified by his first contact with hard children, strict masters and a spartan discipline, he wanted to escape as soon as possible. He remembers the first day, when he was taken to the swimming pool, as symbolic. All the boys were stark naked, in the water, and the master asked him to undress. He refused. A very erratic pupil, he did brilliantly well in some years, while others were disastrous. He got his bachot with ease; and it was at that point that his father decided to put him down for a preparatory class in a religious establishment. It seemed to him that the English experience was about to be repeated a second time. That year his results were truly mediocre. When he received his diploma, he entered his father's firm, thinking that it was a matter of 'going to school', then succeeding his father at the head of the business. He felt very bitterly that his father was only interested in humiliating him—scolding him when he was a few minutes late, obliging him to give way to those who were his equals in the hierarchy but had been longer in the business, lending his ear to all the gossip motivated by jealousy, and withdrawing all responsibility and initiative from him. He went through three years of hell at a time when he thought he was making true his childhood dream. Then he made the harsh decision to break off his collaboration with his father. There followed two years of drifting and sinking, during which he lived as a destitute. Then he decided to start a small business himself, which began to give him some satisfaction. He thought he had resolved the difficulties of his existence, but there remained a tension, a sort of ever-present excitement, whose origin he did not know, but whose source he recognized within himself without being able to define it, still less to name it. He thought that it was time to attend to it. But how? A psychoanalysis perhaps, or else group psychotherapy? Did I practise group psychotherapy? Did I revive old emotions?

And this was the second double question that Patroclus put to me: psychoanalysis or group psychotherapy . . . or both? I understood this question as follows: 'I need to undertake a psychoanalytic task, but my psyche is not distinct from a group (or family) psyche. And you must take account of that in your work.' This reminded me of a request for analysis from another patient, who made the following approach to me in his first interview: 'I would like to undertake a psychoanalysis with you, but I am a member of the Communist Party and would like you to consider me as such during my treatment'—in other words, as one part of a great whole.

The altogether classical analysis that we began immediately bore fruit. The more he talked and made an effort to distinguish the thoughts and feelings that motivated him, the more Patroclus gradually emerged from a sort of dream in which he felt himself to be trapped. 'I am increasingly aware that I have been living in a totally imaginary world.' His conversation, which was structured, intelligent and precise, evoked profound truths but *in no way resembled free association,* something that never ceased to puzzle me.

A dream

The analysis took a turn after an unusual series of dreams. One day Patroclus arrived for his session very troubled. 'I don't usually remember my dreams, but today I had one that won't go away. *I was following my father on a country walk, and I was plucking him. I pulled little bits of skin off of him, which I detached delicately in shreds. This skin offered no resistance, like that of a boiled chicken. I think, what is more, that I ate it. A little later in the dream my father let bank notes fall one by one, all of the same denomination.'*

This dream gave Patroclus the opportunity to define the type of identificatory relationship that he had with his father—or, more precisely, the failure of his paternal identification. In the course of this session several series of associations emerged:

(1)   The ease with which he skinned his father still fascinated him at the time when he was narrating the dream. This 'flaying' evoked for him the fragility of his own skin and his tendency to develop pimples, beauty spots and various rashes—excema, urticaria—as well as the very unusual length of time which certain skin injuries had taken to heal.

(2)   But the fact that in the dream he fed himself on his father's skin brought up for him another series of thoughts concerning his own sense of existence:

• Although they had never been short of money—quite the contrary—there was not the same food for the children and the father. At dinner, for example, cheese was reserved for father alone. What Patroclus naturally longed for above all was to share the cheese with his father.

• His father never gave him money. Throughout his childhood, he had never known the system of pocket money and had therefore never been able to play at being 'little Daddy'. Being unable to *do like father,* he did not feel that he existed unless he really was father, unless he was inside his father's skin: *'actually being father or being nothing'.*

(3)   The expression 'being inside someone's skin' evoked a terror for him that stemmed from the depths of his childhood: that of being inhabited by a thing or an animal—a parasite—

that would devour him from inside and to which he would finally give birth. In the past he had dreaded tapeworm. He imagined that the worm would feed itself on his contents until it occupied all the available space so completely that his envelope was no longer anything more than a decoy: a semblance of a man sheltering the worm. The film *Alien,* which he saw a number of times, became a sort of emblem for him. In it, the monster entered through the eyes and laid its eggs, which developed inside the human, who 'gave birth' to them by a brutal ripping-apart of the chest and then died.

Patroclus' skin is therefore a simple envelope whose content is another (Alien); conversely, the skinned father is reduced to his musculature, his edible substance, 'incorporable'. It is obvious that one of the functions of the ego-skin is missing in the elaboration of this dream: that of interface.[1] If Patroclus' dilemma could be expressed as 'being father or being nothing', it is because he shows that it is impossible for him to be 'like father'.

(4) It is easy now to understand the banknotes that detached themselves from his father, like scraps that are reusable piecemeal. His father's protection was no more than an envelope when it was a matter of assimilating his substance. In the same way, the banknotes given to the analyst, all identical, represent the offering of a simple envelope, which allows chaotic contents to be preserved: the real substance.

At this point another memory came back to him: while skiing, he could only proceed if he was in his father's tracks— behind him, as in the dream. He followed him in this way for whole days on end on the most difficult runs. Outside his father's tracks, he was unable even to stand up on his skis.

During the analysis of this dream, Patroclus displayed by turns anxiety, excitement and then depression. At the end of the session he sat on the couch and looked at me for a long time. Then he was seized with uncontrollable laughter. After several minutes he calmed down and said to me, 'That reminds me of a time when I was also seized with laughter like that in front of my father. I must have got terribly on his nerves because he ended up by slapping me in the face. Even though I was eighteen years old. The slap calmed me down, and I began to cry.'

Commentary

The identifications open to Patroclus can be summarized as follows: either *actually to be his father, duplicate him and inhabit his skin,* or *allow himself to be inhabited by him.* It is essentially in this latter alternative that the defect in the function of interface of the ego-skin shows up. What is more, this ego-skin is unable to contain excitement, which inevitably drives Patroclus into a physical shock: banging his head against the wall, getting a slap, and then, during his analysis, having a serious car accident, luckily without physical injury.

Continuing from this observation, it seems to me that one could propose the following hypothesis: the only patients who dream of dismemberment—which one could regard as depicting the ego-skin—are those suffering from a fault in the constitution of their ego-skin. For the others, the skin serves instead as screen for the dream (B. Lewin) and is therefore not represented as contents.

In Patroclus' case, this fault in the constitution of his ego-skin was the corollary of a complete failure in identificatory functioning. His ego-skin was not truly functional—it could not secure the interface between container and contents and was unable to channel excitement, in consequence of which skin complaints appeared—just as identificatory movement was blocked; it was impossible for him to live *as if* ('as though I were my father').

The aetiology of this double defect could also be discussed. If it seems comparable with that of borderline states—episodic failure of the early environment, anaclitic depression—in this case it also includes additional elements. The tone of the transference, the modality of his conversation, his difficulty in giving himself up to free association, evoke the notion of trauma. What is more, his tendency towards mimicry (duplicating his father) had already suggested the possibility of an early trauma, because *if the pedagogic relationship gives rise to the similar, the traumatic relationship produces identity* (Nathan, 1986).

Having experienced a trauma could therefore be represented in the psychic apparatus by a hole in the ego-skin, a hole from which the envelope came away in shreds. This hole would make its appearance in the identificatory system by means of a tendency towards mimetic identification (dual and homosexual by definition), barring access to hysterical identification.

Extensions

The rites of initiation in traditional societies seem to have understood this mechanism, because they consist in the deliberate organization of psychic traumas associated with skin injuries (scarifications, tattoos or sexual mutilations) in order to obtain identity: *initiates*. What is more, in order to achieve this end, rites of initiation systematically resort to the use of the terror which is the specific trauma that produces mimicry (Lebovici et al., 1986).

Subsequent analysis and second dream

A few weeks later Patroclus reported a second dream: '*Last night I was lying down as I am here, and you were behind me, with a greying beard. A friend was present at the session and said, "He is also an instructor," and I said, "You are wrong, he is a therapist". I had a sort of amorous friendship with this lad. Then you opened a trap door under the couch and there were four or five people there. Perhaps they were my brothers and sisters? I remember that in one part of the dream this friend insisted upon attending the session. I replied, "If you like, but there is nothing to see." While I was saying that, a bit of my skin came unstuck.'*

In this dream Patroclus took up the theme and confirmed the interpretations of the preceding dream. The opposition instructor/therapist relates very well to the two types of identification mentioned above: 'mimetic' identification and hysterical identification. An instructor asks people to conform to behavioural models; a therapist investigates and analyses paths of identification. My beard in the dream reminded him of the portrait of Freud which he saw in a book that he leafed through in my waiting room. There is therefore also a similar questioning about my own identification with Freud: mimetic or hysterical . . . derived from a trauma or closely interwoven with my history and my identificatory system? The trap door under the couch recalls the bit of skin that came unstuck—the hole in the ego-skin that I mentioned above. But under the trap door were his siblings, seemingly encased within a single womb or a single skin. And it is here that we perceive a second possible representation of the hole in the ego-skin: the hole itself in the guise of a 'dirty lying tale', the element that would detonate the whole. A skin that assured its function of interface could be represented by a homogeneous group of siblings. The fact that Patroclus was unclassifiable seems to represent a grouping that was neither enclosed nor logical. He was therefore this bit of skin that detached itself from the family harmony, and he felt on his own body the fault starting from which the entire family system fell apart. This is why Patroclus had asked me in his first session, 'Psychoanalysis or group psychotherapy . . . or both?'

(III)   THE FEAR-SKIN:
THE CASE OF 'DEIMOS'

I cannot here recount the progress of a long and complex analysis. By way of introduction I would simply like to give a few landmarks that will make sense of the dream about the ego-skin that my patient reported to me at the end of a year of analysis.

Deimos [Terror, in Greek] is a woman of about 40, the youngest of a family of four girls. Tall, slender, rather elegant, her face was visibly ravaged by anxiety and depression. This was her fifth or sixth attempt at analysis. A consultation with a famous psychoanalyst for her 15-year-old son had persuaded her to undertake a true classical psychoanalysis. She was referred to me with this in view. What is more, she had had to spend several periods in different psychiatric hospitals and clinics and had come away with an anxious grievance against medical personnel: 'They destroyed me. I was fucked up! Medicines, electric shocks, attempts at seduction . . . they did the lot!' During her first session she complained of an emptiness inside, of a mis-match between her feelings and her thoughts, and of a severe and permanent depression. She wept throughout the entire duration of every session, evoking the image of an ever-open wound. She called to mind a dream that she had had several years previously, in which she saw a mummy whose wrappings she unwound, and right at the bottom there was nothing but a drop of blood: for her, an image of her internal emptiness. The psychiatrist she encountered during her first hospitalization, and who gave her an interview every day, ended up by proposing that she should become his mistress. 'He must have been mad, that one! Anyway, he ended up by killing himself.' She made out that she was finished, destroyed by her attempts at therapy with oblivious and incompetent doctors.

Born during the war in a little country village to very unassuming parents, personnel in the service of a noble family, she had experienced traumatic events when she was three or four years old. When the territory was liberated, she witnessed the execution of German soldiers. Her father, of whom she was very fond, seems to have been an eccentric, with the degree of psychopathology that that description usually implies, but also with its degree of richness. She was very fond of this father, who took her on long walks through the woods, holding her little child's hand in his huge rural policeman's paw. From these walks she has preserved the memory of a moment of truth: she felt real, and the world existed. However, this father was alcoholic, and the household regularly reverberated with shouting from the scenes that took place between the couple. Her 'depression' and her psychiatric history began at the age of 18 when her father died. But although she was aware that the two events coincided, she could not connect them.

She agreed to undergo the strict process of psychoanalytic treatment, but, at least in the beginning, she experienced an unbearable emptiness during her sessions: no thoughts, nothing to say, no association of ideas, not even the puns or the delirious play on numbers that had so much interested her previous therapists. 'In contrast with the others, I think you are competent,' she told me; 'but it's too late, I'm done for, there's nothing more to be done for me: too old, too damaged!' 'I always coped so that my therapist would regard me as an exceptional patient, but you, I can see very well that I don't interest you. . . .

On the day when I told her that she could not talk to me because I was not as 'eccentric' as her father or that first psychiatrist whom she had mentioned several times, two childhood memories came back to her which turned out to be decisive for understanding her problematic.

• In the first, she saw her father during one of his crises, lining up the four sisters against the wall and threatening them with his loaded shotgun, yelling 'I'm going to kill one'; but which? 'If only it were me,' she thought . . . or, again, the opposite, 'Pray God that it's not me!' Be chosen by her father but die, or else not be chosen by her father and live in an unreal way, which amounts to saying not live. Here, indeed, was the paradoxical dilemma that Deimos put to me from the earliest moments of the establishment of the transference.

• In the second memory she recalled two games that the four sisters went in for. The game, 'Anything Could Happen', consisted of shutting the eyes and guessing what one of the sisters was thinking might happen—accidents, catastrophes, deaths, but also pleasant events. In the second, 'The Kid', one of the sisters covered herself with a 'kidskin' normally used as a rug and was called 'the wolf', while the others were called 'the kids'. 'The wolf' had to cross a long room with her eyes shut, and 'the kids' must not even brush against the kidskin on pain of being devoured.

When her father died, the family disintegrated, was cut to bits, Deimos included. The father's presence had ensured the coherence of the family group by means of the terror which he periodically made to reign. *Fear was the skin that united the members of the family so as to form a homogeneous group, a body.* Thus, by inciting her therapists to terrorize her, but also by terrorizing them, Deimos had artificially assured herself of a substitute fear-skin. One day, when she was asking me whether I would give her permission to miss a week of sessions so that she could go on holiday, and I was refusing to answer her question, she gave me a look of terror and cried out, '*You frighten me!*' But she was trying just as much to frighten me. For whole sessions on end she would howl with pain and rage against my incapacity to comfort her. 'Shrinks are all the same—words! You make a show, but know nothing. Your science isn't one. You manipulate forces that are beyond you, you can utterly destroy a person', etc. These moments of inducing terror addressed to one or other of us always came about in two types of circumstances: either when for some reason or other I was obliged to change the time of one of Deimos' sessions or when, following a series of elaborations and interpretations, we succeeded in understanding a fragment of her history. It was then that, feeling herself to be an individual, recognized as a person, she was gripped with terror[2] and tried to communicate this terror to me by contagion. On many occasions we together invoked the history of Odysseus, who, on the point of being *devoured* by the Cyclops Polyphemus, made out that he was *Nobody*.[3] I can no longer say today whether this mythological reference came from her or from me.

Two dreams

The *fear-skin* appeared twice in dreams. The first time it was in a simple dream image that escaped from the night: in her dream, Deimos had a little hairy patch on the outer surface of her knee joint, which reminded her of the kidskin in her childhood game. The ideas associated with this image were not very numerous but contributed to understanding to what extent she bore, inscribed on her skin, the need to reunite the four sisters within the double, suspect and paradoxical sights of her father's shotgun. The second appearance of the fear-skin followed a little later, in a complex and subtle dream which she had after a session in which, very anxious, she had preferred to talk with me face to face:

'I had a rather odd dream. It's a sort of present that I am giving you to thank you for the last session face to face. I think you said one vital thing to me: that if I was continuing to make an *aggregate* with my sisters, as we once were under the threat of my father's shotgun, it was also so as not to experience human feelings such as envy, jealousy and others of the same sort, notably with regard to them. In fact, when I do experience feelings like that, I see myself as a monster, a beast, or mad. What is more, during that face-to-face session, when you told me that I would not allow myself to have human feelings, you frightened me. But at the same time I had the feeling that you were giving me back an image of myself. I don't know whether you meant to frighten me by saying, 'You are an empty mummy, but your head is alive!'

Here is the dream: *I was somewhere, perhaps at my old work. A colleague said to me, 'I cannot be there during the news. Could you follow it for me and take notes?' I replied, 'You know very well that I am incapable of taking notes. I only know how to copy down!' Then there was a sort of doctor in a white coat, who passed by and said, 'You know what has been done to you. . . .' they went on to remove the apocryphal patch. It was not easy to find. It was hidden in a place that was difficult to get at: the hypothalamus.*

In fact, a short time before that, after an improvement in her depressive state, she had found herself flooded afresh with guilt at the idea that one of her sisters was very depressed and could not allow herself the luxury of an analysis, and that another had to undergo a surgical operation that was rather disturbing. A cataclysmic anxiety then took hold of her, which made that face-to-face session necessary. During that session she also told me about uncontrollable feelings of jealousy centred around her husband. I had then put to her the idea that the kidskin had indeed served to protect the sisters from their father's aggression, by facing him with the dilemma 'all or none', but that it had also protected her from invasion by jealous thoughts of the type 'Father always hits Brigitte and never me. Does he therefore prefer her? She had then given herself over to listing the damaged organs in each of her sisters: one had a disorder of the womb, another of the intestines, the third, obese, of the oral area; finally, Deimos was afflicted in her head. I was struck by the fact that she was listing the different erogenous zones described by psychoanalysis, including the head in so far as it is the organ of the epistemophilic instinct. It is then that I put to her the formulation 'You are an empty mummy, but your head is alive', because the family phantasy that had been current for many sessions seemed to be the following: the group of sisters formed a psychic body, enveloped by a skin, 'the kidskin'. Each of the sisters represented one of the erogenous zones, and together they formed a group psyche (cf. Anzieu, 1975). Each of the organs specific to a given erogenous zone was alive in the sister who represented it, and that is why the 'kidskin-fear of father' was needed to contain these organs alive. Inside the mummy-wrappings Deimos was empty; she was reduced simply to her mental functioning. Besides, this is what she complained of: the feeling of emptiness and artificiality; empty because she had no body, and artificial because while this specific defense mechanism that consisted in a fusion with her sisters protected her from her own destructive feelings (hate, envy, jealously), it cut her off from her 'humanity'. She immediately understood the relationship between this type of defence and what she called her 'cinema', which consisted in staging 'follies' in order to trigger off reactions in the other party and merge herself once more in a group psyche united by a *skin of fear*.

The flow of her association of ideas led us towards a still more subtle understanding of this mechanism. 'Brigitte has a "nervous patch" on her head where no hair grows. The patch in my first dream was the opposite, because it was a patch of hairs or, more precisely, of fur. Between the two of us we could close the fontanelle.' I had already noticed on several occasions with other patients that the fontanelle naturally represented the absence of closure of the psychic apparatus. In her formulation, Deimos indicated that she could not close her ego-skin without the help of her sister(s). As for the term *apocryphal*, it contained, condensed as though on a scrap of parchment, the following different elaborations:

● Verbal play upon their first names took her back to the scene where she was threatened by her father's shotgun, and to her effort to resolve this trauma in the game, 'Anything Could Happen'.

● But *apocryphal* also led simultaneously to 'secret' (as in the 'apocryphal gospels') and to 'not authentic' (as in an 'apocryphal story'). Deimos astutely summed up these two elaborations in the formula, 'In the dream they removed my *secret*, which is my feeling of *falseness*, of artificiality.'

● Another play on words took up the idea of a global skin, of one skin among four.

● 'Finally,' she said, 'I read somewhere that the hypothalamus contained the archaic and savage part of our person. It was in that place that my patch of skin was situated, as though to indicate that it was to defend me against desires that were savage, as were those of my father when he was drunk and I had to resort to this type of defence.'

● It remains to understand the expression in the dream, 'You know very well that I am incapable of taking notes. I only know how to copy down!' Deimos did not offer any association of ideas on this subject, which should not surprise us because this expression related precisely to the repetition compulsion or, more exactly, to what I called a 'mimetic identification' in Patroclus' case. The trauma of terror triggers off mimetic reactions, which cannot be elaborated and can only be repeated, as Deimos did in the different transferential situations that she got into, miming *anger* and *terror* over and over again without being able to take them on board as her own.

(IV) CONCLUSIONS—HYPOTHESES

The cases of Patroclus and Deimos have numerous elements in common, which prompt me to put forward some theoretical hypotheses.

• Dreams containing an explicit depiction of the ego-skin are admittedly rather rare. They convey a defect in the constitution of the ego-skin, which cannot be represented as closed. These patients have usually experienced states of fusion with their siblings as a defence against archaic emotions, rather like the experience that is usually ascribed to twins.

• These patients seem to show so-called borderline states. That means that to a greater or lesser extent during their analysis it will prove to be essential to retrieve and recognize things that *actually happened during childhood,* whereas in the transference neuroses phantasy elaborations are sufficient to overcome the repetition compulsion. What is more, these patients clearly express in the transference their expectation of fusion,[4] which is also displayed by manipulating the analyst's unconscious personality. They seem to surround the space of their session with a single 'skin', wrapping patient and analyst in a single envelope. This characteristic often leads them into the phantasy of a pair of twins inside the maternal abdomen, surrounded by a single amniotic membrane.[5] When this phantasy is active in the transference, any pathology that might have led the patient to undertake treatment seems to have disappeared, giving way to a fusional functioning, a necessary illusion of a definitive repair to the original damage.

• These patients have usually suffered serious and repeated traumas during their childhood, to which they responded by a mimetic reaction (cf. Nathan, 1986), incorporating the object of fear and episodically merging with it. This 'mimetic' reaction makes heavy demands upon the functioning of the identificatory system and makes sexual differentiation difficult or even impossible in serious cases.

- The mimetic reaction makes it impossible to channel the flow of instincts towards the object, so that they can only be expressed in 'crises'. If 'tantrums' have often disappeared by adulthood, they surge up again during treatment, and patients usually know that they are exposed to them. In the same way, sexual excitement cannot be contained and is expressed in explosive episodes, which manifest themselves as acting-out.

- Finally, the affect of these patients is usually deeply depressive, and their bearing towards their immediate environment is of anaclitic type. It seems that this 'essential' depression needs to be connected with a feeling of having lost their 'vital spark'—or, in other words, their 'soul'. This last observation makes me think that some traditional aetiological theories, in Africa, America and Asia alike, seem to have recognized this mechanism, since they hold that the outcome of a powerful fright is a 'loss of the soul', leaving the body of the patient like a sort of automaton whose only impulsion consists in imitating the first animate object that it perceives.[6] This difficulty can only be resolved in the transference, by involving the analyst, who undertakes to observe and invoke those aspects of the analytic setting that have triggered off the patient's terror, and by so doing to provoke him into resuming his mimetic reaction in the hope of evolving a different way of functioning.

NOTES

1. 'And the need to overinvest the narcissistic envelope in this way certainly seems like the defensive counterpart of a phantasy of a stripped-off skin: faced with a permanent danger of external/internal attacks, he must restore the fortunes of an ego-skin that is very insecure in its functions of excitement-screen and psychic container. The topographical solution then consists in abolishing the difference between the two surfaces, external and internal, of the ego-skin, and imagining the interface as a double wall' (D. Anzieu, 1985, p. 129).
2. Probably terror of being devoured—see G. Devereux, 1967.

3. See T. Nathan (1978), where I report a clinical case that is structured around the same mythical representation.
4. On the characteristics of these treatments see the works of D. W. Winnicott, Masud Khan, D. Anzieu, A. Green, etc.
5. On the amniotic membrane as a representation of certain types of psychic envelope, see T. Nathan (1983, 1986).
6. See the discussion of the Siberian *Myriatchit,* the Malay *Latach* and the *Imu* of the Ainu of Japan in G. Devereux (1970); but also the *Susto* of Peru, the *Khal'a* of the Maghreb, and even the *Paura,* which is still very common in southern Italy (see S. Lebovici et al., 1986).

BIBLIOGRAPHY

Anzieu, D. (1975). *L'auto-analyse de Freud*, 2 vol. New edition: Paris: P.U.F.

————— (1976). L'enveloppe sonore du Soi. *Nouvelle Revue de Psychanalyse, 13:* 161–179 [reprinted in *Le Moi-Peau*, pp. 159–174].

————— (1983). *Le corps de L'oeuvre.* Paris: Gallimard.

————— (1984). Le double interdit du toucher. *Nouvelle Revue de Psychanalyse, 29:* 173–187 [reprinted in *Le Moi-Peau*, pp. 136–155].

————— (1985). *Le Moi-Peau.* Paris: Dunod.

————— (1986). Cadre psychanalytique et enveloppes psychiques. *Journal de la Psychanalyse de l'Enfant, 2:* 12–24.

Anzieu, D., Bejarano, A., Kaës, R., Missenard, A., & Pontalis, J. B. (1972). *Le travail psychanalytique dans les groupes*, vol. 1 (2nd ed., 1982). Paris: Dunod.

Aulagnier, P. (1980). Du langage pictural au langage de l'interprète. *Topique, 26:* 29–54. Paris: Épi.

————— (1985). *L'apprenti historien et le maître sorcier.* Paris: P.U.F.

————— (1985). Quelqu'un a tué quelque chose. *Topique, 35/36.*

Barande, R. (1975). *La naissance exorcisée, ou l'érotique anale de l'homme inachevé.* Paris: Denoël.

———— (1975). *L'inachèvement de l'homme comme structure de son temps*. Paris: Denoël.

Baranes, J.-J. (1986). Vers une métapsychologie transgénérationnelle. In: Congrès, *Mémoires, transmissions psychiques, transfert*. Paris (31 January–1 February 1986).

Bateson, G. (1979). *Mind and Nature*. London: Wildwood House.

Beckett, S. (1984). *Compagnie*. Paris: Éditions de Minuit.

Begoin-Guignard, F. (1985). Essai sur l'identification projective. *Topique, 35/36:* 173–185.

Bergeret, J. (1974). *La dépression et les états-limites*. Paris: Payot.

Bettelheim, B. (1967). *The Empty Fortress*. London: Thames & Hudson.

Bick, E. (1968). The experience of the skin in early object relations. *International Journal of Psycho-Analysis, 49:* 484–486.

Bion, W. R. (1962). *Learning from Experience*. London: Heinemann Medical [reprinted London: Maresfield Library, 1984].

———— (1963). *Elements of Psychoanalysis*. London: Heinemann Medical [reprinted London: Maresfield Library, 1984].

———— (1964). A theory of thinking. *International Journal of Psycho-Analysis, 43* [also in *Second Thoughts*].

———— (1967). *Second Thoughts*. London: Heinemann Medical [reprinted London: Maresfield Library, 1984].

———— (1970). *Attention and Interpretation*. London: Tavistock Publications [reprinted London: Maresfield Library, 1984].

Bleger, J. (1967). *Symbiose et ambiguïté*. French translation: 1981. Paris: P.U.F.

Bourdier, P. (1972). Hypermaturation des enfants de parents malades mentaux. *Revue Française de Psychanalyse, 1*.

———— (1986). Besoins des enfants, désirs et folie des adultes. Étude clinique comparée de quelques incompatibilités. *Perspectives Psychiatriques, 28* (1): 7–19.

Bowlby, J. (1969). *Attachment and Loss, vol. I: Attachment*. London: Hogarth Press.

Braunschweig, D., & Fain, M. (1975). *La nuit, le jour. Essai psychanalytique sur le fonctionnement mental*. Paris: P.U.F.

Brenman, E. (1985). Hysteria. *International Journal of Psycho-analysis, 66* (4): 423–432.

Castoriadis-Aulagnier, P. (1975). *La violence de l'interprétation*. Paris: P.U.F.

Chasseguet-Smirgel, J. (1973). *L'idéal du Moi*. Paris: Tchou.

Condillace, E. (1754). *Traité des sensations*. Paris: Alcan.

Cosnier, J. (1981). *Nouvelles clés pour la psychologie* (preface by J. Guillaumin), 2nd ed. Lyon: P.U.L.

Couchoud, M.-Th. (1985). La potentialité autistique, un défaut de l'étayage. *Topique, 35/36:* 89–119.

_____ (1986). Refoulement et fonction dénégatrice. *Topique, 37:* 93–135.

Cramer, B. (1985). Fonctionnement mental précoce et interactions mère-enfant. *Topique, 5/6:* 152–172.

David, C. (1971). *L'état amoureux*. Paris: Payot.

David, M. (1981). Les enfants de mères perturbées. *Cahier de l'UER expérimentale de Bobigny, 3:* 43–50.

Dayan, M. (1985). Entre rêve et psychose. *Topique, 35/36.*

_____ (1985). *Inconscient et réalité*. Paris: P.U.F.

Decobert, S. (1985). Spécificité de la thérapie familiale psychanalytique. *Gruppo, 1.*

Dejours, C. (1986). *Le corps entre biologie et psychanalyse*. Paris: Payot.

Devereux, G. (1967). La renonciation à l'identité, défense contre l'anéantissement. *Revue Française de Psychanalyse, XXXI* (1): 101–142.

_____ (1970). *Essais d'Ethnopsychiatrie générale*. Paris: Gallimard.

_____ (1980). *De l'angoisse à la méthode*. Paris: Flammarion.

Donnet, J.-L. (1976). Contre-transfert, transfert sur l'analyse. *Revue Française de Psychanalyse, XL* (3): 443–454.

Doron, J. (1980). L'imagination dans les tests projectifs (chez l'enfant et l'adolescent) au sein de l'examen psychologique approfondi. Thèse de troisième cycle. Paris X (mimeographed).

_____ (1983). Étude d'une nouvelle grille de l'espace. *Psychologie française, XXVIII* (2): 181–186.

_____ (1984). Une rencontre dynamique avec l'enfant, le portrait psychologique. *Enfance:* 131–166.

_____ (1985). Comparaison de l'espace projectif du scéno-test et du dessin. *Bulletin de Psychologie, vol. XXXVIII* (369): 323–333.

Duport Rosan, J.-P. (1986). Morphogenèse du symbole, régulation symbolique et formelle. In: J. Guillaumin (ed.), *Ordre et désordre de la parole*. Lyon: C.T.I.: 57–76.

Éliade, M. (1963). *Aspects du mythe*. Paris: Gallimard.

Enriquez, M. (1979). L'analysant parasite. *Topique, 23:* 37–53.

_____ (1984). *Aux carrefours de la haine*. Paris: Épi.

Faimberg, H. (1981). Une des difficultés de l'analyse, la reconnaissance de l'altérité: l'écoute des interprétations. *Revue Française de Psychanalyse, 6:* 1351–1367.

————— (1987). Le télescopage des générations: sur un certain type d'identification. *Psychanalyse à l'Université, 2* (April).

Fain, M. (1969). Ébauche d'une recherche concernant l'existence d'activités mentales pouvant être considérées comme prototypiques du processus psychanalytique. *Revue Française de Psychanalyse, 33,* (5–6): 929–962.

————— (1971). Prélude à la vie fantasmatique. *Revue Française de Psychanalyse, 35* (2–3): 291–364.

————— (1981). Aproche métapsychologique du toxicomane. In J. Bergeret (ed.), *Le psychanalyste à l'écoute du toxicomane.* Paris: Dunod: 27–36.

Ferenczi, S. (1985). *Journal clinique* (January–October 1932). French translation. Paris: Payot.

Fliess, R. (1942). The metapsychology of the analyst. *Psycho-analytic Quarterly, 11:* 211–227.

Fresco, N. (1981). La diaspora des cendres. *Nouvelle Revue de Psychanalyse, 24.*

Freud, S. (1892–93). A case of successful treatment by hypnotism. *Standard Edition, 1.*

————— (1883c). Some points for a comparative study of organic and hysterical motor paralyses. *Standard Edition, 1.*

————— (1893f). Charcot. *Standard Edition, 3.*

————— (1896c). The aetiology of hysteria. *Standard Edition, 3.*

————— (1894a). The neuro-psychoses of defence. *Standard Edition, 3.*

————— (1900a). *The Interpretation of Dreams. Standard Edition, 4–5.*

————— (1910k). 'Wild' psychoanalysis. *Standard Edition, 11.*

————— (1912e). Recommendations to physicians practicing psychoanalysis. *Standard Edition, 12.*

————— (1913i). The disposition to obsessional neurosis. *Standard Edition, 12.*

————— (1914c). On narcissism: an introduction. *Standard Edition, 14.*

————— (1917d). A metapsychological supplement to the theory of dreams. *Standard Edition, 14.*

————— (1920g). *Beyond the Pleasure Principle. Standard Edition, 18.*

———— (1921c). *Group Psychology and the Analysis of the Ego.* *Standard Edition, 3.*

———— (1922a). Dreams and telepathy. *Standard Edition, 18.*

———— (1923b). *The Ego and the Id. Standard Edition, 19.*

———— (1924b). Neurosis and psychosis. *Standard Edition, 19.*

———— (1925a). A note upon the 'mystic writing pad'. *Standard Edition, 19.*

———— (1925h). On negation. *Standard Edition, 19.*

———— (1925i). Some additional notes on dream-interpretation as a whole. *Standard Edition, 19.*

———— (1926d). *Inhibitions, Symptoms and Anxiety. Standard Edition, 20.*

———— (1937b). Constructions in analysis. *Standard Edition, 23.*

———— (1937c). Analysis terminable and interminable. *Standard Edition, 23.*

———— (1950a [1895]). Project for a scientific psychology. *Standard Edition, 1.*

Gori, R. (1978). *Le corps et le signe dans l'acte de parole.* Paris: Dunod.

Gosselin, M.-Th., & Lecourt, E. (1986). Damien ou la 'bulle écholalique'. *La Revue de Musicothérapie, VI* (2): 30–36.

Granjon, E., & Guérin, Ch. (1985). La transmission psychique négative dans le travail thérapeutique avec les familles, approche clinique, théorique et méthodologique. In: La transmission psychique intergénérationnelle et intra-groupale; aspects pathologiques, thérapeutifs et curatifs. Rapport présenté par R. Kaës sur une recherche pour le compte de la MIRE, du Centre de recherche clinique sur les formations intermédiaires, Université de Lyon 2.

Granoff, W., & Rey, J. M. (1984). *L'occulte, objet de la psychanalyse.* Paris: P.U.F.

Green, A. (1979). Le silence du psychanalyste. *Topique, 23:* 5–25.

Gribinski, M. (1982). Personnages archaïques sur la scène. *Nouvelle Revue de Psychanalyse, 26.*

Guérin, Ch. (1984). L'obstacle et le lieu, l'inter-dit familial et son rapport à l'identification dans la famille. In: R. Kaës, M. Dulac, J. De Martino, E. Granjon, M. Thaon, & Ch. Guérin, *Penser la famille. Actes des Journées d'Études de Psychologie sociale clinique* (pp. 29–35). Arles: Hôpital Imbert.

Guillaume, P. (1942). *La psychologie de la forme.* Paris: Flammarion.

Guillaumin, J. (1976a). L'énergie et les structures dans l'expérience dépressive. Le rôle du préconscient. *Revue Française de Psychanalyse, XL* (56): 1059–1072.

———— (1976b). Contre-transferts. *Revue Française de Psychanalyse, XL* (3): 55–482 [also in: J. Guillaumin, *Psyché, Études psychanalytiques sur la réalité psychique*. Paris: P.U.F., 1983].

———— (1977). Le rôle des régulations temporelles (notamment linguistiques) en provenance du milieu dans la formation du Moi précoce de l'enfant. *Bulletin d'Audiophonologie* (Société Association francomtoise d'audiophonolie), 7 (4): 11–27.

———— (1979). *Le rêve et le Moi*. Paris: P.U.F.

———— (1980). La peau du centaure. In: J. Guillaumin (ed.), *Corps Création* (pp. 227–269). Lyon: P.U.L.

———— (1981). La curiosité pour l'inconscient. In H. Sztulman & J. Fénelon (eds.), *La curiosité en psychanalyse*. Toulouse: Privat.

———— (1982). La blessure des origines. *Nouvelle Revue de Psychanalyse, 26*: 217–234.

———— (1983). Prise en compte tardive du contre-transfert de fond dans la cure psychanalytique. In: H. Sztulman (ed.), *Le psychanalyste et son patient* (pp. 139–161). Toulouse, Privat.

———— (1984). Transmettre la présence de l'absent ou la part en tiers. *Revue Française de Psychanalyse, 48* (1): 366–378.

———— (1986a). Fliess, Freud, Ferenczi: Création permise et création refusée, succès et échecs de la transmission dans l'appropriation identifiante du négatif. *Bulletin du groupe lyonnais de psychanalyse*, Lyon.

———— (1986b). Mots en souffrance et attitude d'écoute en psychopathologie clinique. In: J. Guillaumin (ed.), *Ordre et désordre de la parole* (pp. 119–129). Lyon: C.R.I. [also in Les paroles du patient, *Psychiatrie française*, 2 (March–April 1985): 121–127.

———— (1986c). Le préconscient et le travail du négatif dans l'interprétation, 46e Congrès de langue française, Liège.

———— (1986d). Négation, négativité, renoncement, création. *Revue Française de Psychanalyse, L* (4): 1173–1181.

———— (1987). *Entre blessure et cicatrice, le destin du négatif dans la psychanalyse*. Paris: P.U.F.; Champ Vallon.

Guyotat, J. (1980). *Mort, naissance et filiation*. Paris: Masson.

Haag, G. (1984). Autisme infantile précoce et phénomènes autistiques. Réflexions psychanalytiques. *La Psychiatrie de l'Enfant, XXVII* (2): 293–354.

———— (1985). De l'autisme à la schizophrénie chez l'enfant. *Topique, 35/36*: 47–65.

Hall, E. T. (1966). *The Hidden Dimension*. New York: Doubleday.

Hecaen, H., & Robert, R. (1963). Les hallucinations auditives des otopathes. *Journal de Psychologie, 1:* 2.

Houzel, D. (1985a). Le monde tourbillonnaire de l'autisme. *Lieux de l'enfance, 3:* 169–183.

———— (1985b). L'évolution du concept d'espace psychique dans l'oeuvre de Mélanie Klein et de ses successeurs. In: J. Gammil, D. Anzieu et al., *Mélanie Klein aujourd'hui*, (pp. 123–138). Lyon: Cesura.

———— (1986). L'interprétation: métaphore ou analogie. *Journal de la Psychanalyse de l'Enfant, 1*.

Kaës, R. (1980). *L'idéologie: études psychanalytiques*. Paris: Dunod.

———— (1984). La transmission psychique intergénérationnelle et intragroupale. In: R. Kaës, M. Dulac, J. De Martino, E. Granjon, M. Thaon, & Ch. Guérin, *Penser la famille*. Actes des journées d'étude de psychologie sociale clinique (pp. 4–12). Arles: Hôpital Imbert.

Kaës R., Missenard A., et al. (1982). *Le travail psychanalytique dans les groupes, Vol. 2*. Paris: Dunod.

Kafka, F. (1914–1919). *La colonie pénitentiaire*. French translation: *La Pléiade. Vol. 2* 1980. Paris: Gallimard (written in 1914; original German publication in 1919).

Klein, M. (1946). Notes on some schizoid mechanisms. *International Journal of Psycho-Analysis, 27* [reprinted in *The Writings of Melanie Klein, III*. London: Hogarth].

Kohut, H. (1971). *The Analysis of the Self*. New York: International Universities Press.

Kreisler, L. (1981). *L'enfant du désordre psychosomatique*. Toulouse: Privat.

———— (1984). Bébés de mères endeuillées. *Revue du Centre Alfred Binet* (July).

Kreisler, L., & Cramer, B. (1981). Sur les bases cliniques de la psychiatrie du nourrisson. *Psychiatrie de l'Enfant, XXIV* (1): 223–232.

Krull, M. (1979). *Sigmund, fils de Jacob*. French translation. Paris: Gallimard, 1983.

Lacan, J. (1936). Le stade du miroir. *International Journal of Psycho-Analysis, 18* (1).

———— (1978). *Le séminaire, livre II. Le Moi dans la théorie de Freud et dans la technique de la psychanalyse.* Paris: Le Seuil.

Laplanche, J. (1981). L'inconscient et le Ça. *Problématiques, IV.* Paris: P.U.F.

———— (1984). La pulsion de mort dans la théorie de la pulsion sexuelle. In: *La pulsion de mort.* Paris: P.U.F.

———— (1985). La pulsion et son objet source: son destin dans le transfert. In: *La pulsion, pour quoi faire?* Association psychanalytique de France.

Lebovici, S. (1974). A propos de l'hystérie chez l'enfant. *Psychiatrie de L'Enfant, 17:* 1.

Lebovici, S., Rabain, J. F., Nathan, T., Thomas P., & Duboz, M. M. (1986). A propos de la maladie de Gilles de la Tourette. *Psychiatrie de L'Enfant, XXIX* (1): 5–59.

Lechevalier, B., Eustache, F., & Rossa, Y. (1985). Les troubles de la perception de la musique d'origine neurologique (les trois niveaux de la désintégration de la perception musicale considérée comme une agnosie auditive). Rapport de neurologie présente au Congrès de psychiatrie et de neurologie de langue française. Paris: Masson.

Lecourt, E. (1974). Dépression et musique, deux études de cas. *Annales de Psychothérapie, V* (9): 25–33.

———— (1983). Le sonore et les limites du Soi. *Bulletin de Psychologie, XXXV* (I): 360, 377, 382.

———— (1985). La musique, le groupe et l'inconscient, une écoute analytique de vécu sonore, entre parole et musique. Doctoral thesis. University of Lyon II.

———— (1987a). Identité culturelle et création groupale, polyphonique. *Revue de psychothérapie psychanalytique de Groupe.*

———— (1987b). *La musicothérapie.* Paris: P.U.F.

MacDougall, J. (1982). *Les théâtres du Je.* Paris: Gallimard.

———— (1986). Un corps pour deux. In: *Corps et Histoire.* Paris: Les Belles Lettres.

Masud Khan (1971). To hear with eyes. In: *The Privacy of the Self.* London: Hogarth Press, 1974.

Meltzer, D. (1980). *The Kleinian Development: Part III: The Clinical Significance of the Work of Bion.* Strathtay: Clunie Press, 1978.

———— (1984). La maladie psychotique dans le petite enfance. Exposé au Colloque sur l'approache de l'autisme. Monaco (June, 1984).

———— (1985). L'objet esthétique. *Revue Française de Psychanalyse, 5:* 137.

Meltzer, D., et al. (1975). *Explorations in Autism.* Strathtay: Clunie Press.

Meltzer, D., Milana, G., et al. (1984). La distinction entre les concepts d'"identification projective" et de "contenant-contenu". *Revue Française de Psychanalyse, XLVIII:* 2.

Mijolla, A. de (1981). *Les visiteurs du Moi, Fantasmes d'identification.* Paris: Les Belles Lettres.

Milner, M. (1969). *Les mains du Dieu vivant.* French translation. Paris: Gallimard.

———— (1976). *L'inconscient et la peinture.* French translation. Paris: P.U.F.

Missenard, A. (1979). Narcissisme et rupture. In R. Kaës, D. Anzieu et al., *Crise, rupture et dépassement.* Paris: Dunod.

———— (1985). Rêves de l'un, rêves de l'autre. *Psychiatrie, 67:* 4.

Murray Schafer, R. (1979). Le paysage sonore. Paris: J. C. Lattès.

Nathan, T. (1978). Considérations ethnopsychiatriques sur le traitement analytique des psychoses. *Ethnopsychiatrica, 1* (I), 15–42.

———— (1983). *Psychanalyse et copulation des insectes.* Grenoble, La pensée sauvage.

———— (1986a). L'utérus, le chaman et le psychanalyste. Ethnopsychanalyse du cadre thérapeutique. *Nouvelle Revue d'Ethnopsychiatrie, 5:* 17–48.

———— (1986b). Trauma et mémoire. Introduction à l'étude des soubassements psychologiques des rituels d'initiation. *Nouvelle revue d'Ethnopsychiatrie, 6:* 7–19.

———— (1986c). *La folie des autres. Traité d'ethnopsychiatrie clinique.* Paris: Dunod.

Neyraut, M. (1973). *Le transfert.* Paris: P.U.F.

Perez Sanchez, M., & Abello, N. (1981). L'unité originaire. *Revue Française de Psychanalyse, XLV,* (4): 777–786.

Pontalis, J. B. (1972). Rêves dans un groupe. In: D. Anzieu et al., *Le travail psychanalytique dans les groupes,* 1972–1982. Paris: Dunod.

———— (1975). Naissance et reconnaissance du 'Self'. In: *Psychologie de la connaissance de soi.* Paris: P.U.F.

———— (1977). *Entre le rêve et la douleur.* Paris: Gallimard.

Racamier, P. C. (1979). *De psychanalyse en psychiatrie.* Paris: Payot.

———— (1985). Une crise de la métapsychologie, I, *XLIX* (6), II. *Revue Française de Psychanalyse, XLIX* (5).

Rosolato, G. (1977). Les hallucinations acoustico-verbales et les champs perceptifs du corps. *L'Évolution psychiatrique, III* (2): 729–742.

———— (1978). L'ombilic et la relation d'inconnu. In: *La relation d'inconnu*. Paris: Gallimard.

———— (1984). Destin du signifiant. *Nouvelle Revue de Psychanalyse, 30* [reprinted in Rosolato, 1985].

———— (1985). *Éléments de l'interprétation*. Paris: Gallimard.

Rouart, J. (1979). Le souvenir comme annésie organisée. *Revue Française de Psychanalyse, 43* (4): 665–678.

Roustang, F. (1980). *Elle ne le lâche plus*. Paris: Éditions de Minuit.

Ruffiot, A., Eiguer, A., et al. (1981). *La thérapie familiale psychanalytique*. Paris: Dunod.

Sapir, M., et al. (1979). *La relaxation: son approche psychanalytique*. Paris: Dunod.

Schacht, L. (1977). La découverte de l'historicité. *Nouvelle Revue de Psychanalyse, 15. Mémoires* (pp. 69–80). Paris: Gallimard.

Schneider, M. (1980). *Blessures de mémoire*. Paris: Gallimard.

Schur, M. (1966). Some additional 'days residues' of the 'specimen dream' of psychoanalysis. In: R. M. Loewenstein, L. M. Newman, M. Schur, & A. T. Solnit (eds.), *Psychoanalysis—a General Psychology*. New York: International Universities Press.

Segal, H. (1986). De l'unité clinique du concept d'instinct de mort. In: *La pulsion de mort*. Paris: P.U.F.

Serre, C. (1981). *Humour noir et hommes en blanc*. Luçon: J. Glénot.

Serres, M. (1980). *Le parasite*. Paris: Grasset.

Stern, D., et al. (1975). Vocalizing in unison and in alternation: two modes of communication within the mother–infant dyad. *Annals of N.Y. Academy of Sciences, 263*: 89–100.

Thom, R. (1980). *Modèles mathématiques de la morphogenèse*. Paris: Christian Bourgois.

———— (1983). *Paraboles et catastrophes*. Paris: Flammarion.

Velabrega, J. P. (1980). *Phantasme, mythe, corps et sens*. Paris: Payot.

Vernant, J. P. (1959). Aspects mythiques de la mémoire en Grèce. *Journal de Psychologie*: 11–29.

Villier, J. (1982). Des rêves en groupanalyse. *Connexions, 36*: 43–67.

Winnicott, D. W. (1962). *The Maturational Processes of the Facilitating Environment*. London: Hogarth Press, 1965.

———— (1969). *Collected Papers: Through Paediatrics to Psychoanalysis*. London: Tavistock Publications, 1958.

———— (1971a). Mirror-role of mother and family in child development. In: *Playing and Reality*. London: Tavistock Publications.

_____ (1971b). *Playing and Reality*. London: Tavistock Publications.

Woodcock, A., & Davis, M. (1984). *La théorie des catastrophes*, Lausanne: L'Age d'Homme.

LIST OF CASES

Anna O: 140
Céline: 126–128
Damien: 229–230
David: 218–223, 226–227, 229, 230, 234
Deimos: 246–253
Dora: 140
Emma: 30–33
Fanchon: 96–97
Gérard: 9–10, 21, 74–77
Irma: 31–33, 38, 41
Isabelle: 193–195
Jennie: 74–77, 80, 83, 91
Mrs A: 133–134
Mrs G: 123–126, 131, 141–142
Marie: 2–7, 19, 20, 24
Marsyas: 222–223
Mireille and little K: 129–130
Nathalie: 8–9, 10, 25
Noémie: 19
Patroclus: 239–246, 253
RL: 62–64, 68
Sarah (Missenard): 72–73, 81
Sarah (Enriquez): 101–112, 115, 119

INDEX OF PROPER NAMES

Abello, N., 80
Anzieu, A., 21, 121–145
Anzieu, D., 1–25, 28, 34, 43,
    47, 52, 54–55, 57n, 61,
    68–69, 71, 79, 84, 89,
    105, 113, 119, 148–150,
    154–155, 160, 186n,
    187n, 188n, 192, 202,
    212–213, 216, 222, 224–
    225, 229, 235n, 251,
    255n
Aulagnier, P., 76, 79, 119,
    120n, 151

Barande, R., 169, 189n
Baranès, J. J., 76
Bateson, 193, 204
Beckett, S., 21, 95
Begoin, F., 80
Bergeret, J., 187n

Berio, C., 228
Bettelheim, B., 230
Bick, E., 38, 44, 47, 48–49,
    52–54, 79, 222, 229
Bion, W. R., 11, 22, 33, 36,
    44–45, 49, 52, 113, 129,
    132, 188n
Blanchard, A. M., 81–83
Bleger, J., 43, 156, 187n
Bolk, 169
Bourdier, P., 150
Braunschweig, D., 187n
Brenman, E., 125, 144
Breuer, M. 32

Cabibo, N., 47
Cage, J., 228
Castoriadis-Aulagnier, P., 15,
    55, 79
Chasseguet-Smirgel, J., 168

Champollion, F., 148
Condillac, E., 223
Cosnier, J., 188n
Couchoud, M. T., 76, 80, 81
Cramer, B., 93n

Davis, M., 202, 209n
Dayan, M., 67, 113
Dejours, C., 93n
Deutsch, H., 48
Devereux, G., 254n, 255n
Donnet, S. L., 171, 188n
Doron, J., 191–209
Dostoevsky, F., 238
Duport Rosan, J. P., 186n

Eliade, M., 96
Enriquez, M., 95–120, 188n

Fain, M., 156, 187n
Faimberg, H., 151
Fajon, M., 232
Federn, P., 39
Ferenczi, S., 152, 164, 170,
    176, 178, 189n
Fichte, J., 27
Fleischl, von, 33
Fliess, R., 151, 187n
Fliess, W., 29–33, 38, 178,
    189n
Fresco, N., 120n
Freud, S., 11–14, 16, 29–36,
    45, 51, 52, 54, 56n, 57n,
    61–62, 67, 83, 97, 113–
    115, 121–123, 127–129,
    134–136, 137–141, 147–
    149, 152–154, 157–158,
    160, 164, 172, 176, 178,
    186n, 188n, 189n, 245

Genet, J., 104
Gibello, B., 2, 22
Globokar, V., 228
Gödel, K., 56
Goethe, W., 93n
Gori, R., 154, 229
Gossein, 230
Granjon, E., 150
Green, A., 186n, 188n, 255n
Greenson, R., 188n
Gribinski, M., 67
Grisey, 228
Grotstein, J. S., 235n
Grunberger, B., 136
Guérin, Ch., 151–152
Guillaume, P., 191
Guillaumin, J., 83, 147–189,
    224, 225
Gutierrez, Y., 84–88
Guyotat, J., 151, 170

Haag, G., 79, 234
Hartmann, H., 40
Hecaen, H., 233
Henry, P., 228–229
Heimann, P., 43
Hilbert, 56
Houzel, D., 19–20, 27–58

Jung, C., 39

Kaës, R., 84, 87, 120n, 150
Kafka, F., 22
Klein, M., 34, 41–42, 52–53,
    57n, 137, 142
Kobo, A., 8
Kohut, M., 188n, 172, 175
Kreisler, L., 69–71, 80
Kris, E., 40

Krull, M., 178

Lacan, J., 40–37, 44, 57n, 169, 173, 189n
Laplanche, J., 78, 113, 137
Lebovici, S., 122, 245, 255n
Lechevalier, B., 234
Lecourt, E., 211–235
Lewin, B., 244
Löwenstein, R., 40

McDougall, J., 6, 15, 136, 138, 188n
Mahler, M., 46
Mandelbrot, B., 58
Marietan, 228
Marty, P., 163
Masud Khan, M., 21, 255n
Meltzer, D., 21, 48, 57n, 80, 122, 137–138, 225, 230, 234
Mijolla, A. de, 119
Milner, M., 220
Missenard, A., 59–93
Möbius, 20, 45
Murray Schafer, R., 227
M'uzan, M. de, 183

Nathan, T., 77, 93n, 143, 145, 237–254, 255n
Neyraut, M., 120n
Nunberg, 39

Ormesson, J. d', 93n

Pankow, G., 6
Pasche, F., 55
Perez Sanchez, M., 80
Piaget, J., 48, 187n

Plato, 99
Poe, E., 238
Pontalis, J. B., 67, 89, 191
Prigogine, I., 58n

Régis, 233–234
Robert, R., 233
Rosenfeld, D., 46
Rosolato, G., 11–13, 67, 136, 235n
Rouart, J., 120n
Roustang, F., 189n
Ruelle, D., 57n

Sabourin, P., 178
Sami-Ali, 8
Schacht, L., 100, 120n
Schelling, F., 27
Schneider, M., 120n
Schur, M., 30–31
Segal, H., 142
Serres, M., 188n
Shakespeare, W., 21
Spitz, R., 187n, 214, 218
Stengers, I., 58n
Stern, D., 214
Stockhausen, K., 228
Strachey, J., 38–39

Takens, F., 57n
Tausk, V., 176
Thom, R., 45, 57n, 186n, 201, 208
Tustin, F., 46–47, 50, 79

Valabrega, J. P., 76
Vernant, J. P., 99
Villier, J., 89–90

Wilde, O., 238

Winnicott, D., 38, 42, 48,
    54–55, 113, 126, 188n,

199–200, 213, 255n

Wisdom, 176

Woodcock, A., 202, 209n